THE FORCE OF CUSTOM

Central Eurasia in Context Series
Douglas Northrop, Editor

THE FORCE OF CUSTOM

Law and the Ordering
of Everyday Life in Kyrgyzstan

Judith Beyer

University of Pittsburgh Press

Parts of chapter 1 appeared in "Revitalisation, Invention and Continued Existence of the Kyrgyz Aksakal Courts: Listening to Pluralistic Accounts of History," *The Journal of Legal Pluralism and Unofficial Law* 53/54 (2006): 141–75.

Parts of chapter 2 appeared in "Settling Descent: Place-Making and Genealogy in Talas, Kyrgyzstan," *Central Asian Survey* 30, no. 3–4 (2011): 455–68.

Parts of chapter 3 appeared in "'There Is This Law': Performing the State in the Kyrgyz Courts of Elders," in *Ethnographies of the State in Central Asia*, eds. Madeleine Reeves, Johan Rasanayagam, and Judith Beyer, 99–123 (Bloomington: Indiana University Press, 2014), and in "Customizations of Law: Courts of Elders (*Aksakal* Courts) in Rural and Urban Kyrgyzstan," *PoLAR* 38, no. 1 (2015): 53–71.

Parts of chapter 4 appeared in "Ordering Ideals: Accomplishing Well-Being in a Kyrgyz Cooperative of Elders," *Central Asian Survey* 32, no. 4 (2013): 432–47.

Parts of chapter 6 appeared in Beyer and Girke, "Practicing Harmony Ideology: Ethnographic Reflections on Community and Coercion," *Common Knowledge* 21, no. 2 (2015): 196–235.

Published by the University of Pittsburgh Press, Pittsburgh, Pa., 15260
Manufactured in the United States of America
Printed on acid-free paper
10 9 8 7 6 5 4 3 2 1

Library of Congress Cataloging-in-Publication Data

Names: Beyer, Judith, author.
Title: *The Force of Custom: Law and the Ordering of Everyday Life in Kyrgyzstan* / Judith Beyer.
Description: Pittsburgh: University of Pittsburgh Press, 2016. | Series: Central Eurasia in context | Includes bibliographical references and index.
Identifiers: LCCN 2016039764 | ISBN 9780822964209 (paperback)
Subjects: LCSH: Kyrgyzstan—Social life and customs. | Kyrgyz—Ethnic identity—History. | Ethnology—Kyrgyzstan. | National characteristics, Kyrgyz. | BISAC: SOCIAL SCIENCE / Anthropology / Cultural.
Classification: LCC DK917 .B49 2016 | DDC 390.095843—dc23
LC record available at https://lccn.loc.gov/2016039764

Cover art: Photo by the author
Cover design by Alex Wolfe

To Felix and Constantin
with love

It is true, that what is settled by custom, though it be not good, yet at least it is fit.

—FRANCIS BACON, *OF INNOVATIONS* (1740)

CONTENTS

ACKNOWLEDGMENTS

Over the many years of research and writing that have gone into this book, a great number of friends and colleagues have supported me and my work, and I would like to thank them here for their inspiration, assistance, encouragement, and collaboration: Sergei Abashin, Olumide Abimbola, Dirk Ackermann, Gulnara Aitpaeva, Natalia Alenkina, Dirk Bake, Talantaaly Bakchiev, Martin Beck, Ildikó Bellér-Hann, Franz and Keebet von Benda-Beckmann, Andrea Berg, Friedhelm Beyer, Matthias Beyer, Christoph Beyer, Kristian Bettke, Ksenia Bianchi, Malgorzata Biczyk, Christine Bichsel, David Bozzini, Andreas Braun, Suchandana Chatterjee and her family, Eva-Marie Dubuisson, Aida Egemberdieva, Beate Eschment, Birgitt and Bernd Friedrich, Réne Gerrets, Wolfgang and Johanna Girke, Stephen Gudeman, David Gullette, Otto Habeck, Stephanie Hesche, John Heathershaw, Irene Hilgers, Markus Höhne, Ali Iğmen, Lena Ignatova, Gulnara Iskakova, Rano Ismailova, Shabit Inogamov and Zarema Inogamova, Said Inogamov, Sherbet Inogamova, Aksana Ismailbekova, Maksat Kachkeev, Anara Karakulova, Botagoz Kassymbekova, Michael Kemper, Andrea Klein, Gesine Koch, Roman Knee, Herta and Hermann Knee, Kirsten Mahlke, Anja Neuner, Mateusz Laszczkowski, Jürgen Paul, Anett and Ronald Kirchhof, Gulmira Kokesheva, Nancy Köckert, Patrice Ladwig, Wolfgang Levermann, Nathan Light, Aidai Mambetalieva and her family, Bettina Mann, Till Mostowlansky, Beate Neumann, Kathrin Niehuus, Elida Nogoibaeva, Lenara Mambetalieva, Julie McBrien, Winnie Öhrlich, David Montgomery, Laura Newby, Frank Pieler, Armin Pippel, Johan Rasanayagam, Merim Razbaeva, Madeleine Reeves, Jutta Rittweger, Nurlan Sadykov, Merle Schatz, Burkhard Schnepel, Petra Strähle, Julie Theivendran, Anja Titze, Zarina Trapman, Tommaso Trevisani, Baktygul Tulebaeva-Shabdanalieva, Nurkyz Tuiteeva, Tursunaly Tulegenov, Bert and Jutta Turner, Monica Vasile, Larissa Vetters,

Oliver Weihmann, Matthias Wulff, Lale Yalcin-Heckmann, Roberta Zavoretti, and Askar Zhakishev.

Without the help of Aizat Aisarakunova, Zemfira Inogamova-Hanbury, and Eliza Isabaeva, all of whom I met at different times during their studies at the American University in Central Asia, I would have never managed to handle the amount of fieldwork data I collected in Kyrgyzstan. These young and talented anthropologists spent weeks on end with me in Talas, accompanied me on various follow-up trips, meticulously transcribed hours of recorded talks, and provided a great deal of help with organizational matters. But most importantly, they have become really good friends.

A special thanks goes to Brian Donahoe for language editing this book manuscript. His knowledge of legal anthropology and his familiarity with the Russian and Kyrgyz languages as well as the geographical area have made his comments, suggestions, and advice invaluable.

I also thank Douglas Northrop for his continuous support in seeing the book come to fruition, and Peter Kracht for taking it on board at the University of Pittsburgh Press in the first place. I also thank the two anonymous reviewers for their very constructive comments on this manuscript.

Research for this book has been funded by several institutions that I would like to thank for their financial and administrative support: the Volkswagen Foundation, the Max Planck Institute for Social Anthropology, the Graduate School "Society and Culture in Motion" at the Martin Luther University Halle-Wittenberg, the Central Asia and Caucasus Research and Training Initiative (CARTI) of the Open Society Foundations, and the Center of Excellence "Cultural Foundations of Social Integration" at the University of Konstanz.

Chong rakhmat to everyone in Aral and Engels! Thank you so much for sharing your lives with me and for continuing to welcome my family and me in your homes. I owe more than I can say to Baiyz Apa and her whole household: Nasir Baike and Elmira Ezhe and their children Urmat, Takhmina, Sani, Anarkul, and Zhusup. To all of Baiyz Apa's other children and their families: thank you for your hospitality, your interest in my work, and your support, particularly Ydyrys Baike and Zhyldyz Ezhe for letting me live in your house and for taking care of all the small things. Thank you to their children Medina, Tunuk, Ümüt, Baktygul, Zhangyl, and Anarbek for accepting me as part of your family. *Chong rakhmat* to Kudaibergen Ata for teaching me about what it means to be an *aksakal* in Talas, and thanks go to his wife and their children for their hospitality. *Großes Dankeschön* to the late Abaskan Ata and to Kozhoke Ata for telling me about their lives, especially their time in Germany in the 1940s. Thanks also to Abdysadyr Baike and his staff, particularly Kalipa Ezhe, for their tremendous help; to Ainura Ezhe for helping me with documents and for sharing her life story with me; to Kasym Ata for trusting me and for showing me his work, and to his wife for her hospitality; to Syrgak Baike for teaching me about shariat, and to Dinar Ezhe for making *airan* and *borsook*. Thank you, Tülööberdi Ata, for your jokes!

Rakhmat also to Bektur Agai and Shailoobek Ata for what they taught me about the history of Aral and Engels. I would also like to thank the late Sabatar Baike for having been a great neighbor, Muslim Baike for driving us around, the late Askar Ata and his wife for their hospitality, all members of both aksakal courts for letting me take part in their work, Gulmira Ezhe for teaching us Kyrgyz, my dear neighbor Raia Apa for thinking anthropologically, and finally the late Cholponkul Ata for being my soulmate. To all these people and all the other inhabitants of Aral and Engels: *Baaryngyzdardy Kudai koldosun!*

Most importantly, I would like to thank Felix Girke for his steady support throughout all the stages of this book project, for his constructive criticism, and for showing me every day that life is fun! I dedicate this book to him and to our son, Constantin.

PREFACE

When I began research for this book, I wanted to investigate the newly formed courts of elders (*aksakaldar sotu*) in Kyrgyzstan and study their dispute management techniques as well as the kind of law they were applying in their court sessions. Several years earlier, when I was studying law at the American University of Central Asia (AUCA) in Bishkek, the capital of Kyrgyzstan, and conducting research for my master's thesis on the ongoing constitutional reform, I came across a statement by Amnesty International in which a court of elders in the northern province of Talas was accused of having permitted the stoning of a person (Amnesty International 1996). It was the most spectacular case—and remained the only one—where *aksakals* seem to have condoned such violent action. Whereas the exact details of the event were never fully revealed because the whole village decided to remain silent on the issue, I was intrigued by what I perceived to be some form of archaic legal sanctioning. The story made me want to know more about these courts in Talas, and I decided to design a research project focusing on this institution. While this focus provided valuable insights into the relationship between aksakals, state officials, and their respective perceptions of the Soviet and post-Soviet state, in the course of my fieldwork my research focus quite naturally expanded.

After a few months in the field, in early April 2006, I jotted down an experience in my journal, which I used to write in late at night. I had already attended many sessions of the local courts of elders, but I still had a vague sense that there was not enough dispute "going on." This feeling was also triggered by numerous conversations I had with villagers and aksakals, and by what I overheard when people spoke among themselves. "What we need is *yntymak*!" (*Yntymak kerek*!) was an utterance I heard frequently in a wide variety of situations. My field notes even refer to my "horror of yntymak." Most simply, I learned to translate *yntymak* as "harmony" (see figure 0.1).

FIGURE 0.1. Sign at the entrance to the village Aral: *Yntymak eldi kögörtöt* (Harmony allows people to prosper) (2015).

This call for "harmony" could be related to almost every aspect of people's relations, be it within the family, the descent group, the village, during aksakal court cases, or in reference to politics. While I generally wrote down everything I could observe, ranging from how bread was made to the different breeds of sheep in the area, I remember that yntymak was something I did not like to write about. People's emphasis on "harmony" seemed to devalue my data on disputes. I thus had to overcome my preference for "local dispute-watching," which, according to Moore (2005, 350), has "been the principal form of social voyeurism in legal anthropology" ever since Gluckman's focus on court cases. People were emphasizing yntymak so emphatically that I had no other option than to take this emphasis seriously. It was a turning point in my analysis when I realized that yntymak and related concepts such as *uiat* (shame-anxiety), *syi* (respect), *namyz* (pride), and the umbrella term *salt* (custom) were an intrinsic part of everyday life.

The etymology of the Kyrgyz word *salt* is unclear. It is pronounced with an open vowel as in the English word *skull*. To call *salt* "custom" is a deliberate decision, although that concept has been interpreted rather differently within anthropology over time. Geertz ([1983] 2000, 208) has argued that mischief was done by the word *custom* in anthropology, as it was used to reduce thought to habit. The issue is not that "custom includes norms, but is both greater and more precise than norms" or that "law includes custom, but is both greater and more precise" (Bohannan 1967, 46), but that *salt* is regarded as having the capacity to be both: it is a binding obligation one needs to adhere to, but it is also an integral part of oneself.

In this book I try to grasp this "different sense of law" (Geertz [1983] 2000, 187) by focusing on how actors employ and (re)produce *salt* in everyday interactions, even in such seemingly trivial situations as, for example, sitting down with others.

SITTING DOWN "ACCORDING TO *SALT*"

A particularly visible and only partly verbalized instance of how people establish orderliness according to *salt* is how individuals take their seats around a low table or on the floor during any kind of gathering. "According to *salt*" (*salt boiuncha*), the most respected person has the privilege of sitting in *tör*—the place in a room (or a yurt) that directly faces the door. This place is usually offered to and claimed by elders. If guests have arrived, the owner of the house will offer the place to the guest, irrespective of age or gender. Tör is claimed and offered, surrendered and maintained. However, people arrange their seats not only in relation to tör but also in relation to whoever else is present in the room. The respective positions are negotiated through talk, gestures, and glances, through sitting down and getting up, through offering one's place to someone else or by telling a third person to give up his or her seat. Sitting down in a room is a collaborative (re)production of *salt*, and as I was living in two villages, Aral and Engels, in Talas, Kyrgyzstan's northwesternmost province, I became a part of it, thereby even helping to reproduce its validity.

I could always assess my current status among my host family from my seating position, which changed gradually over the course of my fieldwork. Initially I was always assigned the tör position, but later in my time in Talas I was expected to bring plates and teacups and help with chopping onions when we had guests (and thus sometimes not even allowed to sit down at all). The further away from tör I was seated, the more integrated I had become. However, I was not always passively seated by others; as soon as I understood the practice of tör, I actively tried to avoid being seated in this exposed position, where one was the constant center of attention and was also offered more tea and food than usual. To sit in tör, while formally a privilege, can also be an unwanted burden that one must bear, even to the point of trying to circumvent it! Thus, by using verbal and nonverbal cues, I would urge others to take the position. I also pretended not to have heard a person's suggestion that I move to tör and simply remained where I thought my appropriate place was in that situation. I finally succeeded, in the sense that it took less performative effort to assume the place I wanted than it did at the beginning of my stay.[1]

Thus, *salt* not only is found in the rule of tör ("The most respected person sits furthest away from the door") but it is equally used by people who negotiate their positions elsewhere in the room. To escape tör, one would also argue "according to *salt*." While most interactions like the one I just mentioned are not explicitly connected to *salt*, they will trigger reference to this concept as soon as one is asked for a reason or an explanation. To hint at the main argument of this book in terms of this scenario, I can say that it is through *salt* that people order their positions in a room and to one another, and in doing so they help maintain and (re)produce *salt*. The hierarchy implicit in tör is one example of this sense of orderliness. Ordering through *salt*; that is, achieving a sense of normativity and orderliness in one's life, occurs in direct interaction with others, but also when an Other is only imagined. It encompasses verbal as well as nonverbal communication, embodied practices, and discourses. Most basically, I regard ordering as a practice we all engage in by constantly defining and redefining our relations to others. As Rapport and Overing have observed (2000, 40), "Human beings recognize that the world is actually multiple . . . and that any one system of classification is only a pretence at overall orderly encompassment. . . . We classify, we categorize, conscious of the logical impossibility of so doing once-for-all."

I hold that the actions undertaken in the name of or according to *salt* have a strong ordering component, as they are carried out and reflected on with the explicit aim of achieving a shared sense of orderliness. In this book I employ an ethnomethodological approach that orients itself to what people observably do, what they say they do, and what they say they should do, reflecting on their own and others' behavior. *Salt* orders people's lives in particular ways that neither law nor custom alone could do. It is this recognition that guides my exploration of *salt* as a legal repertoire in contemporary Talas, as it is entwined with state law and Islamic law (shari'a, shariat in Kyrgyz) and thereby forms a part of the contemporary plural legal landscape.[2]

By attending to my informants' own models and concepts and by observing how they use them to order (that is, to reason about, reflect on, or justify) their own and others' actions, I trace the force of custom from an emic standpoint. By stressing the necessity to respect *salt*, actors subject their agency to this legal repertoire. By emphasizing the expansion and strengthening of *salt*, they objectify this cultural concept while downplaying the possibility of ignoring or walking away from it. While the "force of custom" is an emic rhetorical strategy that does not require further explanation from the point of view of the actors, the concept of "customization" that I apply in this book can help us understand how the perceived dominance of custom in rural Kyrgyzstan is brought about. By reinterpreting noncustomary law as something that becomes part of *salt* over time, people also come to regard and present historic developments and contemporary social change as no longer alien, but as their own achievements and part and parcel of their everyday lives.

NOTES ON NAMING, ADDRESSING, AND FIELDWORK

ON NAMING

I have decided not to anonymize the names of my informants. The names of the places where I conducted fieldwork are also real. My reasons for breaking with the anthropological tradition of anonymizing fieldwork data is that all of the informants with whom I lived have asked me to use their real names, as they regard the work I have been carrying out since 2005 to be part of their village history. As with my previous monographs (Beyer and Knee 2007; Beyer and Inogamova 2010), I intend to deliver this book to my key informants and to the libraries and schools in my two fieldwork villages.

ON TRANSLITERATION

Most of the people in my fieldsite speak Kyrgyz, a Turkic language. The language was standardized in the early Soviet years and first transcribed by Soviet linguists using the Arabic alphabet. After a brief period of transcribing the language in the Latin alphabet, the Cyrillic alphabet was introduced and has been in continuous use since 1937. The transliteration of Kyrgyz (and Russian) words follows the standard American Library Association and Library of Congress Romanization tables for Slavic alphabets (ALA-LC). As the Kyrgyz language contains phonemes that are absent in Russian, I use the following additions to the ALA-LC standard: Kyrg. ө = ö; Kyrg. ү = ü; Kyrg. ң = ng. The abbreviation "Russ." stands for the Russian language and is used whenever my informants use the Russian term instead of the Kyrgyz, or where there simply exists no Kyrgyz equivalent. Complete Kyrgyz sentences in the footnotes are either proverbs or instances when the word *salt* was explicitly mentioned. For the sake of simplicity and readability, I have decided to use the English conventions *-s* and *-es* to render plural forms of foreign terms rather than transliterating the plural forms from the foreign languages. Thus, for example, for the plural of the Kyrgyz word *aksakal* ("elder," literally "white beard"), I write *aksakals* rather than *aksakaldar* (the Kyrgyz plural form), and for the plural of the Russian word *kolkhoz* ("collective farm"), I write *kolkhozes* rather than *kolkhozy*. Regarding the pluralization of the Russian word *artel'* (work unit), I have decided to omit the apostrophe at the end of the word (which indicates the Russian soft sign) when pluralizing (*artels*) in order to avoid the possibility of confusing the plural with the singular possessive. Throughout the text I use the word *shariat*, which is the Kyrgyz version of the Arabic *shari'a*.

ON ADDRESSING

In the Kyrgyz language people can be addressed by their first names alone only if ego is older than the person addressed. In all other cases, a second name that signifies the social relation to ego is added to the first name. The names mentioned here are indications of how I addressed the respective persons. As most people were older than I was, I used the polite or formal verb ending (*–siz*) and a second name. *Ata* is the way to address a male elder. *Baike*, *Ake*, or *Agai* are the polite forms of addressing someone as one's older brother or uncle. *Apa* indicates an elder female, and *Ezhe* can be roughly translated as "sister" and is used to address a woman somewhat older than ego. While the Kyrgyz have an elaborate system of addressing one another as well as several naming taboos, I was not subjected to these rules and thus do not discuss them here.

ON FIELDWORK

This book is based on anthropological fieldwork in Talas province in northwestern Kyrgyzstan (see figure 0.2). Talas is one of the most remote areas of Kyrgyzstan. It is the smallest of the country's seven provinces: it consists of a single major river valley, and is nearly completely surrounded by mountains.[3] On its northern side, the Kyrgyz mountain range separates the province from the steppes of Kazakhstan, onto which it opens only at its very northwestern end. From the Kyrgyz range, the Talas Ala-Too splits off and marks Talas's southern border with the neighboring Zhalal Abad province, which can only be reached by horse from within Talas. In the southwest the province shares a border with Uzbekistan, but the mountains are impassable

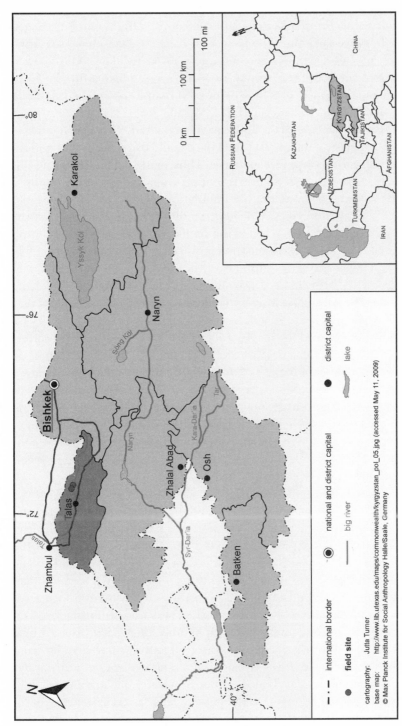

FIGURE 0.2. Map of Kyrgyzstan.

at that point. From other parts of the country, Talas can be reached only by traversing the Ötmök pass at 3,300 meters above sea level, which in harsh winters is sometimes closed for days. The 320 km trip from the country's capital, Bishkek, used to take a full day until major repairs to the previously unpaved road were finished in 2008. Due to this troublesome geography, during Soviet times the province was usually accessed through Kazakhstan. But with independence in 1991, border controls and tolls have made traveling across national borders difficult and expensive. Thus, with independence, Talas province came to be temporarily cut off from the rest of the country.

More than 80 percent of the population of Talas province (see figure 0.3) lives in villages of 1,500 to 4,500 inhabitants. Most people live on what they can grow in the fields and in the gardens behind their houses, as well as on their animals. While they keep chickens and geese in yards behind their houses, sheep, cows, goats, and horses are sent to the pastures during the summer months. Despite the fact that animal husbandry is largely on the increase, only a very few Kyrgyz people at present manage to make a living exclusively on breeding sheep and horses. In Talas, families generally own on average twenty sheep, one or two cows, and one or two horses or donkeys. In recent years, their herds have steadily increased. Animals are a "mobile bank account," as they can be sold whenever cash is needed—mostly in autumn when the festive season starts. After having been portrayed as "backward" during Soviet times, the possession of animals and the activity of transhumance today carry a positive connotation, as they indicate wealth and are cherished as an expression of authentic Kyrgyz culture.

Fieldwork took place in the two villages of Aral and Engels.[4] I spent fifteen months in 2005 and 2006 in this fieldsite and returned three times thereafter for several weeks each time (in 2008, 2010, and 2015). For the most part I conducted participant observation in the course of various aspects of daily life, as well as during official village events such as court sessions, meetings, celebrations, and political campaigns. I also collected the life histories of my main informants, stories and narratives, legal documents, statistical information, and newspaper articles; took photographs and made video recordings; and kept a fieldwork journal. As I arrived with my partner and lived in a separate house, I was considered a married woman leading her own household (tütün). This gave me a considerable amount of freedom. The expectations it encompassed, such as contributing financially to the life-cycle events of the descent line into which I was

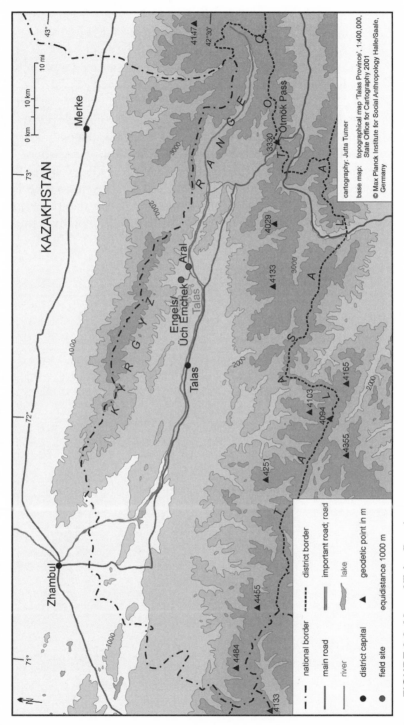

FIGURE 0.3. Map of Talas Province.

adopted, helping to prepare food during these events, establishing good relations with neighbors by visiting them and bringing food over to their houses, and also by paying electricity bills and taxes, helped me to become a member of the village community. I gradually understood how life in Aral and Engels was conducted.

As I lived in Aral, most of my ethnographic data come from that village, particularly from the eighty-eight-year-old widow Baiyz Apa and the families of her eight children. However, I developed closer relations with the imam and the aksakals living in Engels, where I also attended more aksakal court sessions. As the villages are only a one-hour walk from one another (see figure 0.4), I went to Engels on average twice a week and would spend the entire day there in different people's houses, participating in their everyday lives and listening to their stories.

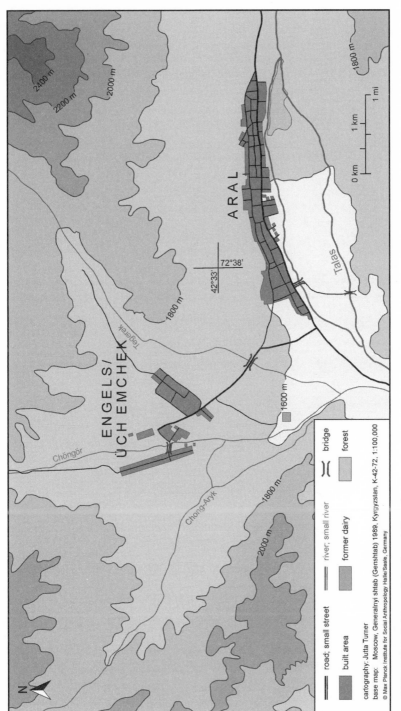

FIGURE 0.4. Map of Aral and Engels.

cartography: Jutta Turner
base map: Moscow, Generalnyi shtab (Genshtab) 1989, Kyrgyzstan, K-42-72, 1:100,000
© Max Planck Institute for Social Anthropology Halle/Saale, Germany

road; small street
built area
former dairy

river, small river
bridge
forest

THE FORCE OF CUSTOM

Introduction

INVOKING CUSTOM

The bus came from Engels and while he was driving, something must have gotten into the driver's eye and he couldn't see. He hit the horse and the bus flipped over. It was the bus from Engels. They called me and I went there. I told the driver, "Driver, you know the rules. You will have to pay for the horse no matter what you say." Then some people said, "Kudaibergen, there are *aksakals* [elders] in Engels, too. He didn't hit it on purpose." Then I said, "All right," and I told my son, "Get a knife and butcher it!" Somebody had a knife. I told the boys, "Butcher it and distribute the meat to the relatives here" [meaning all people present]. That's how you make peace. One needs to trust people. He did not hit it on purpose. But if it had been someone else in that situation and not me, he might have said, "Pay for the horse."

This story was narrated by Kudaibergen Ata in 2006 during a session of the court of elders (*aksakaldar sotu*) in the village of Aral, a couple of days after the incident took place. It sheds a great deal of light on how everyday life is ordered in two adjacent mountain villages in a peripheral part of Kyrgyzstan.[1] For one, we can see that the relations between the two villages seem to be regulated by certain rules, and that these rules cover, for example, what happens if a person's livestock is accidentally killed. It also seems that people view the aksakals—the local village elders—as central figures who are intrinsically related to these rules. However, this story does not specify whether the aksakals are regarded as responsible for the elaboration of the rules or for their application. Also, while alluding to the existence of rules, Kudaibergen Ata (see figure 0.5) did not mention their content. These rules appeared to be self-evident to everyone present that day. While the passengers from Engels paid respect to Kudaibergen Ata by listening to him and by not disputing the "rule" he invoked, they reminded him that "there are elders in Engels, too," implying that those elders deserved respect as much as he did, something that he, in turn, ought to take into account. Finally, the very rules to which Kudaibergen Ata referred in the beginning were not only not spelled out, they were also not adhered to by the aksakal himself. Instead of having the driver give a horse in payment to the owner (who was not present that day), he ordered the slaughtering of the horse in order to make peace among all witnesses of the accident, whom he referred to as "relatives." By accepting the meat that his son distributed among them, the witnesses, who were from both villages, also accepted his decision. While the sharing of food reaffirms the "axiom of amity" (Fortes 1969), the old man also drew attention to his own personality: under the guidance of another elder, the situation might have developed differently.

As the head of the court, Kudaibergen Ata used this example as a precedent. In the court case during which he told the story, he was about to decide on a dispute between a herder who had lost a cow in the mountains and the owner of the cow, who was demanding compensation. The story was told to the disputing parties and the court audience to remind everyone of how good relations are maintained between villagers. The old man thereby emphasized his reputation as a good judge and as someone who is respected not only in Aral but also in the neighboring village of Engels. Kudaibergen Ata was successful in his admonition, as both plaintiff and defendant acknowledged that he had acted properly in the earlier case of the bus driver and the dead horse. This, in turn, gave the old man the opportunity to conclude the court case about the lost cow amicably as well. The herder was told to raise a calf until the following autumn, which he then had to hand over to the plaintiff. In this particular court decision, the poor economic condition of the herder was taken into account. To further bolster his decision, Kudaibergen Ata invoked a proverb—"Take a young goat from the one who owes you and be grateful for that"[2]—which suggested that the plaintiff should be satisfied with a small animal even though he had suffered the loss of a larger one, especially because the herder had not deliberately abandoned the animal in the mountains. On our way home from the court case during which the old man had told the story, Kudaibergen Ata asked me, "Did you see how I did it? I did it in the Kyrgyz way [*kyrgyzcha*]—according to custom [*salt boiuncha*]."

I heard the utterance "according to *salt*" many times during fieldwork, mostly as an ex post statement through which people reflected upon, reasoned about, or justified a particular action. Whenever someone declares that something is (or should be) "according to cus-

FIGURE 0.5. Kudaibergen Ata (2015).

tom," they are formulating what they consider righteous and appropriate behavior in a given situation. This can come at the expense of the people toward whom these utterances are directed. When I asked Kudaibergen Ata whether the owner of the dead horse had agreed with his decision to slaughter the animal and distribute its meat among everyone present, he said, "He screamed at first when he found out. But they have all eaten his food [the horse meat]. His reputation will rise." From the perspective of the aksakal, then, *salt* was something he enforced. From the perspective of the owner of the horse as well as from the perspective of the man whose cow had been lost by the herder, it was something forced upon them. These two nested cases give a vivid impression of how the invocation of *salt* can enable agency—to be able to declare what is "according to *salt*"—and how it can demand patiency—to accord to *salt*.[3] This tension is present whenever people talk about custom in Kyrgyzstan.

Salt has all characteristics that Geertz ([1983] 2000) listed for *adat* (Arabic: *'ada*). Referring to Franz von Benda-Beckmann's (1979) discussion of the Indonesian concept of adat, Geertz presents it as follows: "In his [Benda-Beckmann's] glossary, the word is 'defined' as 'tradition, custom, law, morality, political system, legal system' which, except for the omission of 'etiquette' and 'ritual,' is about the size of it" (Geertz [1983] 2000, 210). Analogous to Geertz's approach to adat, I understand *salt* as a form of "legal sensibility": it is through *salt* that people forge new kinds of relations with one another and reinterpret and adapt existing ones. *Salt* is the product of such relations and interactions as much as it orders them. While *salt* thus encompasses more than strictly legal aspects, it is also law in the strict sense of the term because my informants often talk about *salt* using the same terms that they use in regard to state law or Islamic law: *salt* has "laws" (*myizam*; Russ. *zakon*), and obeying these laws is considered obligatory. Some few elements of *salt* are even codified, so that people can refer to detailed written rules when they manage' disputes regarding land, property, family, and penal issues. I also noticed that when disputes and discussions arose, they arose mostly over the correct interpretation of the rules and principles of *salt*.

How do Kyrgyz order their everyday lives, and what role does the invocation of custom (*salt*) play in it? If we want to understand how people in rural areas of this post-Soviet country conceptualize their world today, we need to pay attention to this key aspect of Kyrgyz history and culture and how it relates to Islamic law (called shariat in Kyrgyz) and state law. Often, these two legal repertoires are precisely what *salt* is compared to or contrasted with; in such instances, it is not a stretch to translate *salt* as "customary law." *Salt* has normative and cognitive elements, and just like shariat, it is also inherently connected to everyday interactions and performed in utterly mundane as well as highly ritualistic ways. As there is little codification of *salt*, people's invocations of it and their efforts to justify or explain situations according to *salt* are often the only observable actions or behaviors whereby people develop and propose new or defend old ways of understanding *salt* and each other. Starting from everyday conversations as the most pervasive mode of interaction in social life, in this book I investigate how people order their social relations through speaking and performing "according to *salt*."[4]

Social relations need to be actively and continuously realized through communicative and performative acts; they require constant work, effort, and maintenance. The invocation of *salt* is used in conversations as a stronghold, providing rhetorical refuge to those who want to evade accountability for their own actions or seek an excuse for not acting in a particular situation. It is a reflexive cultural technique by means of which my informants invoke *salt*'s purported stability while they in fact dynamically adjust its principles and rules, just as Kudaibergen Ata did in the aforementioned dispute. Backed up by the rhetoric of stability and continuity, *salt* is thus constantly "in the making." As Chanock observed long ago: "customary law is not customary" (Chanock 1985, 4). He argues that customs are "among the armoury of arguments" that people put in place in order to deal with social and economic changes: "Claimed custom is sometimes simply ideological, but it is often pragmatic, a claim put forward in a form in which it is likely to be successful. In circumstances of conflict and change where there is an unbridgeable gap between social ideals and the actual ways in which life can be lived, custom, or customary law, cannot be a rule which emerges from, is descriptive of and which governs practice or social system. In this changing world claims about custom were competitive rather than descriptive" (1985, 17).

In these constructions of custom, which are frequently at odds with each other, actors more often draw on normativity than on lived reality, on how things should be and not on how they are. Any discussion of *salt* (and, for that matter, of shariat and of state law), taken out of context, triggers normative definitions of the term and how people should live according to it. Only when discussed in concrete situations—during life-cycle rituals, political events, village court sessions, or within the intimacy of the household—do actors depart from these ideal-typical definitions and get down to the nitty-gritty of the matter at hand. This leads us back to the idea of ordering, which is based on the observation that the world is complex and heterogeneous. Acknowledging inconsistencies in one's own behavior or wrapping one's head around the messy entanglements of lived life and its legal predicaments takes a lot more effort and reflexive thinking than postulating clear-cut tenets. Ordering depends on representation: "It depends, that is, on how it is that agents represent both themselves, and their context, *to* themselves" (Law 1994, 25, emphasis in original). In these contexts, *salt* is often blamed for bringing about more disorder and hardship than order and harmony. Nevertheless, it allows people to disavow responsibility for their actions.

THE BODY OF CUSTOM

The entry for salt in the Kyrgyz ethnographic dictionary (Karataev and Eraliev 2005, 402–3) offers a circular definition of the term. It lists terms such as *ürp-adat, nark, yrym-zhyrym,* and *kaada-salt,* thus specifying one term by referring to others with a similar meaning. In conversations the word salt itself can be used interchangeably with *adat* and the aforementioned terms, even though references to salt are much more common. All of my efforts to delineate these notions and translate them adequately failed, as every person I talked to had a different way of conceptualizing them and their respective differences. It seems, then, that not only for my informants but also for local scholars in Kyrgyzstan it is impossible to define salt in a way that would allow the observing researcher or the involved actors to easily delineate, codify, or otherwise pin it down.

This realization led me to concentrate more on practices and conversations in my efforts to better understand in what situations my informants used any of these terms, and specifically what they achieved when they invoked *salt*. Baiyz Apa, my Kyrgyz "grandmother" to whose extended family I belonged during my fieldwork in Aral, reflected on why she—according to *salt*—needs to participate in certain ritualized exchange practices during mortuary rituals even though it goes against her understanding of shariat: "I will feel sick," she explained. "If others do it, how can I not do it? . . . You have to be with the others. If you do not follow the others, it is not good. They do not even have to cast you out. *Salt* itself leads to it. This is why we don't go astray—we do not want to be left out of *salt*."[5] As this statement shows, *salt* is often presented as a burden or—to stick with the bodily metaphors Baiyz Apa and others often use—as something that makes your body "sick" (*naarazy*) or that can make your "head spin" (*bash alaman*). While *salt* is actively "being done" by individuals, they perform it in ways that often deny their very agency in the matter: they describe *salt* as being "in our mentality" (*mentalitet ichinde*) and "in our blood" (*kanybyzda*), thus claiming that *salt* is an inextricable part of themselves. Such a categorical understanding liberates people from having to reason or justify in each case why something is done in a particular way or why something cannot be done differently: they do not have to reflect on why *salt* is part of their world because it is already part of them. When people in Talas say, "*Salt* is in our blood," they employ a primordialist metaphor and extend a typical symbol of identity—blood—to a notion that people associate with a wide variety of activities, practices, and discourses. To have "*salt* in the blood" is also a claim to *communitas*, as individual bodies are symbolically united with those whose blood also contains *salt*. All those who are involved in this kind of legal socialization are considered to be "one." These are acts of self-persuasion that can serve to provide rationalizations whenever actors need to reflect on and reason about their behavior. To have "*salt* in the blood" signals that one is able neither to think nor act in ways that would contradict this shared normative repertoire. It suggests that actors deliberately deny their agency and subject themselves to the practices and discourses of *salt*. The reference to "blood" suggests that, rather than being a domain of knowledge or even a particular virtue, *salt* is prior to such social constructions, as it moves people's minds and bodies.

This emic perception is accompanied by a creative process or practice that keeps *salt* flexible: irrespective of countless acts of incorporation and silent forgetting of cultural elements, it remains "ours."[6] This is particularly striking when my informants speak of *salt* "swallowing" (*zhutuu*) state law or Islamic law.[7] I refer to this gradual incorporation of noncustomary cultural elements into *salt* as "customization." The term was originally used by Inda and Rosaldo (2002, 16–17) to refer to the process of making "foreign cultural forms" customary. However, it would be misleading to say that my informants incorporate cultural forms of "alien" origin (2002, 19). Rather, the idiom of *salt* allows them to downplay the very "alienness" of noncustomary law, practices, objects, and notions by asserting that they have "always" been "ours." Inda and Rosaldo talk about customization in the explicit context of globalization, but globalization is not the most important backdrop against which to analyze these practices in Kyrgyzstan. People in Talas province, where Aral and Engels are located, do not actively perceive themselves as living in a "globalized" world or being subjected to "global flows" any more or less than during the Soviet period or even before. I suggest that these processes of customization are not a recent phenomenon but are, rather, a more general way of ordering the world. People have applied *salt* in this way for a long time, leaving scholars and policy-makers confounded when trying to get a grip on what seemed to be chaotic modes of livelihood.

Presenting *salt* as unchanging while at the same time engaging in customization provides people in Talas with the opportunity to frame their world as an orderly place. To try systematically and objectively to document *salt* would be to turn a blind eye to the fact that *salt* only maintains its relevance as it remains flexible. To capture and codify its rules and principles at a given moment in time would destroy the possibility of negotiation in future situations.

ENTWINED LEGAL REPERTOIRES

It is widely acknowledged in the literature that a plurality of legal repertoires exists in most societies, and that the history of a system of law is largely a history of borrowing of legal materials from other legal systems (see, e.g., Geertz [1983] 2000, 221; Örücü 2006, 281). The following Kyrgyz proverb is an example of how such legal plurality is locally interpreted in Kyrgyzstan: "The person who assaults his parents has to be stoned—this is the law of shariat."[8] As an established proverb, it belongs to the realm of *salt*, but it refers directly to Islamic law and, somewhat surprisingly, uses the Russian word for law (*zakon*) instead of the Kyrgyz word (*myizam*). This particular proverb thus combines references to three legal repertoires, which gives us the first indication that in the emic conception and especially in observable practice, these legal repertoires are neither clearly delineated nor kept apart. The following examples show how *salt*, state law, and shariat become entwined.

ISSUING FINES

In my fieldsites, villagers usually do not conclude an agreement by writing a document. Written evidence is perceived as spoiling the relationship between two parties from the very beginning. In Talas, agreements are concluded by shaking hands and reminding one another that "*Kudai* [God] is watching," and by the subsequent sharing of food or alcohol. In the following example, however, villagers have decided to write down every spring a set of rules and fines related to animal husbandry. These were "the rules" Kudaibergen Ata was referring to in the opening vignette.

Once a year, a large group of men—aksakals, household heads, herders, and staff of the local administration—gather in Aral and Engels for a so-called *kurultai* or *eldik zhiyin* (people's meeting), during which the following questions are discussed: When shall the herders leave the village with their animals to set out on their spring migration to the mountain pastures? What route will they take to the pasturelands (*zhailoo*)? Who will stay where on the pasture? And when will the herds be allowed to return to the village? These questions are crucial for a number of reasons: as horses, cows, sheep, and goats have to be brought from one place to another, covering distances of more than 150 kilometers, it has to be ensured that no damage to people's fields is caused by the passing herds. The animals should avoid recently sown fields and those with new sprouts, and they should return to the villages only after the potato harvest is in; that is, around the end of September. However, every year damage occurs because some herders ignore these regulations and drive their animals home earlier in an effort to avoid early snowfall in the mountains. This is one of the most severe problems villagers face, as revenues from the harvest represent their only source of cash.

During the kurultai the men work out a list of fines that herders have to pay if fields are destroyed or if animals are lost, stolen, or killed by predators on the way. If a villager suffers such losses, he usually contacts the aksakal court, which then deals with the issue. While writing up a list of fines and other decisions of the kurultai is explicitly "according to *salt*," there is also another option that would render the documentation official: handing it over to the village council (*aiyldyk kengesh*), in whose name it would be issued and subsequently sent to the department of justice in Talas city.[9] The manner in which this option is exercised has changed at least superficially in recent years. In 2006 Kalipa Ezhe, the secretary of the mayor of Aral (see figure 0.6), explained, "If we register these decisions there [in Talas], they become official. If they are registered 'according to law' [Russ./Kyrg. *zakon boiuncha*], they become legal decisions. But somehow we never get around to registering them on time. The registration needs to be done within twenty days after the decision is made here. We know this, but we never register on time [laughing]. So, God willing [*Kudai buiursa*], we will register next year." As is often the case, no reference to *salt* was made in this statement, but it was clear that Kalipa Ezhe was hinting at the fact that villagers had their own way of handling their problems. They did not consider it helpful to "officialize" their issues by transferring them to Talas.

In 2014, however, the practice changed, with the list of fines for the year being published in the regional newspaper *Manas Ordo*, just as any other official document or decision passed on the village level. Doing so turned these customary decisions into *toktom*s—legal acts.[10] When I asked Kalipa Ezhe why the mayor's office (*aiyl ökmötü*) was now making official the fines for trespassing, destruction of planted crops, lost or killed animals, and theft of irrigation water, she first gave an ideal-typical answer at first: "We have to make it official because many disputes are being dealt with in the aksakal court. And from the aksakal court they would go to the regional court. If a case reached the regional court and the list was not official, the decision that we make here [in the aksakal court] would not have any power." But when I later asked her, Kudaibergen Ata, and the secretary of the aksakal court if there had been actual cases that had been transferred from the aksakal court to the regional court, the three could only think of one in the period from 2010 to 2015. A claimant had wanted higher compensation from a fellow villager whose animals had destroyed his hay. The state court, according to the villagers, had backed the decision made in the aksakal court, and villagers had scolded the person for taking things "outside." Kalipa Ezhe then departed from her formalistic description and gave me her opinion on how things are getting done in the village:

> In general, people do not go to the state court. We do it according to village law [*aiyldyk myizam*]. For example, in another case the aksakal court made a decision to fine a person 17,000 som.[11] But that's just what it said on the paper. The person said he could not afford that much money and paid as much as he could afford. The case was concluded and everyone was thankful. The custom, which people have agreed upon among themselves, will not change [*ich-ara kelishken salty kalbait*].

This new practice of publishing village decisions in the form of *toktom*s and in the name of the local village council could be interpreted as an attempt by the state to reinstitutionalize village customary law

FIGURE 0.6. Kalipa Ezhe, working in the Aral mayor's office (2008).

at the state level. In this case, state law has incorporated customary law in order to make it more tractable to state courts and, conversely, to allow villagers who might find themselves deprived of their rights in the village aksakal court to bring their cases to the state courts. But we have also heard that according to Kalipa Ezhe, who is in charge of publishing village decisions, this possibility is generally not realized. I therefore interpret this recent development as an administrative measure that, like so many others in Kyrgyzstan, is followed in principle but not in practice. In 2015, I spent a day on the pasturelands (*zhailoo*) with village herders from Aral who told me that they still do not report problems that happen on the zhailoo to the police. Kudaibergen Ata, however, already knew about them: "There are two cases we have to deal with in the aksakal court," he explained to me in Aral, "but we will wait until autumn when the men are back from the zhailoo." Families who send their animals to the pastures usually do not even report the actual numbers of animals they own to the authorities in order to evade higher taxation. Finally, informal agreements exist that also alter the village rules. For example, herders are supposed to be paid in money, but they often agree to forego wages in favor of being allowed to keep and sell the mares' milk and other milk products to the many drivers who pass by the zhailoo on their way to or from Bishkek. Thus, even when *salt* becomes part of state law, villagers do not seize the opportunity to pursue it outside their village institutions. Within the village, there remains a great deal of flexibility in terms of when problems are dealt with and the possibilities to reinterpret existing rules.

THE PRESIDENT'S FATWA

I visited Nasir Baike, the village imam, at his home in August 2015. We were discussing the most recent changes in terms of his work as the head of his mosque congregation, and he explained that the highest religious institution in Kyrgyzstan, the Muslim Spiritual Board (*muftiyat*), had started paying him and the other three village imams a monthly salary for their services.[12] That led into a discussion of the role of the state in religious affairs in contemporary Kyrgyzstan, and he got up and handed me a document from one of his kitchen drawers. "This is our President's fatwa," he said. "It tells you all about how religion should be."

A fatwa is an authoritative legal opinion of an Islamic expert. It derives its authority from the authority of the person issuing it. What

Nasir Baike gave me was the nineteenth (and final) article of a declaration issued by Kyrgyzstan's Council of Defense, an institution
headed by President Almaz Atambaev.[13] This article concerns the reorganization of religious institutions from the muftiyat down to every
village mosque. It concerns the procedure of regular reporting to the
mufti, attestations for religious leaders under the auspices of state
bodies, the appointment of imams only after "appropriate checks"
from law enforcement authorities, and preventive measures to be
taken by religious authorities and the village administration against
"religious extremism and religious conflict" in cooperation with the
government of Kyrgyzstan.

This caught my attention for several reasons. To call what was in
fact part of an official governmental declaration a fatwa implies that
the country's president is a religious as well as a political authority.
Almaz Atambaev is the first of Kyrgyzstan's presidents who not only
openly talks about his Muslim beliefs but also prays in public and
appeals to both custom and Islam in his speeches. This was only
the most recent decree in a line of legal documents concerning the
state's attitude toward religion. On January 20, 2014, only two weeks
before the "fatwa" had been issued, the Talas regional administration had sent an administrative ruling (buiruk) to my fieldsite, drawing on presidential decrees of March 2012 and December 2013.[14]
In this decree of January 2014, the village administration of Aral
was instructed to form a coordinative council in each aiyl ökmötü in
order to provide religious security, maintenance of harmony (yntymak), and freedom of religious belief. They were also expected to
work out punishment procedures and to improve "tolerance of religion" (sabyrduuluktu chyngdoo). These quite nebulous instructions
had still not been implemented by the summer of 2015, when Kalipa
Ezhe gave me copies of the earlier decrees. Regardless of its limited enforcement at the village level, the document indicates not only
the state's interest in religion but also its approach to "containing"
it by establishing a system of checks and balances. Village imams
are now not only subordinate to higher religious institutions such as
the kazyiat[15] in each province and the muftiyat in Bishkek but also
required to report monthly on their religious activities and subject to
exams in which state authorities play a key role. From the perspective
of the believers, however, the state's engagement with religion does
not seem to create a problem per se. Kudaibergen Ata, for example,
found a creative way to relate shariat and state law to each other:
"Shariat is the law for those who keep the religion. The constitution

is the law of the state. It is written in shariat, in different *hadith*, to obey the *amir*. That means to obey the king. It means to keep and maintain the constitution [Russ. *Konstitutsiia*]. You have to keep the constitution written by the state. As we are not an Islamic state, we have to obey the constitution. I mostly obey shariat, but I also have to obey state law." The imam also had no problem with the recent changes. He simply reframed his work in terms analogous to those of a person who works in the mayor's office and who also gets paid a regular salary every month.

Looking at the "President's fatwa" of February 2014 in its entirety, we can see that in the full nineteen articles, the Kyrgyzstani state paints a rather bleak picture of the state of religion in its country. The document starts out referencing domestic "terrorist attacks" in 1999–2000, as well as "attempts of certain circles to use Islam for their political interests." It also mentions "Islamic funds providing financial support to promote the ideology of fundamentalism and extremism," and warns that "insufficient attention to the religious situation in the country will lead to conflicts, inter-religious clashes and the threat of a split state, as has taken place in several other countries." Moreover, it argues that the present state policy toward religion "does not fully meet the modern challenges of national and regional security, and the needs of a modern, democratic, and secular society." Its authors also observe "the weakening of traditional Islam" and that "the contradictions in the Muslim community lead to a loosening of the traditional Hanafi Sunni Islam." In order to tackle these issues, a "fundamental revision of the principles and methods of the interaction between state and religion" have been put in place, realized through "making changes and amendments to the relevant legislation." The document then lists nineteen different topics, several of which contain up to eight further subpoints, and it does so in the name of "the defense of national culture and national identity" (*uluttuk madaniaty zhana birdeilikti*). In the final two sentences, we find the following stipulation: "it is proposed . . . to appoint only those imams and *kazi*s who know and follow the Hanafi school which is customary [*salttuu*] for Kyrygz Muslims, and to not allow the establishment of foreign behavior, dress, and appearance."

What President Atambaev is promoting is thus a customary version of shariat, one that combines the "right kind" of Islam with the "right kind" of custom. This version of shariat not only is compatible with state law but is also in line with "national culture and national identity." And while Atambaev tries to set an example through his own personal behavior, he also issues decrees to realize this conjunction by means of state law.

CUSTOMARY SHARIAT

Talking to the village imam as well as to other villagers from both of my fieldsites about what these new legal documents mean for the relationship between Islam and *salt*, I encountered a neologism that I had not heard during earlier stages of my fieldwork: *salttu shariat* (customary Islamic law). Nasir Baike, the village imam of Aral, was the first person to mention it to me in 2015:

> Now there is such a thing called *salttuu shariat*. Atambaev, the president, accepted it. Our Prophet also said to practice and use *salt*, which would not harm or violate shariat. For example, men wearing hats, or women wearing long dresses. Starting from the face to the foot, females have to cover all these parts. We had this in our *salt*, too. A long time ago, our ancestors also used to wear long coats [*chapan*] and women had scarves on their heads. It goes well with shariat [*shariatka tuura kelet*]. They also practiced this. Now people have started to wear short clothing, so we go and explain to them that a long time ago we had this other kind of clothing and now we will have it again.

In this statement, similar versions of which I also heard from other villagers in both villages, the "proper" dress code of Kyrgyz people is positioned against those who "wear short clothing."[16] At the same time, however, the imam also distanced himself from those who have recently come "close to religion" (*dinge zhakin*), meaning young men with long beards and women who had begun to wear the hijab instead of knotting their scarves behind their heads. He was thereby demonstrating his agreement with the "President's fatwa." Baiyz Apa, however, described the recent appearance of the hijab among women in her village (and in her family) as being in accordance with both *salt* and shariat: "During our times, we also had covering clothing—when my mother was still alive. It is our *salt*. It is also correct in shariat." We can understand this neologism of "customary shariat" as the customization of shariat or as the Islamization of *salt*, depending on the context and the person asked. In the case of Baiyz Apa, it can be both at the same time. Going back to classical scholarship on Islamic law, we learn that "custom and customary law have coexisted with the ideal theory of Islamic law, while remaining outside its system, in the whole of the Islamic world. As a point of historical fact, custom contributed a great deal to the formation of Islamic law, but the classical theory of Islamic law was concerned not with its historical development but with the systematic foundation of law, and the consensus of the scholars denied conscious recognition to custom" (Schacht [1964] 1982, 63).

Despite previous and novel entanglements, people in contemporary Kyrgyzstan continue to exclaim that *salt* "wins" over shariat (*salt zhenget*), even if some say that it should be otherwise. "We are not letting go of *salt*" (*saltty ketibei atyrbyz biz*) is another common expression, as is "*salt* is changing with the times" (*zamanga zharasha salt özgörüp kelat*). While *salt* is thus watched over so that it remains "ours," the maintenance of clearly separate legal repertoires is difficult. All three—*salt*, shariat, and state law—overlap; which is considered dominant or more legible in a given context depends on the situation and the actors involved. This kind of entwining of legal repertoires is best understood by looking at how these repertoires evolved historically. Many of the current debates go back to developments that occurred over the last three centuries, when it became advantageous to imperial and Soviet politics to postulate the separate existence of *salt*, shariat, and state law.

Chapter 1

HISTORIES OF LEGAL PLURALITY

There are no written records of Kyrgyz customary law prior to the conquest of Central Asia by the troops of the Russian tsar Nikolai in the second half of the nineteenth century. This presents a contrast to Mongolia or even nearby Kazakhstan, where written legal codes exist from the seventeenth century onward (see Levchine 1840, 401; Sneath 2007, 76, 79–80). Thus, we have little information about how everyday life was ordered according to customary law in pre-tsarist times. During tsarist times, however, army officers, ethnographers, and other scholars were sent out on expeditions and fieldwork to investigate the "customary law" (Russ. *obychnoe pravo*) of the new societies of the expanding tsarist empire.[1] Grodekov (1889) came closest to emic conceptions of customary law, investigating what he called *iuridicheskii byt'* (a Russian term meaning juridical everyday life). Additionally, while Russian literature on "the Kyrgyz" abounds, these documents usually deal not with the Kyrgyz of contemporary Kyrgyzstan, but with the Kazakh.[2] By the time the Russians had reached what is present-day Kyrgyz territory, they had already done a lot of research on the Kazakh. The findings of these early ethnographers were later used by the tsarist administration to formalize and codify what came to be understood as customary law, and to subsequently degrade it as "primitive" in relation to the newly introduced "civilized" laws of the Russian colonial empire.[3] Russian officials and scholars in this way "invented" customary law by locating it within a body of customs that they themselves had written up and which might have reflected the customary law of a particular descent group or a particular region, but certainly not that of the whole society. One has to bear in mind that the overarching goal of the tsarist and, later, the Soviet administrations was to understand Central Asian societies in order to change them according to their own ideologies.[4] "Customary law" as formulated by Russian ethnographers thus needs to be understood as a product of Western (legal) thinking as well as a local response to new socioeconomic developments.[5] These biases make it difficult to reconstruct *the* history of Kyrgyz customary law because the Russian sources themselves, as well as their interpretations and local adaptations, are highly contested. This is equally true for the public discourse on custom and customary law in Kyrgyzstan today. In this book, I do not differentiate between an "invented" and an "authentic" or "traditional" way of performing *salt* but, rather, investigate all those instances in which my informants speak of or in the name of this legal repertoire. Hobsbawm and Ranger (1983) have argued, first, that traditions are invented in order to cement group cohesion; second, that such inventions legitimize action; and third, that they occur most often in times of rapid social transformation. Similarly, I have thus far asserted that *salt* binds people together; that by invoking *salt*, people reason about their behavior; and that Kyrgyzstan is often talked about as being in a state of "transformation." However, Hobsbawm and Ranger then go on to differentiate between "invented" and "old traditional practices" and see it as the task of scholarship to delineate the differences between the two (1983, 10). The notion of the "invention of tradition" set off a lively discussion about the extent to which history can be invented at all. Other authors are critical of what they view as an overemphasis on the instrumental use of history within anthropology. Sahlins, for example, rejects the concept altogether, describing it as an "easy functionalist dismissal of the people's claims of cultural distinction" (1999, 399). While I pay particular attention to those situations in which *salt* is explicitly performed in public, I also take Sahlins's critique into account. If one is interested in how the past is consciously and unconsciously "actualized" (Giordano 1996), one has to be prepared to receive seemingly contradictory information. One actor's thick description of the world is not necessarily congruent with another's. Taking such world making seriously means acknowledging multivocality (see Rapport and Overing 2000, 391). Therefore, I weave emic perspectives and oral histories from the people of Aral and Engels into the historical account of Kyrgyz customary law.

People in Aral and Engels delineate time into periods of different rulers. The Kyrgyz past begins with "the time of Manas" (*Manas ubagynda*), which refers to the time before the Russians arrived in the area and dates back to a mythical past when Manas Ata (Father Manas), the epic ancestor of all Kyrgyz, ruled. The time of the Russian conquest is remembered as "the time of Nikolai" (*Nikolai ubagynda*), in reference to Tsar Nikolai [II]. "Soviet time" (*Sovet ubagynda*)—also called "the time of the kolkhoz" (*kolkhoz ubagynda*)—is often further delineated according to who had been the respective First Party Secretary chairing the Union (e.g., *Khrushchev ubagynda* or *Brezhnev ubagynda*). The contemporary era is referred to as "the time of Independence" (*Egemendüülük ubagynda*). The period up to 2005 is today known by the term "the time of Akaev" (*Akaev ubagynda*), referring to the first president of the country, who had to flee during the so-called March Revolution in 2005.

"THE TIME OF MANAS"

In former times the basic economic and territorial unit of the Kyrgyz was the encampment (*aiyl*), composed of several yurts set up by "children of one father" (*bir atanyn baldary*) (Abramzon 1971, 183; Schmitz 1990, 73). They formed a social and economic entity in the sense that during the winter months people lived together in one encampment in the valley (*kyshtak*), and in the summer months herded together on a common pastureland in the mountains (*zhailoo*). As the translation suggests, the "children of one father" not only shared a territory but were perceived as agnatic relatives from the same descent line (*uruu*). However, the encampment was probably a much more flexible arrangement where not only agnates and their families but also cognates and non-kin resided together.[6]

Each uruu is said to have been led by an elder (*eng uluu aksakal*; lit. "the oldest whitebeard"), who presided over the activities of the unit and acted as mediator in cases of dispute. During larger gatherings (*kurultai*), councils (*kengesh*), and life-cycle rituals such as births, marriages, and deaths, people could put forth their problems to be discussed among these leading old men. Kyrgyz society was highly stratified before the Russians arrived. In the Manas epic, the Kyrgyz hero is described as having descended from a line of kings, and Kyrgyz society as thoroughly aristocratic.[7] In addition to the *aksakals*, there were other individuals responsible for dispute management, such as the *biis* (also *bais*) and the *manaps*. According to Khazanov (1983, 175), the bii was a hereditary leader who ruled his own land and had his own followers. Radloff (1893) noted that biis exercised administrative and legal functions over their subjects. Brusina (2005, 230) differentiates between the activities of aksakals and biis by saying that the tasks of biis were larger, as they mediated between encampments as well as within and between descent lines. In addition to the biis, Russian ethnographers described the manaps as hereditary leaders who, according to Radloff (1893, 533), had "almost despotic power over their people." In order to maintain control and accumulate wealth, manaps imposed taxes on their followers for the use of pastures or for driving a herd through the manap's land.[8] They undertook raids on neighboring encampments in order to take their land and exact tribute from them, and they enlarged their herds by stealing others' livestock. Recent research by Daniel Prior (2014) has shown, however, that we should no longer understand the institution of manaps as one of the traditional aristocratic forms of local authority, as previously argued, but more as a local response by Kyrygz elders to the Russians' search for clearly demarcated political offices. Prior traces the origin of the term *manap* back to the nineteenth century, when it appeared for the first time in the context of negotiations between Russian state officials and some Kyrgyz leaders who, in contrast to the Kazakhs, had no "sultans" to send forth to the negotiation table when the possibility of submission to the Russian tsar was being discussed. Sartori notes that Prior attributes the coinage of the term *manap* to "something like an 'observer effect' or colonial feedback in the decades of political negotiation and accommodation between 1845 and 1864" (Sartori 2014, 16). In the terminology I put forward here, the institution of the manap thus emerged in the context of colonial socioeconomic change and was then customized by Kyrgyz society, which began to conceptualize it as having always existed among the Kyrgyz.

In not quite so mythical times, but still before the Russians arrived, the khanate of Kokand was established in the southern Fergana Valley in 1709–1710 (see figure 1.1). This was of relevance for the Kyrgyz because between 1825 and 1830 the western part of present-day Kyrgyzstan was gradually annexed by the khanate over the course of several battles.[9] While the khans tried to replace earlier Turko-Mongolian laws in the khanate with Islamic law, at no point did jurisdiction, taxation, and education follow Islamic principles exclusively (Babadjanov 2004, 153–54; Newby 2005).[10] In fact, the khans had great difficulty strengthening the position of Islamic law in the khanate. Often they were unable to compete with local interpretations of Islamic practices. By way of contrast, recent historical research has shown that Islamic knowledge was widespread among the Kazakhs in the Emirate of Bukhara, and Islamic principles appear to have gained much more traction in the emirate than in the Kokand Khanate. Allen Frank (2014) depicts the Kazakh nomadic population as being firmly located in the Hanafite school with in-

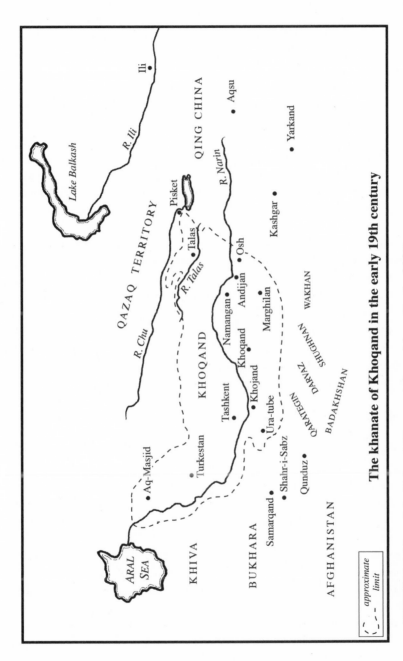

FIGURE 1.1. Map of the Kokand Khanate (adapted from Newby 2005).

depth knowledge of Islamic law, while at the same time applying customary law (adat). It is this "everyday literacy of Central Asian nomads" (Sartori 2014, 19) that requires further scholarly attention, as it cannot be located in the official historical accounts of the Russians who needed to stress that, prior to their arrival, Central Asia had been "uncivilized."

The late coming Kyrgyz themselves, who had migrated to Central Asia as recently as the sixteenth century from the upper Yenisei River area in Siberia, adopted Islam through Sufism, which aligned well with the animistic practices that they also maintained (Schoeberlein 2007, 32). Thus the khanate was not uniformly organized but was, rather, a conglomerate of different sedentary and pastoralist groups. Those who did not want to become subjects of the khanate had to move further north into the inaccessible mountains to which present-day Talas province certainly belonged.

The word *aksakal* appears throughout the records from the time of the khanate, where it refers to so-called head traders that the different rulers of the khanate had sent to all major towns in Xinjiang (China) to administer the affairs of their own merchant communities and to collect taxes for the Kokandian khan (Newby 2005, 65, 69). Those aksakals, however, were not the Kyrgyz elders who headed descent lines and functioned as mediators in cases of dispute, and whom we learn about mostly from Russian records of the tsarist period, referred to by Kyrgyz as "the time of Nikolai."

"THE TIME OF NIKOLAI"

When the Russians arrived in Central Asia in the early nineteenth century, the Kyrgyz were in the process of fighting against the Kokandian rulers. While they initially also fought against the Russian invaders, the Kyrgyz living around Lake Yssyk Köl sent a delegation to Russia to ask for help against the khan. They later allied with the Russian troops, while other Kyrgyz continued fighting against the Russians. The renegade Kyrgyz were eventually defeated and brought under Russian control. In 1867 the tsarist incursions into Central Asia ended with the transformation of Kokand into a vassal state. The so-called Governorate-General of Turkestan was established, which consisted of the two provinces of Semireche and Syr-Dar'ia.[11] The local administration was reorganized on the basis of the "Rules for the Siberian Kyrgyz," which had earlier been elaborated by the Russian statesman Mikhail Speranskii for the Kazakh territory.

These rules called for a territorial and administrative reorganization and promoted the "civilizing mission" of the Russians while arguing to preserve the "native customs" of the locals (Martin 2001, 34–45). At the same time, the Russians tried to stifle the influence of shariat in an effort to disentangle the two legal repertoires, which they knew were in fact intertwined. But at this point in history, "Islam was to be ignored, not destroyed" (Khalid 2007, 37).

Although Russian government officials feared hostile reactions, they introduced administrative changes such as elections to establish some sort of accountability and regularity.[12] The villages or encampments, for example, were supposed to be headed by an aksakal whom the local population should elect for a term of three years. In 1868 a second decree was issued that established military courts for the resolution of disputes between locals and the immigrating Russians, as well as the so-called people's courts, which came to be headed by biis (Brusina 2005; Huskey and Iskakova 2002). Following these reforms, the biis were recast as judges who had to be elected, meaning that their office was no longer hereditary. Their decisions could be appealed or even annulled by the Russian administration (Kozhonaliev [1963] 2000, 68). They had to keep records, and they received an official stamp for this purpose. Generally, they only dealt with minor issues, whereas the Russian courts dealt with serious offenses such as homicide.

All of these new policies, especially having to elect one's representatives, were alien to the region and "something of a fiction in practice" (Sneath 2007, 83). Schuyler (1885, 33) mentioned that as a result of these electoral procedures, discontent escalated into open insurrection in the late nineteenth century. The decrees of 1867 and 1868 also stipulated that customary law had to be written down in the form of regulations (*erezhe*), thereby continuing the codification of what the Russian administration considered "legal traditions." Such regulations were then to be used as precedents in the courts of biis. As the two decrees did not specify the character of the erezhe further, these regulations took various formats, and no consistent codification of customary law was achieved (Kozhonaliev [1963] 2000, 266; Sartori and Shablei 2015). Likewise, the Russians never managed to transform Islamic law into statutory law (Sartori 2011, 301).[13] In the southern areas of present-day Kyrgyzstan yet another institution became incorporated into the Russian legal system—the shari'a-based *kazy* courts.[14] Unlike the aksakals, biis, and manaps, the kazys had to complete a special course of education to be recognized as judges even prior to "the time of Nikolai" (Kozhonaliev [1963] 2000, 39). Studies on the work of the kazy and Islamic law in general appeared only after 1892. From recent historical works we also know that the Russian Empire allowed Islamic judges to draw on and even come up with local "customs." The interdependence of shariat and customary law is also well known from other Islamic contexts. Judith Scheele, in her work on the Touat region of Algeria, speaks of "a system based on inherent contradictions" that defies "all attempts at classification" (2010, 352, 350). She points out that for the local *qadi*s, the maintenance of peace was more important than the strict application of one or the other type of law.

Russian imperial administrators applied legal reforms to differing degrees throughout Central Asia, and it seems that Russian control was exercised to a far lesser extent in the area of my fieldsite in present-day Talas than in the less mountainous areas, such as the region around Bishkek, the Kazakh steppe, and the Fergana Valley. Thus, it is not surprising that my informants' perceptions of these developments diverge from the accounts of the authors listed above. Consider how Kozhoke Ata, an aksakal from Aral (ninety-five years of age in 2015), recalled how his father ran for the position of *bolush* in 1904:[15]

> Kozhoke Ata: They used to collect small stones from the people. Each person gave a stone. The real democracy was during those times. When the elections were over, they used to count their stones. The one who received the most stones got the position he was running for. My father ran for the position of bolush, but he failed because he couldn't collect enough stones.

> Judith: What was the duty of a bolush?

> Kozhoke Ata: A bolush governed the people, taxed them, and settled disputes. We also had a *starshina* [Russian term for elder]—a kind of an assistant, collecting taxes.[16] But the real power was with the bii. His words were law. He was something like the village khan.

> Judith: Why would people want to become bolush, starshina, or bii?

> Kozhoke Ata: They got a lot of "fruit" [earned a lot]. They didn't get a salary, but they used to tax people.

> Judith: When would people turn to aksakals, then?

> Kozhoke Ata: In a village, aksakals are good and respected people whose words have an effect on others. At that time people used to turn to them rather than to biis, bolushes, or starshinas. An aksakal was not a special-

ly appointed person. He would just solve problems as I do now, demanding nothing from people.

Judith: What happened with the arrival of the Russians?

Kozhoke Ata: We still had these positions, but they had to give taxes to Moscow. They would get orders to collect a certain amount of tax. If Moscow said, "Pay one sheep," they would say, "Pay two sheep." Those biis, bolushes, and starshinas, they existed before 1917. Aksakals still exist.

Kozhoke Ata's words give us valuable insight into how contemporary elders conceptualize the arrival of the Russians and the transformation of the administrative and legal positions of their leaders. Kozhoke Ata presents "real democracy" as a characteristic of early Kyrgyz sociality, and his reference to the bii as the "village khan" supports scholarly assumptions about the strong position of the bii in former times. He differentiated between the elected "village elder" (Russ. *starshina*), a position that existed only during "the time of Nikolai," and the less specific aksakal, whom he regarded as different: they were not appointed and "did not demand anything" for their dispute mediation. Of course, one has to take into account that he, as an aksakal himself, might have a vested interest in portraying those aksakals of previous generations in a positive light. However, he was not the only one to do so: aksakals are expected to act in ways that emphasize aspects of giving (i.e., mediating free of charge), and if they take payment in any form, then it is only because others want to show respect to them.

The unintended consequence of the administrative restructuring on the village level was that the elected leaders started taxing their people twice as much as before because they now had to share their "fruit" with the Russians. According to Brusina (2005, 242–43), people also tried to ensure the appointment of their own relatives to the position of bii, using methods ranging from the manipulation of elections to the murder of other candidates. Once in office, the new bii also started "staging" cases and selling decisions.[17] Here we see the beginning of the transformation of the plural legal landscape. As the Fergana Valley was initially less targeted by the reforms, Brusina (2000) reports that northerners brought their dispute cases to the southern kazy courts instead. More often, however, dispute management shifted completely away from the institutionalized courts toward those aksakals who had not been recognized as officials by the administration and who "demanded nothing from people," as Kozhoke Ata said. They commanded the respect and confidence of the local people and to some extent took the place of the biis, who by the turn of the century had already been "russified" (Sabataev 1900, 66–67). These were the aksakals Kozhoke Ata was referring to and about whose roles in rural society we know very little from historical sources (see Wilde 2014, 275).[18] What is well documented, though, is their increasing incorporation into the Russian administrative structure; for example, as tax collectors, in police functions, and as heads of bazaar guilds (Nalivkin 1886, 208; Sartori 2008, 86). These positions were in demand because they came with economic privileges. However, even my oldest informants do not equate the term *aksakal* with any of these positions, as Kozhoke Ata made clear.

Recent research on imperial rule suggests that the most common form of interaction between the colonizers and the colonized was accommodation rather than indifference or resistance (Burbank and Cooper 2010).[19] However, in their own accounts people in Talas stress that *salt* was only partly affected by Russian influence, despite policies that, especially during Soviet times, aimed at the eventual eradication of "customary law" (see below). These oral histories tell us how people in Talas remember history today, in its localized and certainly idealized version; they are "modes of telling" that "tell us at least as much about day-to-day ordering struggles as they do about 'real' history" (Law 1994, 52). According to these stories, *salt* was (and continues to be) inextricably related to everyday life and is seen as embodied in those aksakals who were not incorporated into the Russian administrative system in the first place. Thus, in their accounts, villagers make an effort to clearly delineate "our" custom from "their" policies. As aksakals were not necessarily noblemen or leaders but simply heads of their families and their encampments, they likely might have escaped the scrutiny of the reform measures. This policy of underestimating "old people" did not change during the "Soviet time."

"SOVIET TIME"

After the October Revolution in 1917, it was two years before the so-called Turkestan Commission was sent to Central Asia as the plenipotentiary of the Communist Party (Haugen 2003, 3). Renamed several times, the task of the commission was to accomplish the national delimitation that was to completely reorganize Central Asia and which would ultimately lead to the establishment of the "Kirghiz Autonomous Soviet Socialist Republic" on March 7, 1927. The same year, along with many other sweeping reforms, the Soviets tried to clean up the plural legal situation they had found, and they officially abolished what they had come to understand as institutions of customary law. At the same time, the people were forced to settle down in their winter encampments on a permanent basis and urged to give up transhumance. In contrast to many other areas of northern Kyrgyzstan, however, people residing in what is today Aral and Engels did not have to hand over their land to incoming Russian settlers (see Brower 2003, 126–27). Both Russian and Kyrgyz scholars started to depict the former Kyrgyz leaders as exploiters of their own people, and pre-tsarist history as one of "nomadic feudalism" (Vladimirtsov 2002; see also Sneath 2007). With the first phase of collectivization, the property and cattle of the "class enemies"—the rich manaps and biis—were confiscated.[20]

Government officials then started to enforce state atheism by destroying mosques (and churches in other parts of Central Asia) and intimidating believers.[21] Thus, along with the eradication of "backward" rituals and customs of the people and the targeting of the property of feudal overlords (Russ. *kulak*) came the forceful displacement of Islamic values from the public eye. Masalbek Ata, an aksakal and former history teacher from Engels, recalled some of the changes that occurred during this period:

> With the formation of *artel*s [Russ. (small) work units; sing. *artel'*], sedentarization started. In 1937, *moldo*s [Islamic teachers], *kulak*s and *bai*s [rich people] were sent away. They were called "counter-revolutionaries." They [the Russians] destroyed our mosques. The first secretary of the district committee came from Yssyk Köl [another province] to us and said, "Kyrgyz don't need mosques." The Communists were like this. They were against religion. They used to make fun of those who fasted and said, "There is no God." And they ordered us to burn our mosques. During the Soviet time *moldo* was just a word. They drank vodka like the others. The real moldos were sent away to Siberia or did not dare to leave the houses that people had started building here in 1938.

In the nineteenth century the Russians had allowed legal plurality to exist in order to facilitate their indirect rule. They had also artificially separated customary law from shariat. But with the advent of Soviet rule, state officials not only (physically) removed the feudal leaders as well as the heads of the mosques (the imams) and Islamic teachers (moldos), they also used other "techniques" to transform everyday life, such as the emancipation of women, the education of the youth, the empowerment of the poor, and more generally the enforcement of secularism vis-à-vis both customary law and religious law.[22] But while the Kyrgyz biis, manaps, kazys, and bolushes were muzzled in the early Soviet period, the aksakals seem not to have been targeted by Soviet policies.

Remembering the official position toward the elders, the former head of the aksakal court in Aral recalled, "They said 'those old people should rest.'" He was referring to the fact that, officially speaking, aksakals had no duties in the kolkhozes. They were simply not recognized by the administration as politically or legally relevant actors, although toward the end of the tsarist empire notice had been taken that people were increasingly turning to aksakals for help, and they continued to settle disputes in their roles as elders of descent lines (uruu) throughout Soviet time (Brusina 2005, 249; see Beyer 2006 for examples). In 1943 the Soviets established the so-called Spiritual Directorate of the Muslims of Central Asia (SADUM), which was officially free from the influence of state officials but was in fact under the authority of the Soviet state apparatus.[23]

Just as state ethnographers and military officials had codified "customary law" earlier, "religion" also became a state matter. Soviet officials wanted to keep the practices of Islam and customary law separate because they considered the intertwining of the two repertoires hostile to the official Soviet Muslim hierarchy that staffed the clerical administrations and the mosques.[24] By issuing legal opinions (fatwas) and by setting up a tight and highly elaborate administrative structure, the SADUM tried to regulate Islamic doctrine, despite often not realizing the complex interrelation of customary law and shariat. SADUM officials advocated an ideal-typical notion of Islam, cleansed of the seemingly deviant cultural variations that they simply declared "un-Islamic."

As in other regions, however, the proclaimed superiority of Islamic law over customary law did not take root in Talas: people continued to practice customary law alongside shariat and the newly introduced Russian civil law.[25] Massell even states that new legal institutions were "traditionalized" as soon as they came into contact with the Central Asian population. Even the use of force and the removal of village imams did not lead to the renunciation of customary law for the sake of "Soviet-sponsored mobilization" (Massell [1968] 1980, 231–32).[26] While trying to keep Islam under control, SADUM officials found themselves increasingly fighting "customs" whenever these practices acquired a religious aspect, such as in the case of funeral rituals. High-ranking officials in particular had to observe strict secular etiquette and could find themselves denounced if they were caught conducting religious rituals (Kandiyoti and Azimova 2004, 331). The main means of this fight, the SADUM-issued fatwa, resembled ordinary Soviet bureaucratic decrees in structure and style, only with added religious citations from the Qur'an or the *hadith*.[27] Accordingly, most people seem to have rejected the theological validity of the fatwas, treating them just like other documents issued by a distant bureaucracy (Babadjanov 2004, 168).

In addition to the establishment of a new judiciary, so-called comrades' courts (Russ. *tovarishcheskii sud*) were formed on the kolkhoz level. These courts were responsible for keeping peace within the village and for mediation between villagers. However, it was the local party secretary who nominated persons for membership in this court, selecting those who were most active in the kolkhoz. The party committee would then appoint these individuals. The comrades' courts could not make any decisions in dispute cases and were not even allowed to impose fines.[28] In that regard, they resembled the tsarist-era "people's courts," which were equally constrained and also set up in a top-down manner. By 1936 more than five hundred of these courts already existed in the kolkhozes throughout Kyrgyzstan, together with other new institutions of local self-governance such as the village council and the women's council (Nurbekov 1981, 83). As Massell has argued:

> The new legal system in Soviet Central Asia constituted a fundamental challenge to the structure and life-style of local communities. . . . [I]t called into question the basic assumptions underlying the prevailing belief and value systems, and thus invited radical skepticism about the moral basis of society; . . . it threatened a *total* abrogation of the primordial status system, beginning with the structure and hierarchy of sexual [*sic*] and generational roles; . . . it negated ancient paradigms of solidarity and trust, sanctioned the abrogation of traditional social controls, and cast grave doubt on the justice, utility and hence legitimacy of the entire social order. (Massell [1968] 1980, 241–42, emphasis in original)

If we take Massell's statement at face value, we can understand why since 1991 scholars have come to argue that history in Central Asia (and the other so-called postsocialist countries) is currently being "(re)invented": it is commonly perceived as having been perverted, undermined, and destroyed during Soviet times.[29] But it was not their "entire social order" that the Kyrgyz called into question. While the Soviets tried to establish "religion" and "customary law" as separate domains, people's attachment to their practices, which made no such formal distinction, only grew (see, e.g., Hirsch 2005; Northrop 2004; Shahrani 1984). While the public infrastructure and the *ulama* had been destroyed and persecuted, Islam continued to be practiced within families, where it became part of custom. The fact that even today essential parts of life-cycle events are conducted at night, such as the Islamic marriage ceremony *nike*, shows how people managed to carry out rituals that were officially forbidden and punishable during Soviet times. On the kolkhoz level, these activities were well known to the low-level officials, many of whom were actively involved in these rituals themselves. In addition to these acts of silent resistance, another process was taking place: that of customization, by means of which people gradually reinterpreted new developments as "ours," merging them with already acknowledged aspects of *salt*. Current state and religious officials continue to struggle with the entanglement of religion and custom in the same ways that their predecessors did, and their personal roles are as complex as those of previous leaders.

As customary law officially no longer existed after its abolition in 1927, no further Soviet-era publications dealt with this topic. The only publication about Kyrgyz customary law was by Kozhonaliev, who simply compiled already existing ethnographies and reports. A second edition of his book, *Obychnoe pravo Kyrgyzov* (The customary law of the Kyrgyz), came out in 2000 and was financed by the Soros Foundation. After not having been of interest to Soviet historians and ethnographers, Kyrgyz custom and customary law seems to have regained importance in what Kyrgyz call "the time of Independence."

"THE TIME OF INDEPENDENCE"

Kyrgyzstan declared independence from the Soviet Union on August 31, 1991. It largely took over the Soviet legal system, which was then subjected to various reform initiatives, sometimes referred to as "legal transplants" (Knieper 2010), which were coordinated and financed by Western states and international organizations. Law reforms were considered a necessary aspect of the "transition" from socialism to democracy, from plan to market, and from rule by decree to rule of law (see Beyer 2004 and 2005a).[30] A constitution was adopted on May

5, 1993, which has been amended several times since then, most recently in 2010 (see Beyer 2015a). With each constitutional reform the rights of the president have been extended, including increased power over the judiciary. In accordance with these rights, the country's first president, Askar Akaev (1990–2005), suggested the establishment of the "courts of elders" (*aksakaldar sotu*). They are mentioned for the first time in the Kyrgyz constitution of 1993 and are supposed to settle dispute cases according to "the historically established customs and traditions of the Kyrgyz," as stipulated in articles 2 and 3 of a separate "law on the aksakal courts."[31] With an aksakal court being set up in every village (see figure 1.2), almost every tenth person over the age of seventy has been turned into a "wise elder" (Ibraeva 2007, 7). Similar developments can be observed in Kazakhstan, where courts of biis and courts of elders have been created anew and where customary law has come to be recognized as the source of state law in the civil code and several other codes (Kenzhaliev 2005, 340). The Uzbek state tried to restore the neighborhood community (Uzb. *mahalla*) to its purported precolonial role, where elders (Uzb. *oqsoqol*) play an important part as well. The setup of the aksakal courts in Kyrgyzstan was meant to support Akaev's nation-building project, furthering decentralization and giving villagers a subsidiary stake in local self-governance. Campaigns proclaiming the "uninterrupted" existence of the Kyrgyz state for 2,200 years and asserting that the *Manas* epic represented the history of all Kyrgyz served to build a sense of national identity (see Van der Heide 2008). While he published a series of books about the Kyrgyz state, Akaev struggled at the same time not only to reform the country's economic, political, and legal system but also to define what it meant to be "Kyrgyz" in the first place. For this purpose, Akaev not only elevated the significance of certain places and historical figures but also related these to contemporary challenges that independence had brought with it. He addressed this in a speech to aksakal court members in February 2005, emphasizing the aksakals' strong links to their forefathers, the inherent "Kyrgyz" character of the institution, and its suitability for modern reforms:

> While I was writing my book *Kyrgyz Statehood and the National Epos "Manas"* I had to read and review the history of the Kyrgyz people through the whole 2,200 years of its existence. I determined that Kyrgyz people were a united force back then. They not only built on their spiritual nomadic civilization, but also knew how to govern them-

FIGURE 1.2. Elders attending a meeting with state officials in Talas (2005).

selves. The Kyrgyz aksakals and their courts played a big role in this regard. This becomes clear when reading Kazybek's poem.[32] He said: "One word was said to those who overstep the limits. There were not any courts and no police, just aksakals working together, admonishing each other." . . . Since last year we have been working on local self-governance. This does not mean that we are copying Western countries, as some people think. These principles of self-governance were in the history of the Kyrgyz people. There have never been aksakal courts in the history of other countries.

Kyrgyzstan has seen the rise and fall of various institutions involved in dispute settlement by means of "customary law." At all times the relationship between state-making projects and what officials perceived as a "competing social (or legal) order" has proved difficult: customary law was never easy to pin down, either for government agencies or for scholars. While devoted to understanding the "juridical everyday life" (Grodekov 1889) of the Kyrgyz, Russian and early Soviet authors codified some of its rules and incorporated some of its institutions into the Russian legal system, but they never really grasped how "custom" ordered everyday life. Nevertheless, in every phase of Kyrgyz history the distant center acknowledged this "other" kind of law existing alongside and being entwined with Islamic law and state law, a recognition that became manifest most recently in the establishment of the aksakal courts and in the way they are supposed to operate.

By means of "customization," my informants in Kyrgyzstan present history not as something that happens to them but as something they make happen. This became evident in the statement of Kozhoke Ata, who termed the pre-tsarist era as the time of "real democracy" and who described the Russified biis as "village khans," the Russian starshinas as having existed "before the Russians came," and the kolkhoz directors as the new "heads" (*bash*). Officials seem to have always had trouble compartmentalizing that which the people consider a single entity. They tried to fight "customary law" with "noncustomary law" but never managed to grasp exactly what they were fighting: *salt* was too deeply embedded in practice to be codified, and too strongly embodied in people to be institutionalized.

Chapter 2

SETTLING DESCENT

When I returned to my fieldsite in the summer of 2008 after almost two years away, the most visible change to the landscape was a bronze monument erected on the main street leading into the provincial town of Talas in the northwesternmost province of Kyrgyzstan. Guarding the entrance to the valley in which the two villages where I carried out long-term fieldwork are located, there is now a statue of Bürgö Baatyr. Vested in full armor, the hero is sitting on his horse with two tigers at his feet, baring their teeth. The installation is more than six meters high, including the brick base. A granite plaque is affixed to the base, depicting a spear supporting a flag adorned with small ornaments, as well as the numbers "XVIII–XIX" engraved into the lower left-hand corner of the plate: the centuries during which Bürgö Baatyr lived. This hero is the ancestor of Kudaibergen Ata and Baiyz Apa. Listening to their stories and participating in their lives, I have inevitably come to associate the villages Aral and Engels, as social and physical places, with them. It was also due to their financial contribution that the statue of Bürgö Baatyr was erected in the spring of 2008, manifesting their efforts to imprint the self-image of their descent line (*uruu*) onto the landscape (see figure 2.1). The term *uruu* has often been equated to "tribe" in English and *plemia* in the Russian literature. Another Kyrgyz term, *uruk*, is often translated as "clan" in English or *rod* in Russian. Sometimes, however, *uruk* is also translated as "lineage." In any case, it is quite likely that *uruu* is derived from the genitive form of *uruk*, indicating a specific person's *uruk*, although the terms have taken on slightly different meanings over time.[1] As the term *uruk* is not used in my fieldsite, I do not deal with this nuance here. According to my informants' accounts and their own (written) genealogies, an uruu is made up of a group of agnates who view themselves as having descended from a common ancestor. Uruu is thus a

FIGURE 2.1. The statue of Bürgö Baatyr (2015).

relative term because its range of significance depends on ego and refers to various depths of genealogical descent. In the case of the Bürgö uruu, for example, grown-up males describe themselves as being five generations removed from their ancestor Bürgö Baatyr. An uruu has therefore all the characteristics of a lineage as defined by Evans-Pritchard:

> A lineage in the sense in which we generally employ this word is a group of living agnates, descended from the founder of that particular line. Logically it also includes dead persons descended from the founder—and we sometimes use the word to include them also—but these dead persons are only significant in that their genealogical position explains the relationships between the living. It is clear from the context whether the word is used in a more or less inclusive sense. Clans and lineages have names, possess various ritual symbols, and observe certain reciprocal ceremonial relations. (Evans-Pritchard [1940] 1963, 192)

Note that this definition of lineage, as well as others Evans-Pritchard proffers throughout his book, does not regard lineages as corporate groups. He explicitly refers to a lineage as "*a relation* between a number of smaller units" (Evans-Pritchard [1940] 1963, 115, emphasis added; see also Gudeman and Rivera 1990, 184). I thus understand

FIGURE 2.2. Women and men of the Bürgö uruu slaughter animals for the *tülöö* ritual (2006).

"lineage" as a model that helps to conceptualize relations of difference and the organization of common practices.

Lineage membership plays a material and practical role in everyday life, away from the politicians' stages on which it has so often been instrumentalized since the country's independence.[2] This is visible, for example, in the way people alter and relate to the landscape. I use the expression "settling descent" to refer to a dialectical process in which people alter and make claims upon a physical landscape by performing relatedness (as the people did in erecting the statue of Bürgö Baatyr), while their relationships are simultaneously shaped by their perceptions of place. While both genealogy and landscape appear to be self-contained and eternal, they are in fact not only deeply entangled with each other but also constantly recreated anew over the course of time.[3] The phenomenon of "customization" (discussed in the previous chapter) becomes particularly relevant in the way people in Kyrgyzstan relate to the Russian-induced policies of enforced sedentarization and the structuring and organization of formerly nomadic kin groups into villages and collective farms. It is also manifest in the way they carry out and reflect on their contemporary rituals and practices.

PRAYING FOR RAIN

In May 2006 I took part in a ritual called *tülöö*. The whole day, cars from Bishkek, the capital of Kyrgyzstan, kept arriving: sons and daughters-in-law were coming home for the event. The villagers had been busy throughout the previous two weeks with the planting of their seed potatoes and wheat. Now rain was needed. Early in the morning of May 14, I noticed that people were making their way by horse-drawn carriage down to the river, which flowed by only a few hundred meters from my house. I watched how the first fires were lighted and the smoke of samovars began rising up through the air. I saw yet more people spreading out along the riverbank further down in the direction of the main valley and noticed that the people from my neighborhood stayed together as they walked down from their houses to the river in preparation for the ritual. They were all from the same descent line: the Bürgö uruu. I proceeded down to the river shortly afterward to join "our" group, which had occupied a spot on the riverbank. Women from my neighborhood had spread out table-cloths on the grass, and I observed how newly arriving daughters-in-law added more food to the bread and cookies already laid out. Such food is called *tasmal*, and every household usually brings it to any kind of festivity. I also saw women helping to clean the intestines of the freshly slaughtered animals that younger men were busy butchering (see figure 2.2).

Kudaibergen Ata, the head of the local court of elders and a neighbor of mine, arrived and joined my adoptive grandmother, Baiyz Apa, in giving commands to the women to bring cups, get the samovars going, and tear the large pieces of bread into smaller ones. Baiyz Apa started telling me about the event in which I was about to take part:

> People conduct this tülöö each year in order to ask Allah to give much rain so that there will be enough for the land. We do it once a year in May. We also ask for harmony [*yntymak*] and peace [*tynchtyk*] for the people. Every year different households slaughter [livestock]. This year seven households slaughtered animals. It is a holiday for the village. There are other tülöös there [pointing further down the river where I had seen the fires before]. Another father of yours is there [meaning Kozhoke Ata, another elder]. We separate into uruus today. Kozhoke Ata is Aksak Börü; we are Bürgö. We [Bürgö] are different and they are different.

Baiyz Apa paused, then added, "We used to conduct it together each year. But this year we're doing it separately. I think this father of yours [Kudaibergen Ata] can also tell you why we are doing it separately this year." Kudaibergen Ata, who had listened to what Baiyz Apa was telling me, joined the conversation. Like her, when he used the pronoun "we," he was usually referring to the major descent line, Kaimazar, which included four uruus: Bürgö, Kodol, Chürpö, and Aksak Börü:

> We did not do it together every year. It was like this from the beginning and it is still like this. We have always been doing this. Soon we will unite. Before, when there were only a few people, they used to have a common tülöö, but now the number of people has increased. Before, when we were all united, we were only fifty, sixty, a hundred people. Now when we all come together we are four hundred people. That's why we have it separately. But we all pray for the same thing. We ask Kudai [God] for good things . . . rain, peace. . . . The request as well as the goal of all tülöös is the same. But we need to unite generally and conduct it together. It would be nice to have it together. There is nothing bad about uniting. Over there [pointing down the river again] two uruus are separate: Kodol and Aksak Börü. So we pray in three places today. [Pause.] It was like this before. [Pause.] But we all pray for the same thing. We ask good things from Kudai for people — harmony [yntymak]. This request is the same. It is *salt* coming from Islam. It is obligatory for believers in Muslim countries to ask Kudai once a year, when the year renews itself. It is a good thing.

Baiyz Apa had presented the event as one of coming together, as a "holiday of the village" and as occasioned by the necessary call for rain and the wish for harmony. The term *yntymak*, which Baiyz Apa refers to here, describes an ideal relationship between individuals. It is perceived and presented as being in constant need of manifestation, most often through the presence of elders. Yntymak is not an abstract category, but an explicit demand or diagnosis made by my informants themselves in concrete interactions. The concept is emically understood as a matter of practice as well as of ideology: it is practiced when behavior, whether by individuals or by collective actors, is publicly characterized as communitarian, conciliatory, and in accordance with custom. Baiyz Apa emphasized that in previous years the ritual had been stronger because all the uruus had celebrated together. Kudaibergen Ata, on the other hand, argued that people had organized separate tülöös along uruu lines "from the beginning," a clear statement of the importance of the uruu principle. He then acknowledged, however, that in principle celebrating together "would be nice." His reference to the growing number of uruu members, as well as his description of the ritual as *salt* coming from Islam," may well have been rationalizations produced to deal with the dilemma he was facing; namely, how to reconcile seemingly contradictory interpretations of the event that only surfaced because I was asking.

That the tülöö was conducted separately by each uruu that year prompted the two elders to tell me more about the general delineations along descent lines in the village:

KA: We are Bürgö. Those [pointing downstream] are Kodol. Kodol are the same as we are [in size]. But they only slaughtered three animals, and we slaughtered seven. Aksak Börü are many. Today they are celebrating together with Chürpö. There are only a few Chürpö. So these two uruu united today. In the lower part [of the village] there are more people. In the whole village, there are two *chong uruus*: Zhetigen and Kaimazar.[4] Zhetigen are divided into thirteen smaller uruus. And all those uruus in the other part of the village derive from Zhetigen. From the *kontora* [Russ., referring to the former kolkhoz headquarters in the village center] onward they are Zhetigen, and here and there [pointing toward the mountains behind us in the direction of Engels] live Kaimazar. People from Engels are all Kaimazar. There are only two chong uruus here: Zhetigen and Kaimazar. And from these two uruus people branch out.

BA: They multiply.

Here, Kudaibergen Ata qualified his earlier claim that Kaimazar had split up into uruus this year, celebrating the tülöö separately. Aksak Börü and Chürpö, as it turned out, were celebrating together. When I later joined that group, which had set up camp upriver from the Bürgö uruu, they told me that since there were only a few households of Chürpö in Aral it would have been too boring for their elders to sit alone. So they shared their food and held the event together.

In his comment, Kudaibergen Ata further explained the basic division along descent lines currently prevalent in Aral. According to him, the village is divided in two parts: the four uruus of Bürgö, Kodol, Chürpö, and Aksak Börü all descend from a major descent line whose common ancestor is called Kaimazar. They occupy the "upper" part of Aral, that is, the western part, up to the street leading to the kontora, where today the mayor has his office. The "lower" part of the village, the eastern part, belongs to the thirteen uruus of the

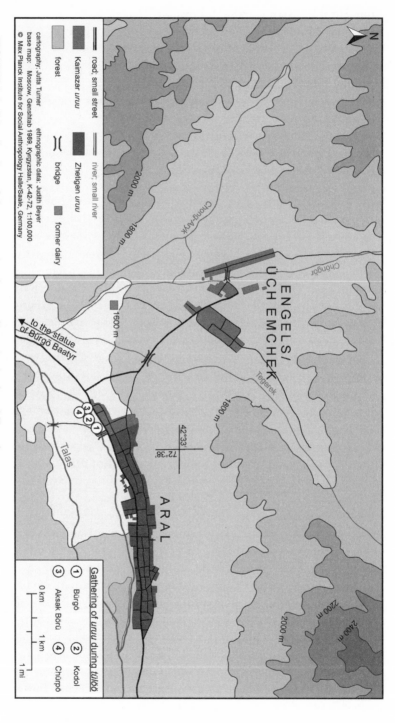

FIGURE 2.3. Distribution of the two major descent lines in Aral and Engels.

Legend:

road; small street

river; small river

Kaimazar *uruu*

Zhetigen *uruu*

forest

bridge

former dairy

cartography: Jutta Turner
base map: Moscow, Genshtab 1989, Kyrgyzstan, K-42/72, 1:100.000
© Max Planck Institute for Social Anthropology Halle/Saale, Germany

ethnographic data: Judith Beyer

ENGELS/
UCH EMCHEK

Chong-Aryk

2000 m

1800 m

Chongör

1600 m

to the statue
of Bürgö Baatyr

Tegerek

1800 m

Talas

ARAL

42°33'

72°38'

2000 m

2200 m

2400 m

Gathering of *uruu* during *tülöö*

① Bürgö   ② Kodol

③ Aksak Börü   ④ Churpö

0 km   1 km   1 mi

N

major descent line named after Zhetigen. Kudaibergen Ata also revealed that all people from the village of Engels are Kaimazar, which means that people from the "upper" part of Aral share a common descent with them. That Aral is split into two parts is also visible in the fact that there are two schools, two pharmacies, and two mosques in the village—one for each "side." We can thus see that the delineation along uruu lines is reflected in the physical layout of the village (see figure 2.3).

While I was listening to the two elders elaborate on the two major descent lines in Aral (Zhetigen and Kaimazar), I became confused. I had recently read a book about the genealogy of Aral written by Bektur Isakov, a local historian who lives on the other side of the village. Isakov describes the principle of an uruu thus:

> Every uruu in Aral helps its members in conducting all kinds of festivities: when there are celebrations, when there are funerals, when there are other events. Best of all, for this kind of help no one will ask for money. Everything is conducted according to equality and everything is done in such a way that every member of the uruu will have an equal share. This is according to *salt* and goes back centuries. . . . The meaning of uruu has never been lost. Collectivity, friendship, yntymak, and help have been important throughout socialist, Muslim, and Buddhist times, as well as during the era of Chingiz Khan. (Isakov 2001, 16)

Nobody in Aral would object to this (idealized) characterization of the uruu. He goes on, however, to note that the two major descent lines in Aral are Zhetigen and Kushchu. The name Kaimazar does not feature in his book. When I pointed out what appeared to me to be an obvious contradiction between Isakov's interpretation and what the two elders had just told me, it came as no surprise to the two elders themselves. They were aware of the contingency of their own and others' interpretations:

KA: Since Bektur himself belongs to Zhetigen, of course he has to praise Zhetigen.

BA: There are many Kushchu too.

KA: In Talas province there are only two [chong uruus]: Kushchu and Saruu. There is no Zhetigen [on the provincial level]. Kushchu and Saruu, only these two. Saruu live on that side [pointing away to the main valley] and Kushchu on this side [sweeping his arm around in an inclusive movement]. But he [Bektur Agai] does not even belong to Kushchu. Zhetigen come from Iran and Iraq.

BA: Yes. It seems they are descendants of the prophet.

KA: Yes, descendants of the prophet. That's why all of them talk like prophets [both laugh].

From this communication we can see that while there seems to be agreement on the importance of the uruu principle as such, the elders accepted that others have their own interpretations of the details of how the uruus break down and what the major divisions are. Kudaibergen Ata revealed his personal understanding of the descent details and did not reproduce the generally agreed-upon discourse. While he explained that, at the level of the village, Kaimazar and Zhetigen are the two main descent lines, he acknowledged that, at the provincial level, Kushchu and Saruu form the hierarchically appropriate opposition. Bektur Agai, on the other hand, had set Zhetigen up against Kushchu. He thereby not only established Kushchu as another commonly shared ancestor of all Kaimazar and therefore as the larger, more encompassing descent group but also elevated his own uruu, Zhetigen, to the status of major descent line, equal to Kushchu, thereby dismissing Saruu as a relevant major descent line in the area. While I had a hard time understanding this move, the two elders did not seem to be confused at all. They had even more examples about how people differed in their accounts on this issue. Kudaibergen Ata suggested that I consult a book on Bürgö Baatyr written by another villager for clarification: "There is a book called *Bürgö Baatyr*. Read that instead. And in that book there is only half a page about Zhetigen," he said, laughing. "Of course everyone praises his own uruu. For instance, Germans praise Germans and not Swiss or Dutch, right?"

We should treat objects such as statues, names, written genealogies, and books about uruu ancestors as valid and relevant interpretations of the general uruu principle as described by Isakov at the beginning of his book. That these objects are clearly influenced by early Russian scholarship and Soviet representational practices and are today used by Kyrgyz politicians in their nation-building efforts should not lead us to treat them simply as instances of "invented traditions." Such influence from "outside" is obvious, particularly in that the practice of codifying genealogies by rendering them in written form, for example, is at odds with the traditional practice of *sanzhyra*, whereby particular elders, the so-called *sanzhyrachy*, recite genealogies orally. Moreover, such codified genealogies are visualized in the form of kinship diagrams and referred to as *genealogüasy*, the Kyrgyz calque of the Russian word *genealogiia*. The fact that such written documents exist is then brought up in conversation whenever people perceive that their personal accounts need further support, although the actual text of the documents is seldom consulted. Customization allows people to sustain the importance of the uruu by creative, new (that is, originally noncustomary) means. In doing so, politicians as well as the general population sustain *salt* as a repertoire to which they can resort when trying to explain how life should be ordered. These different practices and objects are valid even if they are recognized as partial, such as the books of the well-respected village historian. While everybody acknowledged his intellectual scholarship, the two elders were far from accepting his version of the genealogical topography of Aral for themselves. They were in the end very clear about the fact that Kaimazar had been in the area first. When I asked, "And where did Kaimazar come from?" after they had attributed Isakov's uruu origin to "Iran and Iraq," both laughed:

KA: Kaimazar come from here. They have always been here.

BA: Yes [nodding].

KA: They have *always* been here. In Budenyi there is a white monument. It is a big monument of Kaimazar. We came here and owned Zulpukhor Ata [a stone mausoleum located in the Aral graveyard just outside the village]. And later Zhetigen joined us. When they asked for permission to stay, we let them stay. We said, "All right, you may stay."

Through the production of such "prior occupancy" rhetoric, which builds on phrases of domination, references to material objects in the landscape, and emphasis on the strength of one's own uruu, the two elders merged their descent ideology with an ideology about a particular place. I understand this alignment of descent and place as part of a person's or a group's "geographical identity."[5]

It was through attending to the two elders' lives that I understood how such a geographical identity was formed. In telling me about their childhood in the mountains, Soviet policies of sedentarization and subsequent collectivization, working in "the time of the kolkhoz," and about today's ongoing privatization, they also outlined the various periods of "reformation," starting from the 1920s when Russians first entered the area and began to lay down their laws upon people's land.[6] While from an outside perspective, older forms of settlement and administration were enclosed or "stacked" within newer ones like *matrioshka* dolls, villagers each time customized these "reforms" and related to them anew, eventually claiming them as part of their geographical identity. And while these "reforms" were imposed on them as part of a colonial technology, intended to transform a landscape the Russians perceived as "savage," "empty," and in need of "civilization," villagers constantly incorporated these new forms of settlement and organization as part of their own way of living. They altered the imperial landscape, which made it possible to perceive it as "theirs."[7]

THE GRADUAL END OF TRANSHUMANCE

Baiyz Apa grew up in the main valley, about forty kilometers from Aral. In the winter months she lived in an encampment (*kyshtak*) and in the summer months she lived on the pasture (*zhailoo*) where her grandfathers, her father, and her uncles herded animals. She remembers that time fondly:

> I was born in the mountains where people used to set up their yurts. In the wintertime we used to live in the valley, and in the summer we would move [to the pasture]. If one got used to it, it was a nice and interesting life. We used to make good food: in the wintertime, *kymyz-közhö*; in the summer we had *airan* and *kurut* [all dairy products]. Food was good then. Every day we had *besh-barmak* [handmade noodles with meat]! . . . We used to keep in touch with the neighboring yurts. If, for instance, our house was here [pointing], the brother of my father was there [pointing]. He had three children. We used to call him grandfather [*chong-ata*]. There were only a few people in the mountains. And the place of my maternal grandfather was a bit further—three kilometers away from us. There were another three, four yurts. They used to call it *aiyl* at that time. We lived in the yurt for six months. And then we packed our things when it started to snow. In the lower part we also had relatives. We kept in touch with those people. The zhailoo is good! Every day it's like a holiday there.

From Baiyz Apa's nostalgic comment about growing up in the mountains, we can see that her paternal relatives herded their animals together in one place, with her maternal relatives living close by. Recalling her childhood in the mountains not only brought back memories about who had settled together but also references to the homemade dishes and especially the abundance of meat. The good life on the pasture is seen by her as inextricably related to the good food people had.

The first Russians had already arrived before Baiyz Apa was born. While she did not experience the earliest encounters herself, she recalled the stories her parents had told her:

When my mother was a daughter-in-law [kelin], Russian soldiers came and took our animals for food. If they liked a horse, they would just take it. Girls and kelins used to run away from them. They even took our girls and kelins. My mother was a young kelin at that time. I remember my father and my mother saying that Russian soldiers came and that they escaped and hid from them. And if they saw guns, they would take them, too. So that's how Russian soldiers invaded [kaptap ketishti; lit. "flooded"], I don't know which year that was. My mother used to tell me that this happened when she was young. Many people lost their property then. This happened when I had not yet been born.

In 1946 Baiyz Apa was brought to Aral, where she married one of the few men who had not been conscripted into the Soviet armed forces to fight in the war. She described how she was turned into a family member and a member of Bürgö uruu:

I came here after the war. My husband was sixteen years older than I. He was born in 1911 and I was born in 1927. After the war there was a shortage of men [laughing].[8] Life was very difficult. My maternal uncle arranged my marriage, saying to me, "You will go to him, or I will kill you" [laughing]. And it was like he said. It was good. He [her husband] did not beat me a single time. I came here in January of 1946. Six of us came with three horses. We came at night. My maternal uncle had bought me a coat, boots, and a dress. So I was wearing these new things and I thought: Where am I going? What kind of life will I have? I was afraid, thinking what would happen when I got here. When I arrived, many people were in this house [in which she is still living today]. My father-in-law was an aksakal and very respected. Everyone came to welcome me. They organized a feast, invited this house and that house, saying, "Our daughter-in-law has arrived." They made the father of Kainarbek my godfather [ökül-ata]. He had gone to the war and never came back. So they named him ritually. The mother-in-law of our neighbor Raia was my godmother [ökül-ene]. We had a good relationship. So this is how I became a relative and a member of Bürgö. We still had a yurt here then. Once I went in and immediately sat down in the place of honor [tör] [laughing]. When they called me "daughter," I thought I was their daughter and so I sat down in tör. Later I was very embarrassed. My mother [mother-in-law] could have scolded me, but she didn't. I started realizing that the life of a married woman is different. Childhood was gone. I learned living here by working. They told me how to be a daughter-in-law, saying, "You will get up early in the morning. You will make a fire. You will bow" [in front of her parents-in-law]. My mother-in-law was a good person. I did not even call her *kainene* [mother-in-law]. This person made me forget my mother. She welcomed me very well. I never had a conflict with her.

Baiyz Apa "began to belong" by performing her new role as daughter-in-law, by acknowledging her godparents, and by respecting her mother-in-law, who treated her in a way that "made her forget" her biological mother. Through the institution of godparenthood she was incorporated into the descent line of her husband. Bürgö Baatyr, thus, had become her "grandfather." We can also see that while a godfather was needed in order to become an uruu member, no direct interaction with this person was required. The fact that he had not returned from the war and remained unknown to her was not important. The relationships she developed with her godmother and her mother-in-law, on the other hand, were based on constant interaction. It is to these two women a daughter-in-law should turn first with her problems. Baiyz Apa portrayed her mother-in-law in particular in the most positive terms. However, this is also required of daughters-in-law: they are expected to loosen their ties to their parents' house. Sleeping over "at home" after getting married, for example, is not appreciated. Relations with in-laws (*kuda*) are supposed to be conducted only in highly ritualized ways. They require proper performances and involve elaborate exchange practices that are often presented as being motivated by shame-anxiety (*uiat*—see chapter 6).

Kudaibergen Ata, who was born in 1939, remembered stories from his parents about how the first Russians arrived in the area, and he retold the words of his father to me as though he himself had experienced those years:

> We had joined Russia before 1917, when [Tsar] Nikolai was thrown from his throne. And in 1930 they turned the winter encampments into *artel*s. We had five encampments here [in what is now Aral village]: Kara Choku, Taldy Bulak, Terek, Aral, and Birinchi Bolushtuk. You can write them down. And each uruu composed an artel'. You can say an artel' was something like a farmers' association [*dyikan charba*] today. Later we were united into *birikme*s [work units larger than artels]. Ours was called Aral. This was in 1936. We had five birikmes: Zhangy Turmush, Taldy Bulak, Terek, Aral, and Pionir.

Even other Kyrgyz would find it difficult to fully comprehend Kudaibergen Ata's account of how institutional forms and settlement names were constantly changing. As an added complication, he explained the arrival of the Russians in terms of a voluntary alliance. His way of talking about the landscape of Aral and Engels after the Russians came is a perfect example of how descent and new forms of settlement and administration have become entangled and exist alongside one another today.

Since "the time of Manas," the five original winter encampments (*kyshtak*) that Kudaibergen Ata referred to were spread out along a branch of the Talas River over an area of about twenty kilometers. They carried the names of distinctive features of the landscape.[9] Aral, for example, means "island" and refers to a territory surrounded by two branches of the Talas River. This was where the four uruus were celebrating their tülöös in May 2006. It was in these encampments that the different uruus lived in the winter months and to which they returned after a summer spent in the pastures up in the mountains.[10] The westernmost encampment must have had a different name in "the time of Manas," but people only recall the name Birinchi Bolushtuk (literally, "first district"), which hints at the fact that Russians had named it during "the time of Nikolai." Elders recalled that while the first Russians had already come to their valley in 1904, the first foreign families began settling there only in 1912, bringing apples, potatoes, chickens, and vodka with them. The Soviets' decision to rebrand the encampments as artels in 1930 appears to have had little direct impact on the population at that early stage. The most significant change occurred in 1936 when the artels were transformed into birikmes, which villagers sometimes also referred to as "small kolkhozes." It was at that time that the first houses were built for the Kyrgyz inhabitants. In 1937 a large household survey was carried out. This survey not only identified all individuals in all households according to age, sex, and their degree of literacy (almost everyone was recorded as "illiterate" in the survey) but it also noted the number of animals belonging to each household, as well as the crops they planted and the amount of land they owned. A year after this survey was carried out, people had to sign their livestock over to the birikme.[11] Later, in 1955, the inhabitants of Zhangy Turmush, Birinchi Mai, and Oktiabr' had to leave their houses and were forced to move westward, toward the territory of Aral and Pionir, where Kolkhoz Kommunizm was established. The population of this kolkhoz was thus recruited from people who had been living in five encampments-turned-work-units.

THE MAKING OF KOLKHOZ KOMMUNIZM

When the kolkhoz came into being, transhumance was officially forbidden by officials who were by this time not Russian but Kyrgyz who had received training in Kazakhstan or Russia. When I asked Baiyz Apa whether she remembered the practicalities of establishing Kolkhoz Kommunizm, she told me the following:

> There was a district committee. They organized a meeting and then just united us, saying, "Now you are united." At that time there were five birikmes, and they became Kolkhoz Kommunizm. [Pause]. People are like stones in the river. They did not say anything. They agreed to everything. So they united us and mixed us together. Among ourselves, however, we did not get used to each other easily. We kept saying "our village," "your village." And then they united us under Kommunizm. So many heads [bash] came to Kommunizm. I worked in their times, too. They used to give us awards on the holidays, but they also used to force us to go to work.

Other villagers told me that the local residents had asked the architect from Talas, who had been responsible for designing the kolkhoz, that they be allowed to stay together and live as they had lived in the previous encampments-turned-work-units. Their wish was granted, so the story goes, and this is why the setup of the village structure of Aral still reflects the five encampments and therefore also the uruu divisions. Within the two parts of the village, the various neighborhoods were also identified as belonging predominantly to one uruu, although this pattern had been transformed in recent years because people had moved and new houses were being built. Two years after the kolkhoz was established, Kolkhoz Engels was "added" to Kolkhoz Kommunizm.[12] And again villagers had to get used to their new neighbors. Baiyz Apa described how people from Aral felt when the "Engels people" joined them in 1957:

> Everything changed again. When the Engels people were added to us, their land was less [than ours]. Our Kommunizm had more land. We had started to build barns and storage houses as well. And these three [Örnök, Kuugandy, and Özgörüsh] had only stones and mountains [laughing]. But then good leaders came. . . . When we had a

good head, our plan was implemented well. And if we had a bad leader, then work would stop. Order [*tartip*] was very strict then, but that order was not harmful. We were living together really well in the end.

When Kolkhoz Engels joined Kolkhoz Kommunizm, the villagers of contemporary Aral had already come to identify with "their" kolkhoz in a way that made them perceive even their own uruu members from the neighboring village as intruders who did not contribute anything to the community. Baiyz Apa attributed the final coming together of the two villages to the "reign" of certain new "heads": the kolkhoz directors. The commoners were told whom to work for and what to do. They did not receive payment, but they were taken care of and protected. While Baiyz Apa likened people to "stones in a river" when she recalled how nobody protested when the collectivization process started, she went on to present this kind of leadership in a positive light. The kolkhoz blossomed and owned about forty-five thousand animals in its best years, which villagers regarded as "average" when considered on the national level.

In many ways, socialist concepts of administration seemed to correspond to precolonial modes of governance: villagers "began to belong" by working in the artel', the birikme, and the kolkhoz under the leadership of a "head." In their accounts, they portrayed the way this new elite ordered their subjects as similar to how the *biis* or the *manaps* had acted in former times. They thereby customized entire new modes of governance, making them "ours." By continuously "pushing" people of different encampments-turned-work-units into one location from the 1940s onward, the Russians "stacked" not only different residential units within one another but also people of different uruus. But in this process, different geographical identities continued to coexist, albeit less noticeably to outside observers. To put it differently, into Soviet times people continued to identify themselves not exclusively as *Homo Sovieticus* but as having been born in a particular encampment, as descendants of a certain major and minor uruu, as inhabitants of a village, and as workers of a working unit. When at the end of "the time of the kolkhozes" Aral and Engels had become "almost like one," as Kudaibergen Ata said, this did not mean that villagers' geographical identity came to be defined exclusively by the kolkhoz. This was evident in the way that privatization was carried out forty years later; that is, along the previous uruu-oriented organizational forms of residence.

THE UNMAKING OF KOLKHOZ KOMMUNIZM

In 1993, when the members of Kommunizm agreed to privatize the kolkhoz, Kudaibergen Ata headed the commission that was responsible for dividing and allocating the common belongings, land, and animals. Before becoming the main agronomist in Kolkhoz Kommunizm, he had received his technical education in the Kyrgyz capital, at that time called Frunze, where he was also first introduced to the Russian language. He was an eager student and finished his studies with a thesis on the diversity of plants in Talas. He was then first assigned as a land specialist to a kolkhoz in southern Kyrgyzstan, temporarily leaving his family in Aral behind. After long stays in different places, being transferred from kolkhoz to kolkhoz, he finally moved back to Aral at the end of the 1980s, where he worked until the dissolution of the Soviet Union.[13] Here is how he recalled the privatization process of Kolkhoz Kommunizm:

> Only two years after Kyrgyzstan had become an independent nation-state, we decided to split the kolkhoz between the two villages [Aral and Engels]. Do you know the bridge separating Engels and Aral? Everything that is on the other side of the bridge belongs to Engels. When it was called Kolkhoz Engels, Engels used to be part of us. All of the people from Engels are Kaimazar. While Engels formed a new, separate kolkhoz and called itself Üch Emchek, we [Aral] were one of the very first villages in the whole country to undergo complete privatization.[14]

Thus, the first step toward privatization occurred along the former kolkhoz lines—between Kolkhoz Engels and Kolkhoz Kommunizm. After having been shown a kolkhoz in the eastern part of the country that had been privatized already, the two villages started separating from one another, forming new organizational units: Engels turned into Üch Emchek and formed a new, smaller kolkhoz. The other half of Kommunizm was named Aral and continued with the privatization process by itself, as Kudaibergen Ata explained:

> We privatized by dividing everything we had. We thought this was better than renting. "Mine" [meniki] is better than "ours" [bizdiki]. We divided all public buildings, machinery, and animals. Kolkhoz Engels got its share of property and technical equipment. The military station [where soldiers live to guard the border with Kazakhstan]

and other large buildings were divided between Zhetigen and Aral.[15] Then the commission divided the other property according to the number of people living in each birikme. Aral got four tractors, five cars, and two combines.

The next step in the privatization process was to distribute the large shares of commonly owned buildings—the military station, the sawmill, the mill, and storage houses—"between Zhetigen and Aral" (that is, Kaimazar), or, in fact, along the two major descent lines. Other property such as machinery was divided "according to the number of people living in each birikme." Thus, smaller property was allocated to the former encampments-turned-work-units. In the next step, the collective's livestock was privatized:

> KA: Everyone got five sheep from the kolkhoz's stock of animals, and every ten people received one horse. For example, Bürgö received three barns full of sheep. At that time we were 239 people.
>
> BA: More than ten years have passed since then. We [our numbers] have probably increased.
>
> KA: Now we are probably around 300. When we organized a *dyikan charba* [farmers' association], there were 239 of us.

As in the case of the distribution of property, the official allocation of animals was realized by handing over livestock to the various uruus in proportion to the number of members. The sheep of Bürgö uruu were initially kept in the barns that had been allocated to Aral birikme. By 1995 all kolkhoz animals had been distributed in this way. The final and most crucial step, however, was the privatization of land. The land was officially distributed among individuals, who were given usufruct agreements for ninety-nine years: "From every newborn baby to every old person we were given twenty sotik of farmland and fifteen sotik of grassland," Kudaibergen Ata explained.[16] The allocation followed uruu lines again: villagers were given land plots in those areas of the former encampments where their ancestors had lived (Klijn 1998, 61). The land plots were administered by the household head, usually the male elder who was in possession of a document listing the number of individuals belonging to an organizational unit called a *dyikan charba* (farmers' association). These were usually all of his sons, irrespective of whether they still lived under his roof or in their own houses, which, according to *salt*, parents have to build for them.

As land was also distributed to those individuals who had been born in Aral but lived outside the village today, household heads were often in charge of several hectares of land, as they pooled the land plots of their sons and decided on their usage.[17] This practice continues today and still leads to disputes within the households, particularly between fathers and sons (see chapter 4). Klijn describes how at the end of the 1990s several of these *dyikan charba*s had pooled their manpower and cultivated their land together. However, after two years, they split up because larger families, which could provide more labor than smaller families, started demanding more of the produce. There were also complaints that some families were lazy while others worked hard, and this led to a great deal of dissatisfaction (Klijn 1998, 65ff.). In addition to the difference in family size, differences in herd size was another bone of contention. Large herds needed more of the collectively produced fodder than did smaller herds (Klijn 1998, 66). By the time I started fieldwork, this arrangement no longer existed. And while most household heads possess a document identifying them as the head of a farmers' association, in many cases their sons, who live in their own houses, no longer cultivate their land or raise their animals together with their fathers. The birikmes, however, were still partly active during the time of my fieldwork. These units go back to the early encampments and have undergone a series of name changes throughout the course of time, as well as several incorporations into larger units (see Klijn 1998, 64). While these birikmes administered the commonly owned property and the animals of those uruus who belonged to the birikmes, they initially also functioned as intermediaries between the government and the families, for example by collecting land taxes for the government. Klijn mentions that they "also helped families out with funerals," for example by paying for the tractor that transported the body to the graveyard. Since the birikmes were partly formed along uruu divisions, this kind of help needs to be seen as inextricably related to uruu-internal regulations and not simply as existing in addition to them. I learned from people in my neighborhood that there had been a gradual decrease in the number of birikmes in recent years: in the mid-1990s, four units had been active in Aral: Kashka Zhol, Aral, Zhetigen, and Terek.[18] In the year 2000 Zhetigen and Terek dissolved their birikmes, whereas Kashka Zhol and Aral merged into one. When I was conducting fieldwork, there was only one birikme left, Aral birikme, which was located in my neighborhood and consisted of Kaimazar uruu members only. Here is what the two elders had to say about "their" work unit:

KA: Out of all those birikmes only ours survived, only Aral. The other birikmes, they don't have anything any more. It is better to have common property than to have private property. It is bad if we sell our property— then we will also suffer like the others suffered.

BA: When we separated after independence [in March 1993], it was a problem for [the people from Engels]. They had to come here for our mill, to the mayor's office . . . so they had this problem. Everything was here. It was the center here. And now they've gotten used to it.

KA: Little by little [the villagers] destroyed the common kolkhoz build-ings, sold the machinery and spare parts or used them for their [private] houses. They took everything that was not nailed down [laughing].

BA: We had built barns here in the Soviet times, and then most barns were destroyed after independence.

While this observation is far from equating privatization with pros-perity as so often occurs in the writings and discourses of Western scholars and Kyrgyz politicians, it also shows that the elders attribut-ed the agency of this process of "unmaking of Soviet life" (Humphrey 2002) to the villagers themselves: they were the ones tearing down what they had built and taking back what they thought belonged to them. And while Kudaibergen Ata mentioned that it is "better to have common property," it was he who had earlier decided on "com-plete privatization." By partly reversing the steps that had led toward collectivization, villagers remained fully in control of their assets. As seen by the two elders, privatization was not something that hap-pened to people in Aral but something they deliberately decided upon, as Kudaibergen Ata had made clear. While my fieldsite was a latecomer to the collectivization process when compared to other areas of Kyrgyzstan, it was, at least in the elders' perception, one of the first to decollectivize. And while the initial steps were regulated and encouraged by the government and international organizations in the frame of various programs, the later steps were inextricably re-lated to internal organization such as the role of the uruu and inter-generational dynamics that state officials could in no way influence, especially as they themselves were subjected to them in their roles as family and uruu members.[19]

The elders, too, remarked that in the early independence period they were already left to their own devices and had to make their own decisions: "In all of Kyrgyzstan we got the smallest amount of land—only twenty sotik per person. This was the minimum. Akaev [the country's first president] made the mistake of giving land, but he did not take care of the peasants. The first years were hard. People ended up eating their animals or selling them in order to survive. Many people did not work on the land, but moved to Bishkek or left the country. Only for the last two or three years now is everyone working on the land. We are coping with it quite well now."

Thus, while the elders attributed agency and the establishment of order in Soviet times to "good heads," they emphasized that after independence, when Akaev turned out to be "too soft"—this being the major accusation villagers brought forward against him—they had to develop alternative strategies. While some villagers migrated away, others continued to privatize their holdings and activities in order to raise the cash that was increasingly necessary because of the economic "shock therapy" that was introduced in an effort to hasten the transition from a command economy to a market economy. Privatization was still going on when I returned to my fieldsite in 2008: the Aral birikme was holding a meeting in my landlord's sawmill to discuss the selling of the still jointly owned storage house. As in most of the cases before, the highest bid came from a rich villager who did not live in Aral anymore but returned frequently to make sure that his property was administered well by those whom he had appointed as his deputies. While I never managed to talk to him directly, I saw him in action during village meetings and life-cycle rituals. He was undoubtedly one of the new heads of the village, and while there were also undertones of envy when villagers talked about him, he seemed well respected as someone who "takes care of people," as they put it.

Over the course of the last century, various social and spatial transformations have shaped villagers' self-perceptions. The landscape of Aral and Engels, as presented by the two elders, has genealogical as well as topographical features through which villagers anchor themselves in an environment that is "pregnant with the past" (Ingold 2000, 189). The past is conceptualized as a lived experience in the way uruu membership is envisioned and performed and in the way the landscape has been altered. Every part of the landscape of Aral and Engels can be envisioned as "a knot of stories" (Ingold 2009, 41) that references different time periods, forms of organization, and identity. These, however, only gain relevance when they are invoked in the performances and conversations of those who inhabit that "knot."

Descent is essentially tied to the landscape. It has been "settled" in a literal sense: during the tülöö, in the statue of Bürgö Baatyr, in books about village genealogy, and in the stories of the two elders about their village. By closely attending to these material narratives, I traced the intertwining of descent and various forms of organizational orderings throughout the last century and up to the present. People's geographical identities have been sustained through the customization of the different Russian- or Soviet-imposed settlement patterns and modes of organization. From the two elders' accounts of sedentarization, collectivization, and privatization, we see how people managed to relate to the ever-changing modes of settlement and organization, learning to acknowledge as "ours" what used to be "theirs." Today, they refer to places in the landscape by using various alternative toponyms. While villagers gradually customized what Russian "reforms" brought into their lives, they did not forget or deny their uruu identity, as became obvious in "the time of Independence," when privatization was not carried out on the basis of individuals or households but along the lines of the descent groups that had mutated into production units in the Soviet period. In the course of the tülöö in May 2006, this very uruu membership was made visible, and identification with a particular uruu was reasserted.

In the afternoon of that day, the food that the women and men had been busy preparing all day was finally ready to eat. Sitting in groups of three, people ate noodles with boiled meat out of large white aluminum bowls usually used for serving food or for preparing bread dough. After the food had been eaten, an aksakal gave his blessing (*bata*), which people accompanied by holding their cupped hands in front of their faces and murmuring wishes into their hands about how rain was needed that year. As soon as the blessing was over, women proceeded to clean the aluminum bowls and pile them on top of one another. I was surprised because they normally guard their personal household items attentively, making sure that their dishes do not end up in another household. I asked my landlady, Zhyldyz Ezhe, the older daughter-in-law (kelin) of Baiyz Apa, "How do you know which bowl is yours?"

"I don't," she replied. "They are all ours." Elmira Ezhe, the younger kelin of Baiyz Apa, explained further by pointing to the bowl in Zhyldyz Ezhe's hand. "See?" she said, showing me the small hole that had been punched into its rim. "Our bowls have this hole. So everyone knows they belong to Bürgö." The other uruus had different ways of marking their bowls, they told me. I found out that while over the course of the last several years almost all property had been privatized, new utensils had been pooled together and are today regarded as Bürgö property. This is also the case for the cauldrons in which meat and noodles are boiled for rituals. All of these dishes are kept together in one place at a neighbor's house.

When I returned in 2015, further amendments had been made to take into account the growing number of members within Bürgö uruu. In general, the lineage is split up into six different subgroups, of which only two—Sarytai and Torutai—live in Aral. After an aksakal of Sarytai had died, a wealthy family member bought a new yurt and then donated it to Sarytai so this group might use it for further common occasions. The group also purchased a new set of dishes and cooking utensils and began pooling money for festivities on a regular basis. In 2015 Torutai followed suit. I received a list from my neighbor Raia Apa (see figure 2.4), who explained that Torutai was also about to purchase a yurt and other common materials for future festivities and funerals. The list shows that in 2014 Torutai consisted of forty-two households (tütün), of which sixteen were located in the village, twelve in Talas city, nine in Bishkek, and five in the neighboring villages Chat Bazar and Chong Tokoi. It then lists specific rules regarding how money will be collected to purchase collective household items, as well as who is going to take care of guests from outside the village in the case of a funeral (see also chapter 6).

When I asked Raia Apa whether this meant that Bürgö uruu was splitting up, she said, "Yes, but only for occasions such as funerals or festivities. We have grown and there are too many leaders, so it was difficult to keep order. There was no order anymore and that's why we separated into two parts. . . . But we are still holding the tülöö together every spring and take turns slaughtering animals." For this spring ritual, the two subgroups are still using the old common dishes but will both pool from their new respective group items once these have worn out.

In this case, villagers have customized *salt* to reflect demographic changes and to take into account the fact that some of their group members no longer live in the village, albeit without altering the important rule of sharing food with one's relatives on festive and sad occasions. It is a familiar suggestion that food in general and eating together in particular may be "an important mediator between the concepts of identity through locality and identity through descent" (Strathern 1973, 33). The communal preparation of traditional food in dishes owned by descent groups during the tülöö ritual is a powerful manifestation of villagers' efforts to once more perform as uruus, as they ritually imprint their group identity onto the landscape at the place where their previous encampment had been.

FIGURE 2.4. Raia Apa (2015).

Chapter 3

IMAGINING THE STATE

"We don't have a state here anymore!" This was a common expression among the villagers of Aral and Engels. The claim referred back to Soviet times, when their joint kolkhoz had been part of a dense network of agricultural units that spanned the country. As the two villages were subject to the policies of Communist Party officials in Moscow and Bishkek, "the state," apparently, had been there but must have left some time after the country became independent. While state institutions have never gained access to the private sphere of the household in rural Kyrgyzstan to the extent that has been reported for other postsocialist settings, "the state" was a dominant and present actor in daily kolkhoz life, manifest in its officials, its bureaucracy, and its institutionalized means of enforcing order (*tartip*). Looking back at the Soviet state, my informants stressed that there had been order because there had been strong individuals in the kolkhoz who "made people work." After independence, many people in the village complained, the kind of order that existed in Soviet times was never restored. Not only have the labor opportunities in the kolkhoz disappeared; the controlling and nurturing state has also vanished. State officials have little to offer to the village population these days if they are not financially affluent. In order to sustain their own positions as heads (*bash*), they either need to cooperate with businessmen, become businessmen themselves, or tap the resources of international organizations. While the state is increasingly perceived as absent, villagers invoke its presence situationally by appropriating language, rituals, and symbols that they associate with it. In this chapter I investigate these invocations and performances, focusing on the role of state law in relation to customary law (*salt*). Since the state is "an idea" more than "a system," as Abrams (1988, 75) and Graeber (2004, 65) have convincingly argued, I investigate how and where these ideas about the state are voiced and performed by exploring village bureaucracy as "official pronouncements where personal identity and state authority are aligned" (Herzfeld 1992, 37; see Das and Poole 2004, 6).

In the *aksakal* courts, for example, the elders phrased their perceived statelessness in terms of the lack of interest state judges had in their activities. Feeling left to their own devices, they had to handle their new role as judges by themselves. In court sessions they tried to create the appearance of a state court and introduced procedures they claimed were derived from state laws. They also invoked the state as a threat, specifically when people did not want to heed their decisions. While the institution of the aksakal court had been explicitly set up in each village of the country to allow adjudication according to *salt*, an imagined state law nevertheless played an important role in the institution.

INTRODUCING THE AKSAKAL COURTS

Since 1993 the aksakal courts have been mentioned in all versions of the country's constitution. Their assignment has been amended several times: from being incorporated into the judiciary in 1993, to forming a part of the local self-governance structure in 2003, to being subsumed under the section on "citizenship" in 2007, where they remain in the most recent version of the constitution (2010).[1] Article 39 of the 2010 constitution postulates that citizens have the right to organize aksakal courts, and then it refers to a separate law on the aksakal courts.[2]

The law was made more specific in 1995 after disturbing news reached the Kyrgyz public and international organizations about a number of serious offenses involving some aksakal courts. In Talas, a Kyrgyz citizen was allegedly stoned to death by fellow residents after the local aksakal court pronounced him guilty of extortion. In other places aksakal courts had permitted the whipping of culprits. Amnesty International was furthermore concerned with "extra-legal militias operating under the authority of aksakal courts [that] have subjected people to illegal detention and ill treatment and have administered punishments handed down by the aksakal courts" (Amnesty International 1996, 7). Since then international organizations have called for effective supervision and monitoring of aksakal courts and for special protection measures to ensure that aksakal courts fully apply the principles and provisions of international rights.[3]

Local NGOs, on the other hand, demanded the immediate abolition of the institution (e.g., Anon. 1996). One of the leading activists of that time recalled the beginnings of the institution in an interview that I conducted in Bishkek: "It was a big mistake. They were really hastily organized because it was an initiative from above. And awful things started happening. They started putting people in *zindani. Zindan* was the kind of prison people in Central Asia used to have in the Middle Ages. They are usually deep in the ground. They used to keep people there."

While this example refers to one particular case only, the activist presented the instance in a way that reflects the general resentment among activists in the 1990s toward the aksakal courts. Intensive lobbying by local NGOs and the pressure of international organizations elicited a reaction from President Akaev. But rather than abolishing the courts as some organizations had urged, he redefined the limits of their jurisdiction in a separate law and continued to lobby for them. The "law on the aksakal courts," which underwent revision in 1995 as a result of these incidents, consists of eight sections and thirty-seven articles. Article 1 defines aksakal courts as "societal organs that are formed voluntarily and on the basis of elections and self-governance." Articles 2 and 3 emphasize that aksakals should be guided in their decision making as well as in the instructions they give to the people by "historically established Kyrgyz customary law." The court is supposed to consist of five to nine members (Art. 8), who are elected for a period of three years. Court sessions are scheduled on demand. Each municipality can have one aksakal court. In towns, one court for every twenty-five thousand people should be established. The courts have to be registered with the local administration (Art. 12). A judge is not allowed to preside over cases that involve direct relatives (Art. 13). Aksakals are allowed to decide over family disputes, property issues, and disputes involving irrigation and overgrazing (Art. 15). Having established the guilt of an accused, they can issue a verdict and by way of punishment take one of the following actions: (a) issue a warning, (b) require a public apology to the victim or victims, (c) administer a public reprimand, (d) require the guilty party to compensate for material damages, and (e) fine the guilty party an amount not to exceed the equivalent of three months' salary at minimum wage. They can also sentence the guilty party to community service. If the court cannot reconcile the parties in a property- or family-related case, it makes a decision on the question under consideration. If necessary, the aksakal court is empowered to hand materials over to the regional courts.

According to the law, court sessions are supposed to be free of charge for the disputing parties (Art. 23). A judgment made in the aksakal court must be based only on the evidence obtained during the court session (Art. 26), and it is legally binding when a simple majority has been reached (Art. 25). The case is to be transferred to a state court if the required quorum of judges is not present (Art. 16). The decision of an aksakal court can be appealed by the losing party or by other persons participating in the case within ten days of the day the verdict was issued. Appeals are submitted to the raion or city court that has jurisdiction over the territory on which the aksakal court was established.

The cases, the session minutes, and the judgments need to be recorded in writing (Arts. 24 and 27). At least once a year the aksakal judges must report to state judges (Art. 35). References to the jurisdiction of aksakal courts can also be found in the penal and civil codes of the country, as well as in a number of other laws.

Following this attempt to clarify the legal position of the aksakal courts, negative reports about them have ceased to reach the public. In 2004 the aksakal courts, initially only a rural phenomenon, were established in the capital, Bishkek, and in the southern city of Osh as well. While in most rural areas the courts are staffed with male elders only, women form a large percentage in the city aksakal courts in Bishkek.[4]

Akaev's promotion of the institution of the aksakal court must be understood in the following context: aksakal courts were established as part of the decentralization efforts of the government, as they constituted an alternative to state courts. The Kyrgyz government, with the financial and logistical help of the United Nations, has carried out various reforms aimed at decentralizing the state administration and thereby transferring responsibilities and rights to local regions. This policy started in 1996 when a new administrative unit, the municipality (aiyl ökmötü), was introduced in order to strengthen the regions' capacities to govern themselves. Nowadays, each aiyl ökmötü has one aksakal court. However, this policy, which is officially framed as "more rights to the regions," can just as easily be interpreted as "less work and expense for the central state." Regarding the aksakal courts, this has meant less work for the police and the state courts, especially the regional courts, to which claimants had addressed their problems before. The possibilities for citizens to apply to the legal institution of their choice have thus been limited. Issues that are regarded as "minor" by the police or the courts are now being sent, without the consent of the claimants, directly to the aksakal court of the claimant's home community. Even when claimants have managed to access state courts, the cases have often been sent back to the villages, thereby depriving actors of formal judicial expertise.[5] In this way, villagers were forced to interact with this institution first if they wanted to have their cases considered by state organs at all. Moreover, the promotion of the aksakal courts allowed Akaev to use the institution as one of several tools in his nation-building efforts (see chapter 1). Finally, the establishment of aksakal courts also provided Akaev with advantages in dealing with international organizations, which had been highly critical of the courts in their initial years but more recently had started to refer to them as "democratic and responsible to their constituents."[6] They therefore came to be regarded as potential tools that could be used to meet the objectives of international organizations (see UNFPA et al. 2003, 5). According to these organizations, the courts were easily adapted to village life because their working principles were assumed to be based on "pre-Soviet traditional clan-based customs" (Simpson 2003), which were now being channeled through the institution of the aksakal courts. While international observers emphasized that "customs are slowly changing, but customs are more important than law in the villages" (Giovarelli and Akmatova 2002, 19), Akaev himself also aligned the courts with human rights discourses: "To my mind this unique national court system plays a great role in the development and the realization of the conception of the national idea that Kyrgyzstan is a country of human rights. . . . As you know, our constitution says that basic human rights and freedom are guaranteed for everyone. Thus we put human rights above all" (Akaev 2005).[7] From this quote it becomes particularly clear that the existence of aksakal courts in today's Kyrgyzstan is presented as much more than just a "survival": aksakals are of significance for modern state reforms because, according to Akaev, they had been institutions of local self-government long before Western reformers deemed them fitting for the country. Especially with regard to the current popular approach of alternative dispute resolution (ADR), aksakal courts could be presented as mediating bodies and effective dispute management institutions.

One month after he gave a speech at a festive event in Bishkek where he publicly honored "the best aksakals in the country," the president had to flee Kyrgyzstan. On March 24, 2005, a large group of protesters gathered in front of the president's administrative building and eventually took over the complex.[8] Kurmanbek Bakiev became interim president and—on July 10, 2005—the new president of the country. Former president Akaev had planned to further extend the responsibilities of aksakal courts in the years to come and even promised to pay them a salary (Akaev 2005). These possibilities have been discussed under the presidency of Bakiev, but no changes in legislation have yet been made. At present, aksakal judges still work for free, except in Bishkek, where they operate under the control of the city administration.

In all these accounts, the institution of the aksakal court is either characterized by referring to the "customary law" that it presumably applies or viewed in terms of its compliance or noncompliance with human rights. In my fieldsite, however, the institution was until recently predominantly associated with the state. Thus, while state officials expropriated the language of "custom" and presented aksakals as the "bearers of tradition," aksakal judges appropriated official state rhetoric in order to accentuate their competence and their public role as officials. The state and state law are invoked as part and parcel of aksakal court performances, but at the same time written state law is never consulted in aksakal courts and is even for the most part unknown to the aksakals.

"THERE IS THIS LAW . . .": A DIVORCE CASE

I was sitting in the house of Kasym Ata, the head of the aksakal court in Engels, along with my partner and my research assistant Eliza. We were having tea and chatting about the latest village news. When I asked Kasym Ata if any new disputes had arisen during my two-week absence from the village, he suddenly remembered a letter of complaint (*aryz*) to which he had not yet reacted, and he decided to resolve the case that very day.[9] The fact that the petitioner was in the hospital and currently not in the village did not bother him: "We will summon her brother since he wrote the *aryz* in her name." He explained that the case was about the divorce of Ainura and Emil.[10] The couple had two sons and a daughter, Mairam, and had been living with Emil's parents for nine years. Ainura, however, was mentally ill and was often incapable of caring for her husband and her children. Finally, Emil sent her back to her parents' house. He kept their two sons, whereas Ainura decided to take their daughter with her. Emil then found a new wife, who had already moved in with him and his parents.

Ainura's family now wanted Emil to divorce officially, and to give them Mairam's birth certificate and her share of the land. They were claiming neither land for Ainura nor the payment of alimony. Emil did not react to the demands, and thus the family turned to the head of the aksakal court for help. We left Kasym Ata's house to pick up Ainura's brother, but as he was not home, we took his wife, Sura, with us instead. Then we picked up Tülööberdi Ata (referred to in the following conversation as TüA), another aksakal court member, who had not been informed of the case. Together we visited Emil and his parents. There, on the street in front of their house, Kasym Ata (KasA) started talking to Emil and his mother (EmilMo). Askar Ata, another aksakal and a neighbor of Emil, joined the group.

KasA [approaching Emil]: I received a message from the policeman about you. I will save you. You married another woman without divorcing your wife. Do you want to go to the regional court? Or do you want to come to the mayor's office instead, so that I can save you [from the possibility of imprisonment]? Choose one of these options and be quick.

TüA [to KasA]: I will also divorce. Will you save me too? [He laughs.]

KasA [ignoring the comment; to Emil]: Did you understand me?

Emil: When?

KasA: Now.

Sura: And bring Mairam's birth certificate.

KasA: If you don't agree, I will just send my decision and the note from the policeman to the regional court and you will go there. The regional court will deal with you. [To TüA] He married another woman without divorcing his first wife and left her with three children.

TüA: When was this?

Sura [to Emil]: Generally one should get married *after* getting divorced.

Emil: I have my two sons with me.

Sura: You have them, but who will take care of your wife now?

KasA [to Emil]: Who gave birth to your children?

Emil: Why are you threatening me? I don't care. I can even die [in prison].

Sura: Who is talking to you like this? Are you stupid or something?

KasA: Hey, come on! I will save you peacefully.

EmilMo [to KasA]: Dear relative, I am halfway to my death and so is my husband. Don't talk bullshit. How long will you torture this guy?

Emil: I am ready to die.

Sura [to EmilMo]: Dear relative, let him divorce legally.

EmilMo: What do you know about legal things? He might die.

Emil [to both aksakals]: I can die and I will take one of you with me to my grave. I promise if I die, I will kill one of you two.

Sura [to EmilMo]: Dear relative, I have told you that we need to separate them in the aksakal court. That's it.

EmilMo: Shut up. Since then [when her son left his first wife] I feel really bad and so does my husband.

KasA [to EmilMo]: Relative, who is talking bad to you? Let's do it like this: send him and I will give him a paper that says he is divorced. I want to save him.

EmilMo: Yes, okay. He is in your hands, in the hands of our relative.

TüA: Let's just make them divorce.

KasA: Let the new daughter-in-law live normally.

Sura: Yes. We don't have any ill will toward his new wife.

Kasym Ata started the case with a threat. Should Emil not be willing to have his case considered by the aksakal court, Kasym Ata would have to inform the state court. The note he allegedly got from the policeman was invented in order to frighten Emil. This shows that the first image of the state that the aksakal deployed was a threatening one, and Emil was definitely daunted. But it also shows that the aksakal needs to invoke the figure of a policeman in addition to his own presence in order to ensure he gets his message across. The role of the local policeman is particularly important in this regard: on the one hand, he embodies the state, his police uniform visibly marking him as an official responsible for enforcing "law and order." On the other hand, it is through him that the absent state can be contacted. Here, the state is envisioned as residing somewhere outside the village in an institutionalized form such as the Talas city court.

When I did fieldwork in 2005–2006 there was no permanent policeman in the two villages. Instead, a young man traveled to the two villages when he was "invited" by the respective mayor to levy taxes or to be present at an aksakal court session. The two villages had been promised their "own" policeman in 2006, but they had to wait until the summer of 2008 for such an official to permanently assume residence.[11] Invoking the presence of a policeman, as Kasym Ata did in the divorce case, or having him attend court cases was a measure frequently taken by the aksakals in order to give their performances an official appearance and to emphasize that they acted as judges who have state officials at their disposal (cf. Das and Poole 2004, 20; Friedman 2003; Fuller and Harris 2001, 25).

In the lower village, Kudaibergen Ata is less confrontational. He simply informs the disputing parties of their "right" to have their case considered in the state court. But all participants know too well that this "right" is not enforceable for two reasons. First, according to *salt* it is considered inappropriate to engage non-kin in one's problems. Villagers usually try not to let their disputes "come out" (*chyktyrba*); that is, they try to keep them "inside" (*ichinde*). This was also a well-known strategy during Soviet times, when villagers hid their affairs from Soviet officials.[12] While "inside" refers to the sphere of the household within the village, it extends to the sphere of the village once state courts come into play. Thus, what is perceived as "inside" and what as "outside" changes according to the situation (see Vite 1996; Yurchak 2006, 118). Transferring a dispute case to the state courts triggers expressions of shame-anxiety (*uiat*—see chapter 6) in villagers, and might cause those responsible to be stigmatized afterward. Moreover, state courts are very often directly associated with imprisonment, as we have seen in Emil's reaction. Consider how a city judge from Bishkek presented the public image of state courts: "People are afraid of state courts. They always think of the iron cages [where defendants sit during trials] and that it is uiat to go there. It is also expensive—you need a lot of documents, you have to travel there . . . all this is expensive. Here, in Kyrgyzstan, the aksakals decide. This is how it has been done since ancient times" (see figure 3.1).[13]

The second reason that villagers do not enforce their right to bring their problems before state courts is not related to notions of appropriateness but to practicalities such as those mentioned by the state judge: most villagers simply cannot afford to have their cases considered in state courts. Not only does the registration of a case require payment but the procedure as such is also known to bear hidden costs.[14] The documents I collected in my fieldsite also show that, particularly in the early years, state judges sent cases that they considered "minor" back to the villages for (re)consideration in the aksakal courts. These cases dealt mostly with animal theft, grazing transgressions, and land disputes—issues of fundamental importance to villagers who live off their land, from their animals, and with each other.[15]

FIGURE 3.1. Aksakal court session in the upper village. Kasym Ata (on the left side, sitting) listens to a fellow villager pleading his case (2005).

While Kudaibergen Ata in the lower village knows of all these obstacles and therefore does not even threaten to transfer cases to state courts, Kasym Ata's style of conducting court sessions is based on his estimation that villagers nevertheless fear state courts as such. However, in this particular divorce case, he underestimated Emil's aggressive reaction—his counterthreat to take Kasym Ata or the other aksakal present with him to the grave should the case be transferred to the courts.

Emil associated state courts directly with imprisonment, and imprisonment with having to die. This was not the aksakal's intention, although he certainly provoked Emil's reaction by saying he would "save" Emil. Emil's mother felt equally threatened by Kasym Ata's behavior. She reacted very emotionally, appealing to the fact that she and her husband were old and near death themselves, and that they and the aksakal were relatives. When Sura tried to clarify things, she was told that she did not know about "legal things" and that Emil would indeed die if his case were sent to the state court. Only after several attempts at pacification was Emil's mother finally willing to put her son's fate in the aksakal's hands.

Kasym Ata's performance, in the end, was successful, and the accused party agreed to follow him to the mayor's office. While the old men led the way, it was Askar Ata, a neighbor of Emil, who accompanied Emil and his new wife to the mayor's office. The two looked intimidated. Since all the offices in the building were locked, there was no room to sit down to discuss the case. The aksakal and Sura took a seat on the window ledges in the foyer, and the couple crouched on the floor. It was cold and windy even inside the building because some of the windows were broken and the door did not close properly. The aksakals made sarcastic remarks to each other about these working conditions. Nevertheless, the court session began.

Kasym Ata first read the letter of complaint aloud. After a couple of questions about its content, the aksakal again explained the need to divorce first before getting married again. When interrogated, Emil was told to stand up in front of the court. After having answered, he was told to "sit down." After the accused was made aware of the issue at stake, Kasym Ata again emphasized that there was no need for a conflict, and that after he signed the paperwork their divorce would be legal and Emil could officially marry his new wife. Ainura, on the other hand, would then be able to receive the childcare allowance for her daughter because she would then be a single mother. The couple asked whether they would be allowed to register their marriage in Talas after the proceedings, and the aksakal confirmed that they would. Later, Kasym Ata wrote a note stating that Ainura and Emil had decided not to live together anymore, and that the aksakal court had taken notice of their decision.[16] The court session ended amicably and everyone got up to leave the hall.

Although the surroundings in which the court session took place were in no way comparable to a courtroom, the procedures that the aksakal applied mimicked state court procedures. Having the accused brought before the court, reading out the complaint, asking the couple to stand up when being questioned, and telling them when to sit down—all this was highly reminiscent of state court procedures. In this case as well as in other cases I took part in throughout fieldwork, it was precisely the procedural state-court-like appearance the aksakals wanted to create. The legal basis on which they made their decisions mattered little. To further associate their work with the imprimatur of the state, court sessions usually take place in the mayor's office and not in a private setting. The mayors join these events and take an active role, thereby giving the event additional official sanction.[17]

In the lower village, Kudaibergen Ata makes his elevated role as judge visible to everyone by claiming the mayor's leather chair for himself, while the mayor sits in a regular chair (see figure 3.2). Having the right to sit where the mayor usually sits is in itself an important procedural element of the court session. During the court sessions it is not the mayor but the head of the aksakal court who is the most important individual. A court session starts when the head of the court has arrived and when at least one individual from one of the disputing parties is present. I have witnessed court sessions where either the plaintiff or the defendant was absent. In these cases, their relatives show up to substitute for them, which never seemed to pose a problem, as we have seen in the divorce case. Kudaibergen Ata also often told me that it would be good if everyone stood up when he entered the room (as people do for state judges), and if only they had robes—he used the Russian word *forma*—they would be respected even more: "Then people would see me as a real judge." He also showed me the official stamp and seal of the aksakal court, which the mayor's secretary, Kalipa Ezhe, keeps locked in her drawer in the aiyl ökmötü building.[18] Kudaibergen Ata also always opens the court with a formal statement, as he did at the beginning of a court session in July 2008: "In the presence of the people involved in this case and in the presence of the policeman, the mayor, the deputy, and the members of the court, I declare the aksakal court open. I remind you that according to the law, we will fine you 200 som if you speak about things not related to the case or disturb the process by misbehaving.[19] You can only speak when it is your turn and only about things related to the case." In this statement Kudaibergen Ata invokes the policeman—who since 2008 has also regularly taken part in the court sessions—as the personification of the state. However, the policeman usually sits quietly through the session without getting involved unless Kudaibergen Ata or Kasym Ata directly asks him for his opinion, in which case he generally agrees with what the elders have said before. This serves to underscore the notion that aksakals claim and are granted all the authority in the court room, including the authority to control other people's communication and to dominate the proceedings with their own talk. Although the ideal image of aksakals prescribes that they should express themselves in a humble manner, in court they often raise their voices and sometimes shout down the parties should they behave inappropriately by interrupting or screaming at one another.

In the divorce case discussed above this was not necessary. Emil and his new wife were intimidated not only by having been brought before the aksakal court without notice but mostly because they were accused of not having their documents in order. The divorce case, as

FIGURE 3.2. Kudaibergen Ata claims the mayor's chair for himself at a court session. The mayor (without hat) sits in a regular chair next to Kudaibergen Ata during these events (2008).

many other cases brought before the aksakal courts, centered on the presentation, discussion, and invocation of documents: a birth certificate that Emil's ex-wife needed to apply for child benefits; the letter of complaint written by the brother of Emil's ex-wife, who acted as her guardian; an extended discussion about what documents the new couple needed in order to be officially married. Villagers in my fieldsite encounter the state through documents such as identity cards; application forms for child benefits, pensions, and veteran's benefits; birth and death certificates; maps of land plots; written complaints; and tax forms. These documents bear the double sign of the state's distance and its penetration into everyday life (Das and Poole 2004, 15; see also Ssorin-Chaikov 2003). While such written evidence of the state stood at the center of the discussion during this and other court sessions, none of these documents (with the exception of the letter of complaint read out by the aksakal) was visible as such. This suggests that while documents are considered extremely relevant as a means of arguing and legal reasoning, as well as of establishing the state's presence, it is not the actual presentation or the exact nature of these documents that is of importance but the verbal invocation of them.[20]

In Kudaibergen Ata's opening statement above, another important procedural element is mentioned: the right of the aksakals to impose a fine. In this case, Kudaibergen Ata is talking about 200 som. Three years ago it was 150 som in the lower village, but in the upper village, it has always been 100 som, and in a village on the opposite end of Talas it was already 300 som in 2005. While these fines are presented as being fixed according to state law, the amount charged is different in each aiyl ökmötü, and sometimes changes from case to case. Being able to fine others is a plausible way of performing "law and order" in the aksakal courts, where the ability to enforce decisions becomes visible in the financial transaction between the defendant and the aksakal. In addition, this can also be seen as a way of "paying respect."[21]

By drawing upon the resources, strategies, and rituals of state officials, aksakals try to create the atmosphere of a state court in their sessions, aligning their performances with what they imagine state judges would have done in their stead. People associate all these procedures and measures with the state because of how they remember the Soviet state. This, however, is not meant in a negative way: when they refer to the state as such, they very often compare the current government to previous socialist ones and complain that there is no order (tartip) these days. In Soviet times, order, with a positive connotation, was established through strict control and pressure by officials. Rather than criticizing this, people see in it the reason for the success of the kolkhoz: the stricter the heads of the kolkhoz were, the better people worked. Material well-being and success are directly linked to strict surveillance. This kind of disciplining order does not naturally emerge among the population but needs to be created and maintained by an individual head—in the past this was the bii, the manap, and the uruu elders. During Soviet times it was the kolkhoz directors, and today it is the mayor, the governor, and the president. However, when the head of a given unit is not capable of establishing and keeping order, "work stops," as one of my informants said.[22]

In light of the perceived statelessness, aksakals have come to invoke the state by conjuring images of "law and order." Several aksakals of the two courts told me that they initially thought themselves incapable of doing "the job," as they were comparing the new institution to a state-like court. They did not know about "law" and did not consider themselves "real judges." They emphasized that they did not have "the right knowledge" it takes to be a judge. Kudaibergen Ata, at the beginning of my stay, frequently told me that there had been only one judge in Talas province who "knew the law" (i.e., was a trained lawyer), and that all the other aksakals were only "honest people." They saw themselves as experts in the technical, agricultural, or educational sphere, who merely happened to be in good positions when the institution of the court was formed in the lower village in 1995. When they were "elected," they could continue working as part of the state at the same time that they were dismantling the kolkhoz.

That their self-image has obviously changed became evident to me after the divorce case was over. As the relieved couple was leaving the building, the head of the aksakal court approached the couple's neighbor, Askar Ata:

KasA [to AskA]: After court one has to pay 100 som. There is this law [Russ. *zakon*].

TüA: [to KasA]: Now how will you explain this? Do you have this law?

KasA: That guy [Emil] has to pay 100 som.

AskA: All right, I can tell him.

TüA: Yes, tell him.

Judith: Why does he have to pay 100 som?

KasA: For our work. I will give thirty som to the mayor and with the remaining seventy som I will buy something to eat for the aksakals.

TüA: I don't know whether it will work out or not.

KasA: We will make it work out.

Judith: I have not heard about this law.

TüA [to me]: There is such a law. Write down this law.

We left the hall together. The accused and his wife were sitting in front of the building, waiting for us. Askar Ata started to explain:

AskA: There is a law of theirs. I will explain it to you. Since the decision was made in your favor, you will get the decision [the document] after having paid 100 som.

KasA: Thirty som for the mayor.

AskA: You will pay for the mayor.

KasA: And seventy som for me.

AskA: For the court's labor.

TüA: Then that's it.

As usual, the participants in the court session wound up in the small contractor's shed left over from Soviet times, which some villagers had rebuilt into a store and a place where men often sit down together to drink tea or vodka. The head of the aksakal court ordered tea and cookies for everyone and vodka only for himself, as the other aksakal did not drink alcohol. These things were paid for by the couple.

Emil went home immediately, while his wife stayed to serve food and drinks to the group, as a good daughter-in-law is supposed to do. Later, after she had left as well, the mayor of the village, together with the tax inspector, arrived from a meeting in Talas. They got to hear about the new law:

KasA: [to the mayor] Hey! From now on it will be like this: One has to pay 100 som before a court session starts. Thirty som for you and seventy som for the document.

Mayor: [looking irritated] Hmm?

Tax inspector: Before each court session starts?

KasA: Yes. Until one pays, the court session won't start.

AskA: He says that he has this law before opening a court session.

KasA: It is written inside the back cover of the book that I got from Akaev.

TüA: Do whatever you want, but don't forget to buy something for us.

KasA: Aren't you eating something right now?

TüA: But you started it only today.

Tax inspector: Yes, it would be nice to have tea after the court session.

Mayor: There needs to be tea after court, but I don't know . . .

KasA: From now it will be like this: people will pay. Only then will we start a court session.

This is the third image of the state, invoked after the court session was over. It centered on the invention of a new law allowing the aksakals to impose a fee of 100 som for their services. Whereas the aksakals involved in the divorce case knew that there was no such law, no one really challenged Kasym Ata's assertion that there was. The fact that he was once invited by the former president to receive an award for being one of the most successful aksakals in the country boosts his standing among his fellow aksakals and the village administration. He alone owns a copy of "the book," given to him by Akaev himself, on the back cover of which the law in question is supposedly written.[23] The head of the court was therefore playing both on the fact that you have to do what the law (i.e., "the book") tells you (which exonerates him from personal responsibility for his decision) and on the fact that he is the only one in possession of a copy of it. In the divorce case, however, Kasym Ata also employed language associated with the state. Immediately after the session he explained to his fellow aksakal that a fee had to be paid to the court, and that the money would go to the mayor and to himself to pay for their food. Later, however, he told the mayor that the fee is to be paid before a court session begins, and that the money would be for the mayor and for "the document."[24] In presenting the law and the distribution of fees differently to the mayor than to his fellow aksakals, he may have been trying to accommodate the mayor's skepticism about the new law. The mayor, in this case, represented the state because he forms part of the local administration and was usually eager to remind villagers about state laws that enabled or "forced" him to do certain things (e.g., levy taxes). Thus, the head of the aksakal court explained his new law in terms that sounded as impersonal as possible.

Kasym Ata, however, does not have much to fear from the mayor, who once was his pupil. Their teacher–pupil relationship in many ways has not changed, and thus the mayor often keeps quiet instead of voicing his opinion. The position of the other aksakals is also interesting. They sometimes ridiculed Kasym Ata and his way of running the court, knowing that his standing was largely based on the villagers' lack of knowledge about the state. But later they allied with him, dismissing my objection that I had not heard about this new law. Of course, they also stand to profit from it. The new law in the former president's name allowed Kasym Ata and the other aksakals to at least have tea and cookies after their work. By telling me to write down this law, they assigned the codification of the new law to the anthropologist—an appropriate thing to do given the fact that this had been the role of anthropologists in Central Asia throughout the history of the Russian conquest.

Aksakals "represent at once the fading of the state's jurisdiction and its continual refounding through its (not so mythic) appropriation of private justice" (Das and Poole 2004, 14). While the former president set up the aksakal courts in an effort to establish *salt* as a viable alternative to state law, those who were supposed to enact *salt* on the basis of this law chose instead to invoke and imitate state law. These performances eventually led to growing confidence among the

FIGURE 3.3. The mayor and his staff (2008).

court members, who began aligning their role as aksakals with those of state judges, thereby merging *salt* with state law.

"STATE JUDGES DON'T KNOW A LOT"

The aksakals in my fieldsite have managed to turn the two courts of elders into an institution that is increasingly accepted by villagers as a substitute for state courts. Whereas a couple of years ago villagers were disappointed when their cases were sent back from state courts to the aksakal courts, today they do not even try to go to Talas for reasons I have outlined above. This general tendency of not waiting for state officials to take care of them is also reflected in an increasing acceptance of their "state of statelessness." This is not only the case for the staff of the local administration and for state officials from the district but equally so for average villagers like Baiyz Apa's son, Nazir Baike, who works as a farmer. He explained to me why he does not care about the work of the local administration in the village anymore: "We do not care. They can do what they want because we do not get salaries anyway. They do not work for people. If the aiyl ökmötü functioned well they would bring diesel for the people to harvest wheat. We do not care if they exist or not. People work themselves and survive."

The mayor (see figure 3.3), in turn, had already told me two years earlier that he himself does not rely on "the state" anymore:

> I am teaching people to solve village problems by ourselves. We will not go to the province. We will not go to the government. If they [state officials] want to help, they are welcome. But the rest of the work, we will do by ourselves. We have to fix our roads ourselves. We have to build a bridge ourselves. We have to do other work ourselves, too. Then we need to live in harmony [*yntymak*]. But we pay great attention to attracting foreign investment. We must attract foreign investors and make connections with them. This is my first goal.

That the attraction of foreign investment was important was also the opinion of state officials from the district. During one of the few village meetings in the lower village where officials from the district of Talas were present, villagers bemoaned the fact that the water pumps on the main road were not functioning properly and that they had to use the old-fashioned hand-pumped wells again. In response to their complaint, the district governor replied: "I already told you that you should organize an association through which you could get money. Through an association write a project and try to get money from an international organization. The water pump could also be bought with this money. Our government cannot provide you with water pumps!"

These statements show that the state is increasingly perceived as unreliable, and even in the presence of its officials it remains only "spectrally present" (Das 2004). While villagers have stopped expecting anything from their mayor, the mayor does not expect anything from the district or the province anymore. To justify new regulations that elicited criticism from the villagers, the head of the district referred to the capital. In general, new requirements, laws, or rules are usually presented as coming "from Bishkek," where the government sits.[25]

International organizations are today regarded as the main providers and caretakers in Talas. Indeed, foreign organizations and rich individuals from Saudi Arabia sponsor most of the major renovations going on in the two villages. Villagers consider this new development disconcerting. While they have experience with forming associations, they do not understand why they should apply for money if state officials could do so for them. In their eyes, it is the state officials' task to find money, bring it, and then tell them what to do with it, as they did during Soviet times. In these times of local self-governance, however, this does not happen anymore, and the only individuals "taking care" are rich villagers who reside in the capital or even abroad.

In light of this situation, aksakals were initially disappointed when they were forced to realize that state judges had no interest in educating them about "law," as had originally been promised. As Kudaibergen Ata put it in 2006, "They used to come and invite us to seminars and talks. They used to teach us about the law. But this was five years ago. Nobody has checked my documents since then. Nobody has come to ask me about my work."

The situation in 2008 was similar: state officials had not monitored either of the two courts. Neither the court documents nor the aksakals' styles of decision making or their ways of applying law had been scrutinized. They were also not kept informed of the constant and often significant changes initiated by lawmakers in the capital. It was not in spite of this situation but rather because of it that they had to develop confidence in their new roles as judges and in their ways of attending to villagers' problems. Their performances as judges have slowly come to be accepted as part of customary law in the eyes of the village residents, who are equally disappointed by state officials, as the earlier comment by Nazir Baike has shown. Thus, being "abandoned by the state" has not resulted in disempowerment, as is sometimes suggested in the literature on decentralization (see Francis and James 2003). Instead, it has led to the customization of the aksakal courts. Today, the work of these courts in my fieldsite is considered more effective and legitimate than the work of the state courts. This finding also stands in contrast to how Noori presents Uzbeks' perception of the *mahalla* committee, likewise staffed with *oqsoqol* (Uzb.), as "yet another bureaucracy" that is "unsuccessful in achieving its objectives" (Noori 2006, 155). The aksakal judges' new self-image is most vividly reflected in how they (re)conceptualized their relations with state officials. In 2008 Kudaibergen Ata explained to me why state judges do not come to his village anymore: "They [state judges] do not come here because they were offended by us, because now we deliberate on everything here that was supposed to go to them. Since anyone who goes to the [state] court has to pay, they do not make money anymore. My work, however, is for free, and this is what people like about us—among other things. We also know everyone personally. We even know the person's fathers. State judges don't know a lot."

By portraying state judges as the greedy recipients of villagers' money and as now subject to the will of aksakal judges, Kudaibergen Ata turned the historical hierarchy—socialist as well as postsocialist—upside down: if the state does not give anything to the village anymore, the village might as well not give anything to the state. State officials are presented as craving people's money and as knowing nothing about life in the village. While there certainly is a lot of wishful thinking involved, Kudaibergen Ata's statement reflects not only his general disillusionment with the state but the increasing self-confidence of the aksakals vis-à-vis "the state" and state officials.

CONCLUSION

When people complain that they have no state, as villagers in Talas did during my fieldwork, they were—according to Herzfeld (1992, 10)—affirming their desire for precisely such a source of justice in their lives. While former president Akaev envisioned the court of elders as an institution where "customary law" would be applied as an alternative to state law, the aksakals associated the institution of the aksakal courts with the state. It is precisely because they have been turned into representatives of the state by state officials that they draw upon courtroom ceremonialism and etiquette in their legal proceedings, which usually invest state judges with authority (see Arno 1993; Just 2007, 117). Aksakal judges thus tried to appear as "state-like" as possible and specifically referred to the noncustomary repertoire of "state law" in their court sessions. By combining different legal elements into a new justification scheme, they engaged in combined lawmaking (see Benda-Beckmann 1983; Fitzpatrick 1983). Over the course of time, however, they developed a new self-image by aligning their new role as judges with their way of being aksakals.

This, together with the continuing failure of state judges to take care of villagers' problems and the aksakals' legal education, led to the growing acceptance of the aksakal court in my fieldsite. Today (legal) reasoning, establishing evidence, and making decisions are increasingly carried out according to *salt* in the aksakal courts. This is visible in the elders' frequent invocations of harmony (yntymak), in the sharing of food after court sessions, in the way one head leads the sessions and makes a decision, and in the preference for keeping things "inside."

As if in response to this increasing customization and the general laissez-faire attitude of villagers vis-à-vis state officials, state officials are now trying to enliven the presence of the state in the periphery by transferring policemen to the countryside, paying for the renovation of police stations, donating Russian Niva Jeeps to the most successful mayors (usually those who collect the most taxes), and significantly raising the salaries of the administrative staff in the villages. My impression is that a Potemkin state is being created by piling up insignia of the state in the countryside, demonstrating its presence, while at the same time state officials are increasingly less responsive to villagers' basic needs such as clean water, electricity, healthcare, regular payment of pensions, and childcare payments.[26] These new and shiny images of the state thus do not align with the concrete performances of state officials anymore. Judging from the contemporary situation, I consider it very likely that a few years from now the institution of the aksakal courts will be regarded as an inherent part of *salt* in my fieldsite and as something "that has always existed" among the Kyrgyz. Ironically, this is exactly what Akaev argued when he established the institution after Kyrgyzstan gained independence.

Chapter 4

PERFORMING AUTHORITY

One must respect the elders.[1] This is one of the most fundamental principles of *salt*. Bektur Agai, the village historian of Aral, elaborated on this principle for me:

> One of the laws [*myizam*] we have had since ancient times concerns the relationship between elders and young people. An older man is an *aksakal*, and a younger person should listen to him. The older one rules, governs, advises young people, and teaches all kinds of handicrafts such as smithing, how to train a bird and a dog, how to play the *komuz* [a stringed instrument], how to recite [the epic] *Manas*, how to tell the genealogy. A young man learns everything from the elders. And elders teach everything. Young people listen to the elder and serve him: if he wants to ride, the younger one prepares a horse for him; if he asks to get somebody from a field, then the young man goes; if he asks the young man to slaughter a sheep, the young man does it; if he asks him to sweep the road, he sweeps it; an aksakal orders and the young man implements everything. And an elder is obliged to teach everything.

This comment refers to the ideal aspects of *salt*. Bektur Agai is not talking about actual persons or real situations. Instead, he lists a number of activities an unspecified young man has to perform for an unspecified aksakal. While having to implement what the old man says, the young man benefits in that he receives training and experience. And although he may be very demanding, the aksakal is also presented as being obliged to transfer his knowledge to the young man. Old and young thus both enjoy privileges and have obligations toward one another that bind their asymmetrical yet reciprocal relationship. The differences in age and status described by Bektur Agai become embodied through the performance of specific interactional practices. While young people are compelled to be at the elders' disposal, elders are likewise expected to behave in ways deemed appropriate. Being treated respectfully establishes an individual's claims to authority, which should be understood as the result of such coemergent interactional practices.

DOING "BEING ELDERS"

Elders have to properly perform their "elderness" in interaction with others in order to achieve authority—in other words, they are required to "do 'being elders.'"[2] They have achieved authority when these coemergent practices are not challenged in direct interactions. This perspective does not take being or becoming an elder for granted. Rather, it requires a description of how an individual has to work constantly toward being recognized as, for example, an aksakal. This presupposes that elders who want to strengthen their authority are actively seeking opportunities to display their qualities. The following conversation between Kudaibergen Ata and two other aksakal judges, the late Abaskan Ata (the senior elder of Zhetigen uruu) and Kemel Ata (another aksakal from my neighborhood) exemplifies this argument. I recorded the conversation after two court cases had been decided in the aksakal court in Aral. While the first case that the elders settled was tricky, the second was easily resolved, and Kudaibergen Ata was content. However, on our way out of the mayor's office, where the session had taken place, Abaskan Ata approached Kudaibergen Ata with a complaint:

> AbA [to KA]: Hey, court [*sot*]! The deputy [Russ. *zasedatel'*, referring to himself] was supposed to be given the floor [lit. "a word"], too! You didn't give us a word; you solved everything yourself.
>
> KA: No, I gave you a chance to speak.
>
> AbA: No, in the first case you did, but in the second you did not.
>
> KA: Well, the decision was obvious in the second case.
>
> ArA: You should have given each of us a chance to speak, saying, "Abaskan, do you have anything to say? Kemel, do you have anything to say?"
>
> KeA: That's right . . .
>
> ArA: Then you could have concluded.
>
> KeA: Yes, then you could have concluded.
>
> KA: But the second case was clear to everyone. Our opinions were the same. *Zhezde*[3] [to AbA], I gave you a chance to speak, right?

AbA: No, I didn't say anything in the last case.

KA: Okay. Next time I will give you a chance to speak, *Zhezde.*

While the two aksakals agreed in principle with what Kudaibergen Ata had decided, they would have liked to receive an opportunity to speak, too. But it has become customary in the two aksakal courts of Aral and Engels for the head of the court to decide the cases from beginning to end. In Aral, Kudaibergen Ata is usually directly approached by villagers who come to his house to present their cases. After having discussed the issue with the claimant and sometimes with the accused party, he either settles the case by himself out of court or schedules a court meeting in the mayor's office, asking the claimant to state the problem in writing and bring it with him. It is also he who decides if he needs additional aksakals to be present and how the session will be structured. This becomes evident also in terms of address: when speaking of the respective head of their aksakal courts, villagers of Aral and Engels generally refer not to "our village judge" but to "our village court" (*bizdin aiyldyk sot*)—a term they do not use for the other court members, who are simply called *müchösü* (member). The decisions that the "head" (*bash*) makes might be challenged by the parties involved but never by the other aksakals. The situation in Engels is similar.

At first, Kudaibergen Ata tried to deny the validity of the other aksakals' complaint, but eventually he gave in. In addressing Abaskan Ata with a kinship term (*zhezde*), he acknowledged not only their direct relatedness but also that outside the courtroom he had to respect Abaskan Ata as the senior elder of Zhetigen uruu. The aksakal court members are thus confronted with a dilemma: while they do acknowledge him as *bash* in the court, Kudaibergen Ata has to be careful not to deprive them of opportunities to perform their aksakal-ness in public. By not giving them "a word," he potentially disrespected them himself. But only Abaskan Ata, in his role as Kudaibergen Ata's older sister's husband, could raise this issue after the court session. He got support from Kemel Ata in his objection, although the latter's words are of lesser consequence because he is the youngest of them all.

While being able to perform authority is situationally contingent, it matters a great deal to the actors themselves. They only acquired their status as judges in the mid-1990s, when the aksakal courts were set up, and they use the courts as a setting where others have to attend to them. Thus, in the aksakal court, one very fundamental principle of *salt* is operational: namely, that of having to listen to the head of a unit (*bash*), be it the household head, the head of a descent line (uruu), or another leader, such as a politician.[4] Being listened to is something these elders are accustomed to: in the household, they take decisions regarding their property, land, and animals, and they can to a great extent control the lives of their household members. Within the household, the head will be treated in what is considered a respectful way in accordance with *salt*. For example, he should always be offered the most honored place (*tör*), which is opposite the door. When meat is being served, the household head receives the head of the animal, a practice already noted in early ethnographies.[5] There are other parts of the animal that can be eaten by young household members only. For example, only young people eat the ears because, as the Kyrgyz say, "This way, the young learn to listen to the elders." Respect, in these cases, is the basis of the care and attention that elders enjoy from their children and relatives. Their elevated status also becomes visible in their right to name their grandchildren in the male line and, if they want, to raise them as their own children, who will call them "Father" (*Ata*) and "Mother" (*Apa*), and address their biological parents as "Uncle" (*Baike*) and "Aunt" (*Ezhe*).[6] Such requests by elders can hardly be denied, and in fact I have not come across any examples where parents have refused these particular rights.[7]

Some of the elders in the aksakal court are also the heads of their descent lines (*eng uluu aksakal*) and are used to being shown deference by their uruu members, who approach them for help, moral support, blessings (*bata*), and mediation in disputes. All aksakal court members also held important positions in Soviet times as, for example, kolkhoz directors, agronomists, journalists, or teachers. They are educated and possess a lot of technical knowledge related to land, irrigation, and animals—domains of practice around which disputes frequently arise. They are used to speaking in public and can deal with officials and politicians.

The establishment of the aksakal courts in the mid-1990s provided the aksakals with a new stage on which they could continue to display their competence and knowledge at a time when the kolkhoz, which had provided them with jobs before, no longer existed. By becoming aksakal judges, the kolkhoz elite of Aral and Engels could continue their public lives as professionals. While members of the Soviet elite have often managed to retain their official positions, less attention has been devoted to the fact that these positions then usually required a different performative script (see Geiss 2001; Davé 2007, 141–42). In the case of Aral and Engels, the new task of the former kolkhoz elite was no longer to uphold the interests of the Party or to pursue the future-oriented programs of the Soviet Union, but to judge "according to historically established customs and traditions of the Kyrgyz," as stated in the law on the aksakal courts. This opportunity, given to them by former president Akaev, required a readjustment in terms of their self-image. They were explicitly requested to perform as aksakals, which meant that it was not their previous experience as agents of modernization that made them eligible for the position but, in a complete reversal, their presumed competence in matters of *salt*.

MEETING A "SOVIET PERSON"

The former director of Kolkhoz Kommunizm, who had been the first head of the aksakal court in Aral, resigned in the year 2000 after having held the position for five years. I visited him in his house in the winter of 2005, after I had already been living in Aral for some months. Until then I had heard of him, but I had never seen him at village meetings or other events where aksakals gathered. He told me that he did not go out anymore and explained why:

> Since I got used to speaking, I have to speak when I go out. Some people don't like it [laughs]. I can't shut my mouth. I just got used to that. I worked in leading positions for many years in the province as well as in the region. In meetings I criticize others, and I am used to getting praised. [He pauses]. In the Kyrgyz mentality, if an old person is quiet, then people will say, "He got old quietly, which is good." But if I give speeches in meetings, people will say, "He used to speak before and he is still speaking. He did not grow old well." Our *salt* is like this.

He had tried hard to "become a judge," as he put it, by going to the seminars a state judge in Talas had organized in the first year after the aksakal courts came into being, and by trying to stick to the law of the aksakal courts as accurately as possible. But he became frustrated when he realized that he was not taken seriously by the "real" judges. Not only were his decisions ignored by the state court in Talas, he said that he also did not receive any payment or other recognition for his work. Although he was older than most other aksakals I had met up to that point, he neither looked nor behaved in ways similar to the other elders. I had become used to being called *kyzym* (my daughter) and being kissed on the cheek by elders that I had not met before. This old man, however, was distant and very formal. He was polite and hospitable but never inquired into my family affairs—which was usually the first thing elders did when they met me. He also usually spoke Russian with me despite the fact that my assistant, Zemfira, and I addressed him in Kyrgyz. "He did not have a beard," remarked Zemfira on our way home, noting another minor difference when compared to other aksakals his age.[8] He fit the role of a civil servant, a bureaucrat, and had not embraced the role of the jovial aksakal. We realized that we had met a man who called himself a *sovetskii chelovek* (Russ.: a "Soviet person") and who had difficulties adjusting to the present conditions, which required him to perform as an aksakal and whose new duty it was to embody, speak, and even judge according to *salt*.

Other court members, however, learned to use the new institution as an opportunity to display their knowledge and competence in creative new ways, thereby commanding respect for their work from those who consulted them. Holding court sessions is particularly interesting for these aksakals, not only because the disputing parties approach them in their function as judges but also because they are often a person's uruu elder, neighbor, or former colleague from Kolkhoz Kommunizm. The way elders treat the parties involved thus changes according to who approaches them for what purpose.

Despite the law on the aksakal courts' prohibition against presiding over cases that involve close relatives, judges and disputing parties are always related to one another, and often in more than just one way.[9] This multiplex connectedness is invoked by aksakals in every court session, no matter what dispute is at hand: people's shared histories enter the courtroom along with the actual cases and provide opportunities for the elders to recall the common ancestors, the shared residence, or the communal work experience of all people present. To "professionally" sideline kinship, neighborliness, and amity would go against *salt*. While their strategic position as judges enables the aksakals to summon others onto a stage that was erected by state law, they then draw upon their knowledge as technical experts, war veterans, pious Muslims, wise elders, or any combination of these roles.[10]

While each court session follows a different path, and many are about contentious situations and subject to heated discussion, Kudaibergen Ata usually aims at closing with an appeal to the common bond people share with one another. He evokes *yntymak* by citing well-known proverbs and other generally acknowledged principles of *salt*. Consider the following "closing scene" of the court session during which Abaskan Ata and Kemel Ata did not get their chance to speak. The case was about grazing regulations and involved animals belonging to a person from Engels trampling the wheat field of a person from Aral:[11]

> KA: Okay, relatives, listen! You are two fighting parties, two separate bodies, but we are one people. We are relatives. Now each of us has our own land. We get food from this land. We live by working this land. There is no working kolkhoz or sovkhoz anymore. We [the aksakals] are not saying, "Do not have animals!" as they did in kolkhoz times. We plant things on the land, and we live off our lands and our animals. You can have animals. Be rich! Be wealthy! We really hope that these things will come true for all of us. We are relatives. We need to forgive each other. We need to look after our animals and take care of our lands. Let's try not to accuse each other. Let's live in yntymak! Do not let our relations be torn to pieces because of the land. Land is a bad thing. All of the disputes since ancient times are related to land. Now land is private. Before, all land belonged to the kolkhoz. Now it has become "mine," "yours," and "his." That's why we need to take care of our animals. Am I right [*tuuraby*]?

> Audience: Right [*tuura*].

> KA: Then that's it [*büttü*].

While the question, "Am I right?" at the end of his monologue was obviously a rhetorical closure, Kudaibergen Ata persuaded the audience to affirm his statement. No discontent or criticism was voiced afterward, as people also agreed in this case with what the elder had stated. Although he does not always succeed in ending a session with the disputing parties leaving the room amicably, his explicit performance of *salt* at the end of each case is a clear attempt to cut off further discussion. And indeed I seldom heard any of the disputing parties object to his final words. If something is according to custom (*salt boiuncha*), it neither requires nor tolerates explanation. While Kudaibergen Ata might in fact have only temporarily succeeded in calming the waves, this display of *salt* toward the end of the court session also strengthened his authority as an aksakal: for a couple of minutes he had the undivided attention of the audience, and it was precisely this attention that Abaskan Ata and Kemel Ata had wanted to get their share of when they approached him on their way out of the courtroom. While the case they had just solved had been "obvious" and the opinions of the elders unitary, Kudaibergen Ata had deprived the two other members of their privilege to invoke and thus publicly embody *salt* in their role as wise and respected aksakals.

OBLIGATIONS OF ELDERS

When I asked why aksakals were expressly invited to life-cycle rituals and other festive events (such as birth celebrations, marriages, funerals, and national holidays, as well as election campaigns, political meetings, and demonstrations), I often received by way of an answer the saying, "A beard is needed at a feast."[12] This clearly conveys that the respect people accord to elders is only one side of the coin. While on the one hand an elderly person enjoys privileges during these events, on the other hand they have to fulfill certain expectations villagers have of them: they need to validate the event. While elders can invoke *salt* through their narrations and their embodied behavior, thereby educating their children, daughters-in-law, and grandchildren, their actions are also directed by the expectations of others, as the example of the former kolkhoz director has shown. A former Soviet judge who is now an aksakal explained to me that aksakals have to be generous, quiet, restrained, humble, and compromising. He also emphasized that aksakals are regarded as being responsible for the behavior of young people and those who have misbehaved in their communities. Tülööberdi Ata, the aksakal court member from Engels, said aksakals are required not to lie. Their work for people should be "free of charge" because it is "aksakals' work." "The judges of the aksakal court should not judge fairly because they are judges, but because they are aksakals," remarked Arun Ata, a member of the aksakal court in Aral. This list of guidelines shows how male elders should ideally behave in order to be considered good aksakals.

Female elders, on the other hand, are exempt from such expectations as long as they have a husband. They are also characterized quite differently from the aksakals. In general, women in Talas are considered gossipy, loud, and emotional. This is also what they laughingly say about themselves. While these attributions are surely stereotypical, they are not judgmental. Women can display behavior that would be inappropriate for aksakals, such as screaming and shouting in public, but a shift in behavior is required of them when they become widows and thus the heads of their households. I nev-

FIGURE 4.1. Baiyz Apa overseeing her two daughters and her daughter-in-law as they make carpets (2006).

er heard a widow scream, and seldom did they gossip themselves, although they continued listening to what other women had to say.

Baiyz Apa is such a female *bash*. She enjoys enormous respect not only within her household but throughout the entire village. She is able to keep her household members together, takes a central part in the life-cycle rituals of her extended family, her descent line, and her neighborhood, and has a reputation for being one of the most religious elders of either sex (see figure 4.1). She is even called *moldo* by the aksakals—a title usually given only to pious males—because she has been praying regularly for fifty years now. Baiyz Apa resembled respected aksakals even more in the sense that she was home most of the time, attending to the never-ending stream of relatives, neighbors, and other guests who came to see her and talk to her. And, just as with male elders, along with these privileges come obligations, as the rare female heads are supposed to behave much like aksakals.[13]

In the following example, Baiyz Apa maintained the high moral ground at considerable material cost to her household. In spring 2006, after the seed potatoes had just been planted on Baiyz Apa's land, a thief dared to dig out a large portion of them in order to plant them on his own land. He was caught red-handed and brought to Baiyz Apa's house, along with the sacks of potatoes he had managed to dig out. Baiyz Apa refused to see him and had her youngest son, Nasir, deliver a message to him: "My mother said you should take these potatoes—she will not eat from what a thief has touched." The man was forced to take the sacks and leave. By rhetorically converting the potatoes from returned stolen goods into a nonreturnable "poisoned gift," Baiyz Apa denied the thief's attempt to reconcile. She never dropped another word about this incident. Her *kelin*, Elmira Ezhe, however, went on lamenting for some time, because she was already anticipating the problems lying ahead of her. Potatoes are the main source of income for most villagers in Aral and Engels, after animal products. They need to be sold in autumn at the bazaar in Talas or to Kazakh traders roaming the villages in their trucks. Without this harvest, people do not have enough money to participate in life-cycle rituals that are predominantly held during the autumn months when everybody else has cash on hand.

Doing "being elder" can get the actor entangled in a web of expectations. Baiyz Apa perceived the theft as directed against her personal property, which she, as the household *bash*, was in charge of. She then displayed high moral integrity by sacrificing her and her family's only income, the potato harvest. By depriving the thief of the possibility to make up for his nefarious deed, she indebted him for an indefinite time. The thief was humiliated not only because everyone in the village knew about his failed deed but also because it turned out that he had not stolen from an age-mate—the son of Baiyz Apa, who had planted the potatoes—but from one of Aral's most respected individuals. As far as I could tell from the gossip going on afterward, Baiyz Apa's reputation was strengthened throughout the village, especially because everyone acknowledged that her behavior had been according to *salt*. However, as an elder, Baiyz Apa did not have to worry about the consequences of her deed; it was her daughter-in-law who would have to find ways and money to cover the missing income in autumn when the festive season started.

Elders work at performing their authority in ways that prove them worthy of ancestorhood in the eyes of their relatives and fellow villagers.[14] Raising children, giving them an education, arranging their marriages, building houses for them, taking care of their grandchildren, and maintaining a good reputation in the village are all practices through which an elder can show that he or she has led a successful and morally committed life according to *salt* and will, therefore, be remembered by others.

CHALLENGING THE HEAD

According to *salt*, relations between the young and the old are ordered through a formalized mode of communication: while the young need to pay respect to their elders, the elders need to strive toward complying with an idealized image of being humble and wise, which can come at a significant cost. This social contract, however, can be challenged in several ways. Most frequently this occurs by means of indirect communication: gossiping, vilifying, and reciting proverbs that portray elders in a way that contradicts the positive image of benevolence and wisdom all give the younger generation a means to reconcile outward respect with hidden resentment.[15] Consider, for example, the following proverb: *Sakaly uzun kishinin akyly kyska* (A person with a long beard has a short mind). Another way of expressing disagreement with the commands of elders is to silently disapprove and simply do something else, since directly challenging one's parents would be considered shameful (*uiat*). There is little an old person can do in such cases of tacit disrespect. However, young people themselves reiterate and work to sustain the general principle of having to respect one's elders, because "those who do not respect the old will not be respected when they are old themselves," as I heard from young and old alike.[16]

When children who are socialized in this way submit to their parents' wishes and demands, they know that one day they will be in a position that allows them to command respect from others as well. As they grow older, they learn to dominate their younger siblings, who have to address them respectfully in a formal way, using the second person plural. Thus, the young perpetuate the domination by the elders. At the same time, they learn to shoulder the growing responsibilities of having to take care of their younger siblings. This is to say not only that children learn how to behave properly toward the elders but also that every male individual develops a desire to become a head (*bash*), as only this status gives actors significant autonomy.

While women can also become *bash* once they are widows, they first strive toward autonomy in their roles as wives who can manage their household affairs independently. Being married to a man who is the youngest son, however, is a tremendous burden for a woman. According to *salt*, the youngest son stays with his parents even after he is married and takes care of them. His wife—who is a kelin to her parents-in-law—has to serve not only her family but also all other family members, including her husband's older sisters and her husband's older brothers' wives. If several sons live in one household, as is sometimes still the case, the older kelin usually demands respect from the younger one, who will have to work harder.[17] Eventually, though, many people are forced to challenge their parents if they continue to treat them like children.

The following case illustrates how a son who was nearly fifty years old rebelled against his father, who did not recognize him as *bash*. Arstan Baike had set up his own household with the help of his parents after he got married.[18] He had six children. His oldest son was married, and his son's wife was expecting a child. Officially, Arstan Baike owned forty sotik of land (twenty for himself and twenty for his wife). This is a rather small amount for such a large family, but since all of his children were born after land had been privatized, no land plots had been allocated to them. Even these forty sotik, however, were still under the de facto control of his elderly father. The father, as the head of the household, had made use of his customary right to keep the land of all of his family members after they received their plots in 1993. Arstan Baike wanted to finally claim his right to these forty sotik of land his father had not yet handed over to him. He argued that he had many mouths to feed now and, with a grandchild on the way, too little land at any rate. His father, however, systematically ignored the demands of his son to be recognized as *bash* in his own right, even though the latter was about to become a grandfather soon.

In the spring of 2006 his father again sowed wheat in Arstan Baike's land plot, which the son had already cleared of stones in preparation for plowing. He wanted to plant potatoes. When Arstan Baike saw how his father had crossed his plans again, he first tried to talk to him directly but failed to change the old man's mind. Finally, he approached Kudaibergen Ata, who happened to be a member of the same uruu, Bürgö.

With my partner, my research assistant, and me in tow, Kudaibergen Ata met the son and his mother on the respective land plot outside of Aral. The father had not come. "He does not understand," said his wife simply. Even though Arstan Baike and his father had been fighting within the house, there was no way that the father would bring this family dispute into the open. He could not allow his son to disrespect him in front of others, even if the "others" were kinsmen such as Kudaibergen Ata.[19]

The land dispute between mother and son was a lesson in how respecting one's elders (here, one's mother) can constrain an individual's actions. While the mother screamed and cursed her son, accusing him of disrespecting his father and of being ungrateful for all that he had done for him, Arstan Baike tried to stay calm, not raising his voice and arguing in a conciliatory way (see figure 4.2). He tried to get his mother to acknowledge that he, too, was a head and had to take responsibility for his family just as his father had done. But his mother would not listen. Instead, she compared his six children to the eleven children she had given birth to and kept on repeating that, without his father, the son would own nothing, for they had paid for his marriage and built him and his wife a house:

"May you fall down deep into the ground together with your daughter-in-law! 'My son brought a daughter-in law,' he says. Everyone brings a daughter-in-law! Or do you think you are the only one who has a daughter-in-law? Do you think you did a great job by arranging the marriage of your son? I have ten, fifteen daughters-in-law! We built houses for you all! Die instead of squabbling over land with your father!"

Kudaibergen Ata turned his head away, smoked a cigarette, and waited for things to calm down. He then took the old woman by the hand, saying, "Come here, you have given birth to him," ignoring the next curse the old woman uttered at her son.

He went on, "You know you should have left the land to him and not planted anything. There is no need for conflict here. The government gave land to all of us. Everything is based on laws, you understand that, right?"

She did not answer.

"I am trying to feed my family," said Arstan Baike. "Each person has to fight for his own life." Apparently, he was trying to find a balance between respecting his parents and claiming his autonomy. However, his mother would not listen and instead cursed him again. This went on for thirty more minutes, leaving me standing by uncomfortably.

Finally, the son gave in. "But from next year onward," he said, "I will plant on my land." The only answer Kudaibergen Ata had for him was to remind him that whatever he intended to do, he should not forget that "we are one people," and that such disputes should be kept "inside."[20]

To me he said, "I am glad I did not make this public. People would have gossiped that Bürgö had fought." When I tried to talk with Arstan Baike a couple of days later on the street, he denied further problems, saying, "Everything is calm now."

FIGURE 4.2. Eliza and I try not to get in the way of the conversation about how the land should be divided (2006).

While according to *salt* household elders must be benevolent and not exploitative, things can look different in reality. The father asserted his status as *bash* by not being present. However, he thereby also acted according to *salt*, which stipulates, as Kudaibergen Ata himself reminded the son, that family disputes should be kept "inside." While father and son could not openly resent each other, Arstan Baike's mother did not seem to have lost face by showing up and demonstrating her discontent with what her son had done by screaming at him and even cursing him. Married women can get away with such behavior, but for an old man to act this way—or even allow his wife to act this way in his presence—would have been intolerable. Approaching Kudaibergen Ata was a desperate move by Arstan Baike that, in the end, was not successful. Kudaibergen Ata, likewise, would have had little influence over his absent fellow kinsman, who was also his senior. In fact, Kudaibergen Ata mentioned to Arstan Baike that he himself keeps the land plots of his own two sons as long as they live under his roof.[21]

When I returned to Aral in 2008, Arstan Baike's son had left his household and moved to the town of Talas with his wife and their child. Arstan Baike was finally cultivating his own land plot as he had wanted because his father was getting too old to do so himself. Whereas state law prescribed formal equality between the father and son by categorizing both as landowners, their relationship remained hierarchical, with the father as *bash* deciding over his son's property.

Paying respect to one's parents according to *salt* is a performative act that can have critical material aspects. Arstan Baike could not have approached Kudaibergen Ata at an earlier stage in the dispute, which had been going on since he left his father's house. He needed to become a grandfather in order to finally try to establish his status as *bash*, too. Thus, a male *bash* needs to be acknowledged not only by his household members or peers but also by his own parents. In Talas, however, the situation has become complicated because acknowledging a son as *bash* directly diminishes a man's access to the second most valuable material resource after animals—land.[22]

In this conflict, then, two legal repertoires clashed: while Arstan Baike tried to reason in accordance with the land reform, which advocates ownership on an individual basis, his mother employed *salt* in her argumentation, whereby respecting one's parents also implies not challenging the established custom that land is always administered by one head.[23] After first issuing a token affirmation of state law Kudaibergen Ata, the invited mediator, also came down on the side of *salt* in the end. It turned out that he was also keeping control over his sons' land.

In my fieldsite, such open conflict broke out only seldom. In most of the cases, children had to show patience and tried to please their parents until the parents considered them worthy of being *bash*es themselves. When adult children such as Arstan Baike finally claim their land from their parents—even if according to state law they had this right years earlier—they need to carefully weigh the chances of economic success against the risk of publicly disrespecting their parents. The interactional dimension of *salt* and the duality of agency and patiency involved are particularly clear in this example: while Arstan Baike might have acquired his land sooner if he had openly broken the relationship with his father by appealing to state courts, he might then have lost the possibility of relating himself to the Bürgö uruu. Kudaibergen Ata's comment about not making the dispute public so that people would not gossip about "how Bürgö fought" clearly shows that it was not only land as a material resource that was at stake here but also Arstan Baike's attachment to the Bürgö uruu, which goes through his father. Instead of risking his uruu membership by breaking with his father over land, Arstan Baike sent his son to Talas, thereby avoiding the problem of having to transfer land that he did not yet control to his son.

KASYM ATA

Kasym Ata was the head of the aksakal court in Engels until 2009. Born in 1923, he was one of the oldest aksakals in the village (ninety-two years of age in 2015). He is also the head of his household, which consists of himself, his wife, his divorced daughter who moved back in with her two children to live with him, as well as several grandchildren whom he raises in his house. His youngest son and his daughter-in-law live in the mountains half of the year, where they herd Kasym Ata's large herd of horses, sheep, and goats. His other sons live in the village. Kasym Ata studied in Bishkek during Soviet times and took up a career as a journalist. Traveling throughout the Soviet Union as an active Party member, he was rewarded by the Party for his success in propagating atheism as well as for his journalistic talent. He is a member of the Kyrgyz Society of Journalists and became the director of the village school in Engels in the 1960s, holding this position until his retirement in the 1990s.

Among the older male village population there is hardly a person who has not been educated by Kasym Ata. He is respected (and sometimes feared) by young and old for his impressive career and the strong hand with which he ruled his aksakal court. In court he often used commanding language, which the audience likened to the way he used to conduct his lessons at school, addressing the disputing parties as he addressed his pupils. Befitting this authoritarian style, Kasym Ata—just like Kudaibergen Ata—led the court sessions from beginning to end. The other members of the aksakal court often knew nothing about the case when they heard the call from their *bash* to come to the mayor's office to "work." While he ordered other aksakals of the village around without showing much respect, reminding them that they, too, were once his pupils, I have not come across an instance when the other members—even when annoyed—did not heed his calls. Kasym Ata's perception of the relationship between him and his members was revealed to me once during a conversation I overheard while I was having tea with the elders after a court case. He called Tülööberdi Ata his *sandalet* (sandal), a synonym for a slave. Tülööberi Ata, who is in his seventies, answered laughingly: "So this is how you see us?" Later, when we were alone again, Kasym Ata confirmed that he considered himself above the other members of the aksakal court: "In the end, I decide. What the other members say is not that important." That he is the former head of many current heads in various positions throughout Kyrgyzstan is a strong factor in Kasym Ata's dealings with other aksakals. His most famous student is the former governor of Talas province, who then became the governor of Zhalal-Abad province, served as interim prime minister in 2007, and later became minister of agriculture.

His personal connections as well as his personality have also made it possible for him to deal successfully with state officials and politicians. He often stood up for fellow villagers who could not manage to get necessary documents or who felt unfairly treated by state officials in Talas town. In contrast to the former director of Kolkhoz Kommunizm, Kasym Ata has no problem dealing with state judges. On the contrary, stories of how he had "won" a case against a judge of the Talas city court, whom he accused of having been partial and corrupt in divorce cases, circulate widely not only in Engels but also in Aral. He himself liked to remind others that "even the state judges fear me," and that in contrast to state judges he did not have to be elected. "I am the eternal judge," he once laughingly declared when I asked him about whether there would be elections for aksakal judges in the village any time soon.

So is Kasym Ata a powerful aksakal? People in Talas mostly use the Russian word *vlast'* (Kyr.: *biilik*) when referring to a person's capacity to enforce order (*tartip*). While an individual can have and exercise *vlast'*, the term is mostly used as a synonym for "the state" or the government and always includes the possibility of coercion.[24] Sometimes people also use the adjective *chong* (lit. "big") to describe a person. The term *bailyk* translates as "wealth" and is often used for those individuals who are influential and rich. All of these terms refer to politicians or businessmen; that is, people who are characterized either by reference to their financial means or by being connected to "the state." None of these terms—be they Kyrgyz or Russian—is commonly used for aksakals. Kasym Ata, however, was often described by villagers as "big," rich, and able to enforce order.

Many villagers viewed his wealth as a criterion for his ability to judge fairly because he was not dependent on other people's money. On the other hand, his personality (which can best be described as authoritarian), his personal connection to the governor, and the way he used to boss the other aksakals around as if he were still their teacher made him a bad aksakal in their eyes: he did not behave as an aksakal should. Therefore, most elders in the village did not consider him one of "theirs" anymore, since his behavior in public and specifically toward them did not comply with *salt*. On one occasion, when he was the subject of strong criticism from other village aksakals for being drunk in public, the question of when he would resign from his position was brought up. Kasym Ata, in a smart move, denied his agency in regard to the matter, saying, "Only the mayor can decide on this," a claim that, according to state law, was not even correct. However, what mattered was not what was de jure correct but what was successfully postulated. Invoking the responsibility of the mayor in this regard, who was sitting next to him during this conversation, was a smart move because everyone knew perfectly well that the mayor would not speak up against Kasym Ata, who had been his teacher.

Kasym Ata also prevented his own sons from becoming aksakals. While they had all set up their own households, none of them held full land rights, and when Kasym Ata appeared with them in public, he treated them like children. One son in particular, who was a teacher in the village school where his father had been the director for so many years, liked to spend his time with the other aksakals. He was in his sixties and particularly eager to explain *salt* to me "as an aksakal" by citing proverbs and giving historical examples of how things had been in former times. Once Kasym Ata heard him talking to me and publicly snubbed him. "Why are you talking like that?" he said. "Are you an aksakal or what? Go home!" And his son did as he was told.

In 2008 the rebellious mood among the aksakals had consolidated, and they were even discussing having Kasym Ata removed from the aksakal court because he was often seen drinking vodka and playing cards with young people in the street. But still no one dared to directly address the issue. Asked why they did not dare confront him directly, an aksakal court member said: "He would not quit. We would tell him softly that he is too old be a judge and that he needs to give his seat to a younger person. But he would then pull out his diploma. We would just sit there [meaning that they could not do anything] if he showed it." The imam added a reminder about the former governor of Talas province, who had been Kasym Ata's pupil, and that they were still very close.

When I visited Kasym Ata himself, he did not mention any problems—life seemed normal for him. He once told me that a politician against whom he had agitated during the parliamentary elections of 2005 called him a "wolf" who was "howling" at others. Kasym Ata had basically taken the microphone out of the politician's hands while the man was talking to an audience of aksakals in Talas, telling him to go back to Bishkek where he had come from. The politician, who did not know Kasym Ata, gave up the stage. Instead of being offended by being called a wolf, Kasym Ata seemed pleased and laughed wholeheartedly.

A solitary character who does not show concern about what other people in the village think of him, he is also financially independent and intellectually superior to most other people in Engels. He considers himself a just person fighting for villagers whose voices go unheard in the state court in Talas. Different from other elders, he did not try to talk women seeking a divorce into staying with their husbands "for the sake of the children" or for yntymak. He readily allowed them to separate and helped to secure some property and land for them. Although he clearly possesses some of the characteristics that Shahrani (1986, 264), writing about the Kyrgyz in the Pamir, described as ideal qualities for a leader, such as bravery, wealth in livestock, and the ability to protect the interests of the community against government officials, he seemed interested mainly in presenting himself as a "big man." This was also the basis for others' judgments of him.

While wealth is often characterized as providing the means for power, Kasym Ata neither shared his wealth with others nor put his assets to use in order to bind other villagers to him.[25] He was also not interested in working toward yntymak. He would fight against state officials, thereby protecting his clients against outside forces, but he would also scare these same clients into submission by threatening to transfer their cases to the state court if they did not heed his words. In many instances Kasym Ata did not behave according to *salt* but still managed to retain his central position as the head of the court because people nevertheless respected (and sometimes feared) him for being strong (*chong*).

There is a fine line between being accorded respect for comporting oneself in a proper and *salt*-compatible way and being respected for one's willful, proud, and nonconciliatory performance. Even though Kasym Ata did not engage in "doing 'being aksakal,'" as this would have involved surrendering his autonomy, still nobody dared to challenge him directly. Had the other aksakals removed him from his position as head of the aksakal court, it could have been interpreted by others, especially the youth, as an invitation to do the same: if elders start to disrespect one another, then the young might stop respecting them. This is the downside of what Nader (1990) has termed "harmony ideology": for the sake of yntymak and the possibility of retaining their own authority, aksakals cannot openly criticize one another (and especially not their nominated "head") even in the face of utter disrespect (see Beyer and Girke 2015).[26] Kasym Ata profited from the very regulations of *salt* to which he himself did not submit. Thus, it was less his agency and more the patiency of others toward his actions that allowed him to enforce order.

Kasym Ata resigned from his office as the head of the aksakal court in April 2009 due to his age. By 2015 the aksakal court in Engels was, for all intents and purposes, no longer in operation. The institution had been so thoroughly identified with its first judge that, after Kasym Ata left, nobody could be "the court" any more. However, in its place stepped Yiman Nuru (lit. "The Light of Faith"; see Beyer 2013), a local organization that had been established in 2005. It is composed of all the aksakals in the village and is headed by the village imam, Syrgak Baike. Yiman Nuru has taken over many of the functions formerly allocated to the aksakal court, including the informal settlement of disputes. In addition, the organization also tries to diminish those parts of *salt* it considers not customary, such as the excessive spending of money and the exchange of material items during funerals and the drinking of alcohol during weddings (see chapter 6).

CUSTOM MEETS SHARIAT AT THE MOSQUE

The young and the old continue to order their relations outside the sphere of the household as well. This is particularly the case for interactions between religious officials and elders. The two young imams of Aral and Engels (forty and twenty-three years old, respectively, in 2005) who serve as religious experts to their mosque congregation, which consists mainly of aksakals, had only started to become interested in religion after the demise of the Soviet Union. Syrgak Baike, the imam of Engels (see figure 4.3), recalled how he was "elected":[27]

> The old imam of our village did not want to continue being an imam. At that time I had started to become interested in religion, even started to learn a little Arabic from Bakai Moldo [the head imam of the province].[28] And once during a funeral ceremony I was told to join the aksakals at the grave. There, they told me that I would be their new imam. I ran away. I did not want to become an imam. But then we had another funeral ceremony and Bakai Moldo, my teacher, also came. The aksakals told Bakai Moldo: "This boy knows a little. He knows how to read a little bit and you should appoint him for us to become an imam." People insisted.[29] They were saying that my father and my

grandfather had been religious, too. So it is in our family. When I finally became imam, all of them were supportive and helped me. Aksakals would be together with me all the time. They were teaching me: "You should do this, you should do that." They told me how to wash the body of a dead person. Everything.

The imam of Aral was "elected" by aksakals in a similar way.[30] Another religious head, Nurdin Moldo,[31] who used to work as an imam of a large village on the opposite end of Talas province, recalls an almost identical story: "I would perform *namaz*[32] [pray] and read books. The local imam became old and it seemed that people knew about me. They were deciding who is appropriate and who is not. Then they invited me to a village board meeting and they told me that I would become the new imam. I said I did not want to, but the aksakals who were sitting there elected me. And since according to shariat it is not right to refuse the blessing [*bata*] of those who give it you, I had no choice. I was 'tied.'"[33]

In all these cases, the imam's personal family histories played a role in the decision of the aksakals. In Engels, the imam's father and grandfather had been known as "religious." In Nurdin Moldo's case, his wife told me that his great-grandfather had been head of an Islamic school (*medrese*) as well, and that her husband had become an imam because it was "in his blood" (*kanynda*). This gives rise to the impression that when they "elected" their village imams, the aksakals believed religious competence to be hereditary or at least passed down from father to son through example and teaching. The only two examples I heard of during my first stages of fieldwork when religious officials were not "elected" by aksakals are so extraordinary that they cannot be regarded as normal cases either.[34]

When I returned to my fieldsite in 2015, however, I encountered stories of young imams who decided on their own accord to become religious officials. One of them was Syrgabek, the son of Baiyz Apa's husband's niece. He had been interested in Islam from a very young age, and Baiyz Apa was always eagerly listening to the sermons the then sixteen-year-old gave her and whoever else was present in her house in 2005, repeating what he had just learned at the mosque. When he uttered the phrases and repeated the stories the imam had told the group of mosque-goers, Baiyz Apa was proud of him for his eagerness to learn about Islam. However, she also often giggled in light of his words because she had obviously never thought of her daily religious practices in such formal religious terms. When a new

FIGURE 4.3. Syrgak Baike and his wife, Dinara Ezhe (2006).

mosque was built in his part of the village in 2014, he seized the occasion and became an imam.[35]

Syrgabek, the new young imam, began his vocation against the
wishes of Baiyz Apa, who was afraid that people would think he was
too young. "I told him to wait," she explained. "But he did not listen
to me and they appointed him." As the mosque congregation becomes increasingly mixed in terms of age and thus authority, members must come up with novel ways of justifying and explaining their
religious practices in terms of both *salt* and shariat, and they must
negotiate who has the authority to interpret Islam accordingly. As
it turns out, the goals of the young imams and the aksakals are not
always congruent.

Elders have a particular concern in the affairs of Islam: going to
the mosque, praying, and fasting are practical endeavors through
which elderly people prepare for the afterlife. These practices are
part of growing old (see also Khalid 2007, 103). But for today's aksakals, performing Islam also generates respect and sustains their
claims to authority. Most of the aksakals started to pray only after the
Soviet Union collapsed. Some of them who were active in the kolkhoz administration and the Party describe Islam as a new "ideology"
(using the Russian word *ideologiia*). For others, Islam is simply a continuation of practices they engaged in during Soviet times. However,
the existence of parallel ideologies does not pose a problem for them;

they often relate to both ideologies concurrently, as the following example shows. It brings us back to Kasym Ata.

When I first visited Kasym Ata in 2005, he was the undisputed head of the aksakal court in Engels. He invited me into his living room and told his kelin to bring tea. Kasym Ata himself did not drink or eat with me because it was Ramadan and he was keeping the fast (orozo). While I was waiting for tea to be served, my eyes wandered around the room, stopping at certificates documenting his work for the newspaper Sovettik Kyrgyzstan, as well as a certificate from Soviet times honoring Kasym Ata for his work in propagating atheism.[36] When he came to join me, he told me that he had been a famous journalist in Soviet times, and he went to his cupboard to show me medals of honor the Party had awarded him. Another trait that sets him apart is that he enjoys drinking vodka after his court sessions, while the other aksakal court members drink tea. The incongruence of his earlier efforts to propagate atheism (not to mention his penchant for vodka) and his current observance of Islamic fasting rules was not remarked upon by him or any other villager. It seems to me that he has not so much undergone an ideological change as begun to adapt his everyday practices to those customary ways he had resisted when he had other roles to perform.

When aksakals "switch" to Islam nowadays, they are interested in learning how to perform it. They do not necessarily want to know the scripture-oriented interpretation of it, and neither do they repudiate their nonreligious past. When praying, for example, it is important for them to know which phrases should be uttered at the beginning of a prayer and which toward the end. What these phrases mean is of less importance.[37] According to the villagers, it is more important that the elders know how to pray than it is that the imams know Arabic. In these particular cases the authority of the elders is reinforced: orthopraxy is more important than orthodox knowledge. While the imam is respected because only he can read holy texts in Arabic, elders have authority because only they can interpret the meaning of these texts (see Barnes 1986; Lambek 1990; Watson 1996). During funeral and memorial rituals, for example, the imam starts reciting the Qur'an by heart, but soon the aksakals take over and continue with long and elaborate speeches about the deceased in Kyrgyz. These tasks are not assigned to the young imams, who often do not know the deceased as well as the elders did and who lack the rich oratorical skills many of the aksakals command. Accordingly, attention rests on the elders. In Aral and Engels, it has been predominantly aksakals who attend mosque services, where they learn how to recite in Arabic from the imam, tapping into his expert knowledge. There are also young boys who are sent to the mosque by parents who want their children to be active Muslims, even though the parents themselves do not go to services. In recent years, grown-up men have also joined the congregation; for example Ydyrys Baike, who was fifty years old in 2015. Nevertheless, compared to other parts of the country, the overall number of people who go to the mosque is still very small. There is also no separate space for women in the mosques; they must pray at home. Recently, however, prayer groups that teach young schoolgirls about Islam have been established. In general, over the course of the last decade I have noticed a steady increase in the number of people attending mosque services, as well as growing interest in Islam. Developments that were reported in southern Kyrgyzstan in the early 2000s (see McBrien 2008) are only now, ten or more years later, taking place in the northern part of the country.

As Islam is a text-based religion, the act of reciting the Qur'an can constitute a claim to the authority of the text itself—something that aksakals are actively working on today (see Lambek 1990). They are thereby broadening their already established knowledge base even further by becoming religious experts. In recent years, the imam of Engels told me, aksakals have also started to conduct the opening part of a prayer (*Kuran okuu*) in Arabic. When I asked Kudaibergen Ata after the first months of my stay in Aral whether I could take a look at the inside of the village mosque (where only men go), he said, "Sure. But you have to say *Bismilla ir-rakhman-ir-rakhim*.[38] If you say it, I can take you in. If not, then we will just talk outside." Asking further whether he could introduce me to the imam of the village as well, he replied, "Do you want me to take you to the moldo without beard or with beard?[39] I mean, to the one who reads books well or to the one who does not read at all? If you want to talk to the one who reads, then we will go to the child."

He referred to the young imam as a "child" (*bala*), and he treated him accordingly. When I met Nasir Baike, the imam of Aral, for the first time in 2006, he hardly had a chance to speak to me about Islam because Kudaibergen Ata dominated the conversation. In some instances, when Kudaibergen Ata was obviously ill informed, the imam looked down and smiled forbearingly without correcting the explanation. While the imam addressed Kudaibergen Ata politely as "Kudaibergen *Aksakal*," Kudaibergen Ata called Nasir Baike by his first name only. This seeming condescension is not to suggest that the elders do not need the imam. Many have developed a curious interest in the new "official" interpretations of Islam and consider it necessary to know some phrases in Arabic. The humorous potential in the incongruence of scripture and practice was also exploited in other situations: aksakals in Engels thought it particularly tempting to tease the *davaatchi*s,[40] who occasionally come to the village to teach about "true" Islam, by probing into whether these young, bearded men indeed knew more about Islam than the aksakals. Thus, while encouraging education in principle, aksakals partly dismiss the imams' new perspectives on "proper" Islam: the young men often cannot bring their newly acquired knowledge to bear. They, like everyone else, have to listen to the old men and respect them. "It's not the one who knows a lot, but the one who has seen a lot who is wise," Kudaibergen Ata often remarked.[41]

Aksakals quite consciously coordinate the workings of their imams, be it in the way they spread their newly acquired knowledge in public or in how they represent the mosque congregation, or in making sure that the imams execute those religious practices, that aksakals consider appropriate and important. When these imams try to introduce new Islamic practices, they are obligated to incorporate the aksakals in the procedure.

One Friday morning in 2006 I was talking to Nasir Baike before mosque services. He described to me how he recently introduced a new mode of dispute management as part of his Friday prayers. He told me that twenty to thirty men usually gather during Friday mosque services, and if one of them has a problem to discuss, they all form a council, called *mashbara*, at the end of the service:[42]

> The person brings the problem to the middle and all ask, "How can we deal with it?" Then all of us sit and try to solve the problem. Aksakals in particular are sought for help. They appoint one aksakal who has to make a decision, but still everyone gives his own opinion. That aksakal listens to everyone and makes the right decision as given by Allah. Allah sends a good spirit to this aksakal, and he makes a decision. It does not matter what kind of decision it is, but it has to be executed in a way that is mandatory for everybody. If there is a decision, you have to do it! Even if it might be a wrong decision, Allah will save us from bad luck. There won't be any conflicts after the problem is solved jointly in the *mashbara*.

The imam started out by describing how the *mashbara* was ideally intended to work; namely, as a body of joint decision making, but he then attributed all agency to one single aksakal, whose decision was even backed up by Allah. The final comment of the imam, that there will not be conflicts after a *mashbara* decision, refers back to the importance of yntymak—living together in harmony. By enlisting the young imam and by building on familiar ideas and practices, aksakals bring customary practices into the mosque, while the imam adapts and stretches his understanding of shariat to incorporate *salt*. This points to a local understanding of Islamic law that tends to include *salt*; hence the new terminology that I first encountered in 2015: *salt-tuu shariat* (customary shariat; as discussed in the introduction). As a result, the mosque also gains importance in becoming a legal arena in which "religious" dispute management techniques can be tried out, and where the role of custom and shariat are being debated anew.[43] It will be interesting to see how the imams, who currently acknowledge the limits of their own autonomy, will organize their mosques when the current generation of elders has passed away and when they themselves are of proper aksakal age. Until then, however, *salt* continues to order relations between old and young even in the mosque.

DEBATING RELIGIOUS AUTHORITY

While in the mid-2000s Nasir Baike acknowledged the limits of his own autonomy vis-à-vis the aksakals, by 2015 he had established a good reputation among the villagers of Aral, which also had to do with the fact that the new imams were significantly younger than he. He is the only one who reads the important Friday prayer—a regular event that the other imams and their congregations attend—a sign of respect that reinforces his authority as the "big imam" (*chong imam*). He is also the only one who has completed the now obligatory training course for imams in Bishkek, which he did a number of years ago. Since the "President's fatwa," as Nasir Baike called it, the three younger imams are now also required to do so. When I asked Nasir Baike in August 2015 about the procedure, he explained:

> Nasir Baike: The *muftiyat* summoned all imams. . . . After the examination in Bishkek, the muftiyat decided who had passed the test, and then started to pay a salary to those who have passed. It has been two months already [since he started getting paid].

> Judith: Does that mean that you are now a state official?

> Nasir Baike: Religion and state are two different things. They are not

mixed. But now the state interferes in religion; for example, when there are unacceptable things happening like extremism. Religion cannot interfere with the state and politics. But as imams we have to go to mosque and pray *namaz*. If someone gets sick, we have to heal him or her, and we have to read the *zhanaza* prayer if someone passes away from this world. In some sense, we are, therefore, also state workers and do this type of work. That's why they started paying imams. . . . They also told us to report to the *kaziyat* at the end of each month. We report on how we worked, what the topic of the sermon at Friday prayers was, how many *zhanaza* prayers we read. We prepare a report and send it to them. If the report is appropriate and valid, then they pay us a salary. If it is not good, and no work has been done, then they will reduce the salary. . . . Since the state started to pay a salary, they started to interfere more and check up on us more.

When I asked him what he thought of this development, he described it as positive: "There needs to be control from the top. Imams, *kazy*, mufti, they all have to be elected." Nasir Baike thus embraced the recent changes and also supported the planned election of religious officials, which would establish a break with the traditional procedure, whereby imams were appointed by the aksakals. The fact that the state is again controlling religion more tightly reveals a striking resemblance to Soviet times, with the main difference being that leading politicians themselves are now "close to religion" (*dinge zhakin*)—foremost among them President Atambaev, to whom the imam attributed the "fatwa" of 2014. While on the one hand there is thus increasing control and facilitation from "above" and "outside," on the other hand religion has become a deeply personal endeavor that is immediately visible in the way people are changing their appearance. In 2015 Kudaibergen Ata's four sons, for example, not only attended mosque regularly but also sported "Islamic" beards (see figure 4.4). Their father did not mention these changes, which were quite striking to me, as he had already become accustomed to them.

Baiyz Apa was equally supportive of the fact that some of the young women in her family had started wearing the hijab, a headscarf that is tied not at the back of the neck but under the chin, thereby covering the neck and the ears. One of her granddaughters had begun wearing the hijab recently but encountered criticism from her own parents who associated the hijab with "Arab" countries. Baiyz Apa, however, argued differently, referencing shariat as her own teacher had interpreted it several decades ago:

FIGURE 4.4. Kudaibergen Ata's son Bakyt in his car (2015). Three talismans can be seen dangling from the rearview mirror: one traditional, one Islamic, and one national.

Our moldo, Kyial's [her adopted daughter's] father-in-law, used to say that once every hundred years shariat changes. Now things have changed. The mufti, too, says that women should cover their bodies. Women are not allowed to show their faces. He said people should not scold girls for wearing the hijab. He said it is permitted. During our times, when my mother was still alive, we also had covering dresses—it is our *salt*. It is also correct in shariat. It is moral [*adep*]. . . . It is not right to say, "Don't do that [cover]." They say it is shariat. Shariat will change once in a hundred years.

In neighboring Engels, however, this change of outward appearance in many people was more controversial. What Baiyz Apa deemed "customary," Syrgak Baike, who had been the village imam until 2014, thought of as "foreign": "There are many who follow people with beards in Aral," he said. "We do not really like those who have beards and wear flip-flops and long baggy trousers. They are destroying our national dress and our *salt*. That's why we don't like them. We are against it." His wife supported him: "They are wearing Pakistani clothing or black *paranjas* and you cannot see them. The president and the prime minister are also saying that this is against our *salt*."

Again, it is the authority of the state, embodied in the figure of the president, that is referenced as the ultimate arbiter, but in this case with regard to *salt*, whereas before the president was regarded as a religious expert whose fatwa defined "how religion should be." Among the four different mosque congregations in Aral, it is not only *salt* but also shariat that is being interpreted quite differently. In 2014 members of the religious organization Adep Bashaty (Source of Morality), which has become famous throughout Kyrgyzstan, came to the village to organize a prayer contest (*namaz aituu*) for children, who had to recite *surah*s (verses) from the Qur'an by heart in order to win a prize.[44] Kalipa Ezhe, the village secretary, told me that "some with beards from the mosque in the middle [of the village] said that this is not according to shariat. . . . There are always misunderstandings. They pray in the same mosque, but they have different views because religion has become many-sided [*köp taraptuu bolup ketken*]." If we look at the history of Islam in Central Asia, we could say that Kalipa Ezhe is correct: even before the Russian conquest only very few people were able to explicate passages of the Qur'an or had in-depth knowledge of the traditions of the Prophet: "Rather, communities asserted their Muslim identities through elaborate myths of origin that assimilated elements of the Islamic ethical tradition with local norms and vice versa" (Khalid 2007, 21). This is changing in contemporary

Kyrgyzstan, as textual knowledge acquires a new importance not only for elders but also for the youth, who thereby challenge the traditional means of acquiring respect, namely, through age. But religion has never been one-sided in Kyrgyzstan. Which repertoire gets invoked in what context changes, and it does so more frequently than once every hundred years. In 2015, for example, I noted that Kudaibergen Ata's explanations had shifted register: now he more frequently referenced shariat, whereas in former times he would have emphasized *salt*. Syrgak Baike, on the other hand, who in 2014 passed his position of village imam down to his helper, had become an advocate of *salt*. His final words regarding "religious clothing" were: "We have to put our *salt* in the first place, not shariat. We have to put our *salt* on top." While he might not have been able to say this out loud had he still been the imam, my impression is that this had been his opinion all along. The dichotomization between *salt* and shariat that was built up during colonial and early Soviet times has now again become tangible in the context of debating who has the authority to delimit the boundaries and define the content of these repertoires.

Chapter 5

BUYING AND PAYING RESPECT

Salt not only is performed by elders but is also perceived as being embodied in them. This is particularly visible in the ostentatious presence
of *aksakals* at public events. On national holidays and other festivities,
politicians and rich businessmen officially "pay respect" to aksakals
by inviting them for food and entertainment. In addition, the elderly men receive presents and money from these well-known regional
players. Politicians are regarded as *bash*es, and aksakals understand
their invitations as requests to perform in their role as wise elders. In
contrast to the intergenerational dynamics in the household, not only
is respect paid to the elders but the elders, in their role as *bash*es, have
to respect younger people. When these two groups of actors meet,
respect is mutually exchanged. This is visible in the transaction of objects, money, and formalized speech acts of both groups. These events
always take place both for an immediate audience and in the presence
of the media, who broadcast the exchange of respect widely.

Far from simply going through habitual routines, however, aksakals and politicians creatively adapt and interpret *salt* during these
events, often performing in unexpected ways. The aksakals in particular thus manage to accept the material benefits offered by politicians and businessmen without losing face. In doing so, they not only
follow others' scripts but write their own as well; this often involves
novel ways of expression and contextualization. *Salt* thus shapes the
relations between aksakals and young influential actors, who have
to submit themselves to this repertoire if they want to achieve their
personal ambitions. Beyond the household and the village, relations
between aksakals and younger influential (or influence-making) people are thus equally performed according to *salt*.

OLD MEN ON DUTY

On April 28, 2006, aksakals from Engels and Aral were invited to
come to the town of Talas for an *anti-meeting* (a word used in Kyr-

gyz), a governmental event scheduled to take place in front of the White House (*ak üi*), where the provincial administration is housed. The occasion for this event was to publicly voice criticism of ongoing demonstrations by the political opposition in the capital. Opposition leaders were demanding the resignation of President Bakiev, whom they regarded as incapable of stopping the rampant corruption in the state apparatus. My key informants from Aral and Engels were all asked by their respective mayors to join the anti-meeting to protest against the protestors in Bishkek. The elders acknowledged that not going would be impossible, but they complained that they had to pay for the transportation costs themselves. The anti-meeting lasted two hours and consisted of an opening speech by the governor, speeches by various aksakals from all over the province, and contributions from two women and a delegate from a youth organization. The audience consisted mostly of other aksakals and some passersby.

The governor began by addressing his discontent with the demonstrations going on in Bishkek, but he also used the opportunity of speaking in front of such a large audience of elders (I counted slightly more than 150 aksakals) to mention his success in negotiations with a wealthy Indian businessman who wanted to open a sugar-producing factory. "If we do not stop these meetings and demonstrations [Russ. *piket*], these people will be afraid to come to our country," he warned the audience, who clapped their hands approvingly. After the governor had spoken, some handpicked aksakals were asked to give speeches as well. The elderly men supported the governor in his opinion and emphasized that instead of going to demonstrations in Bishkek one should "stay at home" and give the president more quiet time to do his work. "There is no need for that, one should not go there [to Bishkek] just because they pay you and feed you with *plof* [a rice dish]!" one elder said, referring to the common practice of rewarding "demonstrators" with money and food. While addressing the situation in Bishkek, all elders framed their pronouncements in terms of the need for *yntymak* and *tynchtyk* (peace) in the country. Some people were holding up banners that addressed the need for unity, albeit in the Russian language: "We are for unity!" (Russ. *My za edinstvo!*).[1] After the aksakals had finished, a female speaker addressed the problem that even women were participating in the current demonstrations—something she considered highly problematic. "It is shameful [*uiat*] for women to be on the streets!" she admonished. "We should sit at home and take care of our children!" The event culminated in a free lunch for all invited participants in the town's sports stadium. During this and other meetings, people usually receive some kind of compensation: free food in any case, sometimes also money or presents. Their job is, for one, to be present as an audience but also to speak "just words" themselves. Such words, then, lend additional importance to what has been said in the opening speech, usually held at the outset by an important political actor.

As might have become clear from this description, government officials and the political opposition, whom in this case the aksakals and the governor had accused of spoiling yntymak, act in principle in the same way: they invite people, treat them with food and/or presents, and speak to them about their political projects. Aksakals generally accept these invitations because they are invited by a *bash*—a state official, a ranking party member of the opposition, or a person running for political office. The practical and welcome side effect of these events is that aksakals come together, see one another, enjoy food together, and just have a good time. To fulfill the role in which they are cast, elders will recite proverbs and provide illustrations by drawing on their shared history. The content of these formalized speech acts is characterized by the preponderance of invocations of yntymak, which was the main point of reference in most of the public speeches by elders that I heard. Politicians require "a plethora of empathic images and memories" such as a shared history to create political identification and commitment (Parkin 1996, xxii), and in Kyrgyzstan they call on aksakals to invoke these images and memories. State officials "culturally standardize the organization of feeling" (Stoler 2004, 7; see also Jenkins 1991) by having the aksakals address and embody the notion of harmony in their performances, which appeals to most people's sentiments.

Although officially declared apolitical, aksakals have become deeply entrenched in political action and discourses, even when they purportedly act only according to custom. Spencer (2007, 159) observed that "actors involved in the 'political' deny any political intent—their intervention is always said to be in the 'national' interest." In Kyrgyzstan this denial of self-interest is more often framed in terms of yntymak, understood as an appeal to a moral community. The side effect of politicians deploying such a "traditional" mode of communication via the aksakals is, in the words of Maurice Bloch ([1989] 1997, 29), that the political leader "is taking on the role of acting as the 'father of his people' within a well-ordered system where all responses follow each other, but who, at the same time, needs to act the astute politician, thinking of new ways of discrediting his rivals. This he cannot do within the formalized code because the very fixity of the features of articulation make [sic] it inappropriate for the supple use of language he needs." According to Bloch, formalized language cannot be used to cause alterations in the political situation. In contrast to bureaucrats, who can always seek refuge in the authority of highly formalized, disinterested modes of speech (Herzfeld 1992, 19n3), politicians cannot depend on such bland rhetorical forms if they want to be effective in battling their political rivals (Bailey 2001). Thus, in Kyrgyzstan, politicians have transferred the task of speaking in the "traditional" mode of communication to the aksakals and only rarely apply it themselves. By "inviting" elders they have found a clever solution: state officials can present themselves as being "naturally ordained" (Herzfeld 1992, 20–21); that is, as acting according to *salt*. Their "dirty work" is rehabilitated by the presence and performance of elders. Given the fact that the political situation in Kyrgyzstan has been unstable since the revolution of March 2005 and thus requires a lot of "dirty work" from politicians to stand up to their political rivals, this division of labor has proved to be quite efficient, and both opposition members and government officials continue to "pay respect" to the elders. The aksakals' public display of wisdom and experience is thus appropriated by those who have invited them.[2]

The aksakals' performance during these events is therefore a balancing act: while they are given a platform to display their authority in front of an audience, they have to make sure that they do not become too closely associated with the manipulative techniques of the politicians, as this might pose a threat to their reputations. Should aksakals be caught "talking politics," which necessarily implies straying from *salt*, they could become part of political skirmishes and thus make themselves assailable (see Bailey [1969] 1996, 2).

This danger had already been revealed to me during earlier stays in Kyrgyzstan. When analyzing pro-government and pro-opposition newspaper articles in 2003 in relation to the constitutional reform that was being carried out at the time, I noticed that pictures of aksakals were often placed next to speeches of President Akaev (Beyer 2004). Government-sponsored newspapers emphasized that during the nationwide events centered on the discussion of the new constitution, aksakals had been present and had given speeches approving the new legal document. Simultaneously, in the opposition newspapers, I frequently read the accusation that aksakals were puppets in the hands of government officials. The term I first encountered in this context, but which I came across again later in many other situations, was that of the "old man on duty" (Russ/Kyrg. *dezhurnyi chal*).[3] Next to the idealized image of the aksakal as wise, knowledgeable, detached, and fair, we here find a counterimage of the aksakal as an instrument of political power.

This Janus-faced image of aksakals is well known to my informants. "Aksakals are used as advertisement" (Russ. *reklama*), Shailoobek Ata once said after we went home from an election campaign in Aral where only aksakals had been present.[4] Like the bureaucrats, judges, and officers of Mumbai described by Thomas Blom Hansen, aksakals in Talas are "called upon every day to authenticate, inaugurate and authorize—in brief, to act as transient incarnations of authority" (Hansen 2001, 132). In a more diachronic perspective, such invitations to join politicians are in principle nothing new to the current generation of elders, who were all politically active in the Soviet period and are therefore used to speaking in public, going to political events, and being invited by politicians. As public speeches, parades, and Party meetings were regular occurrences for today's aksakals, they in fact enjoy the occasional invitations from state officials and businessmen because it signals that their presence is still wanted. However, they are invited not in their role as professionals of various kinds anymore but as elders. Just as their work in the aksakal court required an adjustment of self, the invitations from state officials today require a different performance from them than during Soviet times. Aksakals have learned not to address the current political situation directly but to appeal to yntymak instead. This implies talking in a quiet—albeit assertive—way about the necessity of living together "as one," leading a quiet life, and letting others live and work in peace. To symbolically indicate the end of such a speech, the aksakal gives a blessing (*bata*) by holding out his cupped hands and lightly brushing his face with his palms in a downward movement. This gesture is mimicked by everyone present and becomes in the process the embodiment of both yntymak and *salt*.

The difference between an elder speaking about yntymak and an elder giving a speech in what my informants termed the "Soviet style" (Russ. *po sovetski*)[5] became very clear to me at two different public events during which I witnessed an aksakal standing bolt upright in front of the microphone, talking very loudly about the political chaos in the country, praising the president (or governor of the province), and ending the speech by shouting "Hurrah!" Some elders laughingly responded with "Hurrah!" and applauded the speech by the aksakal. Most others just laughed about the anachronistic performance.[6] In any case, aksakals try not to miss the chance to perform; that is, to present what they are expected to say in a way that will portray them as skillful and creative.

PERFORMING YNTYMAK ON VETERANS' DAY

"Come in your suit and tie. The governor is calling us. We need to respect him!" said one veteran of Engels to another after the mayor had announced the upcoming celebration for Veterans' Day. Every year on May 9, the veterans of World War II and the Afghanistan War are invited to various festivities by state officials. The first celebration usually takes place in the elders' village, often in a school, where the pupils sing songs or perform plays.[7] This event is organized by the mayor and the teachers. A second event is organized by state officials from the district. From each of the five Kyrgyz provinces, some elders are picked out and brought to join the national celebration in Bishkek. Every year a couple of war veterans are flown to Moscow to attend the military parade in honor of the veterans, with all expenses covered by the state. During all these events, officials honor war veterans in their speeches and reward them with presents, money, and certificates. In Soviet times, medals (Russ. *orden*) were given out, but this is no longer so. The late Abaskan Ata, who was one of the war veterans from Aral, once showed me the medals of honor he had received, among them medals "for bravery" (*za otvagu*), "for defending Stalingrad" (*za oboronu Stalingrada*), "for the capture of Berlin" (*za vziatie Berlina*), and for being an "excellent artillery personnel" (*otlichnik artillerist*). Such icons of bravery are not only souvenirs but also resources for actors, as the display of these symbols reminds others of having to pay respect. He then showed me how the president, Kurmanbek Bakiev, had paid respect to him the previous year; namely, by presenting him with a watch. He had also received a television set from the head of the Kyrgyz army and an umbrella for his wife.

In May 2006 the festivities were held in Chat Bazar, the administrative center of Talas district. All veterans from the district had been invited and were awarded with money in sealed envelopes (see figure 5.1). The money was distributed by a famous local parliamentarian along with state officials who had organized the event. Before handing out the envelopes, the parliamentarian gave a short speech

FIGURE 5.1. Politicians distributing envelopes with money to ak-sakals during Veterans' Day celebrations (2006).

in which he praised the veterans and announced that each of them would receive five hundred som.[8]

After he had distributed his money, he left right away, saying, "You know there are other veterans waiting for me throughout the province, so I need to move on." The old people thanked him and let him go. After some songs were played, a couple of handpicked elders, among them Abaskan Ata, the senior elder of Zhetigen uruu in Aral, were given the floor. Their speeches revolved around their experiences in World War II. They reminded the audience—state officials, schoolchildren, teachers, and the other veterans—of what they had achieved and how brave they had been. All of them also referred to current political events, such as the ongoing disputes between the government and the opposition. They emphasized the need for ynty-mak and tynchtẏk in the country, and said that the president needed "quiet time" to be able to work well. After the official part of the event was over, another aksakal, without being prompted and to the great surprise of the organizers of the event, got up from his seat. Taking three schoolchildren with him—two boys and one girl—he assumed the place at the microphone (see figure 5.2).

Pointing at the first little boy, he said, "This boy here—he is a hero from Saruu." Pointing at the other boy, he said, "And that one there—he is a hero from Kushchu." Finally, looking at the girl stand-

FIGURE 5.2. Aksakal performing during Veterans' Day celebrations in Chat Bazar (2006).

ing in the middle, he said, "And you are Kurmanzhan Datka." He then addressed the elders: "Between Saruu and Kushchu in Talas there should always be yntymak. We should live in harmony and peace with one another. Let's give *bata*. May the children be happy!"

The aksakals in the audience gave *bata* by saying "*Oomin!*" and brushing their faces with their open hands. The performing aksakal then handed over twenty som to each child and resumed his seat. The elderly men and the state officials applauded enthusiastically. During parliamentary elections in 2005, the two candidates had tried to garner votes by exploiting what they considered to be less than amicable relations between the Kushchu and Saruu clans. The elder also referred to Kurmanzhan Datka, a historical female *bash* from the southern part of the country and not related to Talas. The old man brought up precisely these concepts because he knew that on a national level, *traibalizm* (Russ.) was a major topic for politicians in their campaigns (see Gullette 2010). By stating that between these clans, as well as between north and south (Kurmanzhan Datka symbolizing "the south" here), there ought to be harmony and peace, he was tacitly supporting the politician who had just handed out money to him: this very person had been accused by the local residents the year before of having brought hostility to the province through his political campaigning.

His performance was a demonstration of the old man's creativity and improvisational skills. Performing yntymak, as in this case, allowed the old man to please the state administration by alluding to the political situation in the province. However, the aksakal modified the formal and expected mode of communication by involving three children and the distribution of money to all of them. By speaking in front of the others, he encouraged (or forced) the audience to evaluate his skills and the effectiveness of his performance (see Baumann and Briggs 1990, 73). By giving money to the three children, he reiterated the earlier benevolent actions of the (younger) politician, redistributing some of the money he had just received in the process and highlighting and sustaining the very practice from which he and the other aksakals profit both materially and symbolically. His speech act about yntymak was not offset by his innovative way of framing the performance but, rather, constituted a part of it. His behavior was a self-asserting act: the aksakal switched his role from having been a receiver of (materialized) respect to being a donor, a *bash*, who has to be respected. Apparently, then, while the topics the aksakals have to address during political events might be impoverished, the way they speak about yntymak is not. Or, put differently, while the content of the speech acts might be predictable during these events, the performance as such often takes a surprising turn.[9]

Money has become a major material asset in the interactions between politicians, businessmen, and aksakals during political events. In Talas money is given to elders by aspiring politicians and those who want to retain their position not only in order to secure votes but also to pay due respect, which then gives the appearance of aligning their (political) actions with *salt*. Accordingly, politicians give money to all aksakals, regardless of whether they are related to them or not. Even if a young person has made a successful career as a politician or businessman, he still needs the elders' presence and performance on special occasions. Money is one of the means that allows a young person to "summon" elders to events. Some politicians and businessmen have become quite creative in finding out what their money can buy, spending it generously in ways that seem to be in accordance with *salt*.[10] In this way, money indeed has the capacity to bind people in reciprocal relations. However, this is not because of the fact that it "contains and transmits the moral qualities of those who transact it" (Bloch and Parry 1989, 8) but, rather, because respect not only is being paid but is literally being bought during these events. Leaving aside the question of the intentions and moral qualities of the politicians involved, we can see that these exchanges are carried out in the name of yntymak, which serves to weaken the association of aksakals with being "on duty" or "talking politics." Thus, the idiom of yntymak—along with the image of the generous *bash* and the display of mutual respect—serves to customize the politicolegal events to which the aksakals are invited.

Exploring these processes in relation to how authority is situationally created through coemergent interactional practices is more fruitful than discussing the relationship of old and young in terms of leadership. In reference to the Kyrgyz living in the Pamir, Shahrani (1986, 269) sensibly argued that "we shall begin to think about leadership as a contextually and conditionally assumable or attributable 'state' which a qualified person may claim or attain, rather than a permanent 'position' or office one may occupy." Nevertheless, he leaves the initial categories of "leaders" and "followers" untouched. In my examples, however, it is misleading to try to differentiate between the leader and the followers. Politicians, aksakals, and other actors are in a relation of codependency during these public events:[11] in contrast to the relationship between young and old within the household or the uruu, the relationship between (young) politicians and businessmen and aksakals is based on exchange rather than on domination. What is exchanged are tokens of respect in the form of money (for the aksakals) and in the form of attendance (for the politicians). All this is understood as proper behavior in the name of yntymak and according to *salt*. By paying respect to and buying respect from one another, both sides establish claims to authority from yet another audience that is larger than those who are present, as these exchange processes are publicized by the media.

Another difference between the aksakals' performances at these events and their work in other arenas is that, while the respective event might be the initial motivation behind people assembling, everybody knows that the actual subjects to be discussed, especially political ones, have for the most part been decided upon already or at least cannot be decided solely by the actors present. This is to say that, during such events, aksakals' knowledge will not be put to the test as it is, for example, in the aksakal court when solving disputes. They are, rather, regarded as being "in a position to give official imprint to versions of reality" (Goffman 1983, 17).

These examples show that *salt* is an important performative idiom even in the political field, where state officials, politicians, businessmen, and aksakals act accordingly. These meetings are occasions to produce and perform orderliness for the participants themselves. Money is customized as it is transacted in the name of respect and as a means of claiming authority and of making material and ranking social bonds.

THE OPENING OF A VILLAGE MUSEUM

On a Saturday morning in May 2006, Anarkul, a grandson of Bai-yz Apa, opened the door of our house and shouted, "The mayor is standing at the fence!" I went outside and heard from the village head that on that day a museum would be opened in Engels and that a rich person was inviting aksakals. "Do you want to come?" he asked. I agreed, as I had planned to go to the upper village anyway. Half an hour later, my partner, my research assistant, and I picked the mayor up at his office, where we also met Kudaibergen Ata, who was holding a fifty-som note in his hand. He told me that he had just received the money from the mayor and that he was supposed to give it to a poor neighbor of his. The money came from the rich businessman—the person who was about to open the new museum. In the car on the way to Engels, I found out that the rich visitor had donated money to all poor families in Aral. I also learned that this man, who had been born in Engels and whom everyone just called "our child," was making a good living from his private company in Bishkek, where he resided with his family.

Arriving at the newly built museum, I noticed a large crowd of schoolchildren carrying flowers in their hands. A lot of cars were parked on the dusty unpaved street. Looking at their license plates, I realized that they belonged to state officials from Talas. The mayor introduced me to the custodian of the new museum, and we started filming and taking pictures of the interior while no one else was around. The museum was dedicated to the life of Suiunbai Ata, a famous musician and a well-known person from Engels. Pictures, portraits, and his musical instruments were displayed in the two rooms. While we were looking at the exhibition with the mayor of Aral, a convoy from Bishkek arrived. A group of journalists, mostly young women equipped with cameras, videocameras, and dictaphones, flooded the little house, following a sedate, middle-aged Kyrgyz man dressed atypically casually in blue jeans and a dark T-shirt: the businessman, whom I shall call Nurlan Baike, had arrived.

A group of musicians unloaded their instruments from another car. Aksakals, all in their tall felt hats and their suits with various

Soviet medals and orders neatly attached to the lapels, entered the museum, among them Kozhoke Ata and Abaskan Ata, the two senior elders of Kaimazar and Zhetigen uruus respectively. Later I saw that all twelve war veterans from Aral had been brought to the upper village as well. From Engels, all elders but one had arrived—Kasym Ata, the head of the aksakal court, was absent. The journalists, who had never been to this place and whom I heard discussing how "remote," yet how "beautiful," they found it, were utterly puzzled at first to see us foreigners inside the museum, but they quickly forgot about us as they each headed toward an aksakal to begin their work:

> Female journalist: What can you tell me about the opening ceremony of this museum and about Nurlan Baike?
>
> Aksakal: He is from this place, previously called Engels, now Üch Emchek. So many great heroes, deputies, and other people are from here. If the parents die, there should be a child to continue their heritage.[12] Basically he is a son of a good village and of good people. [Raising his voice] Thank you, Nurlan! He built this museum. He invited people, aksakals, who knew his father well; war veterans like me. And he is showing his respect to us. May our young people be like him!
>
> Female journalist: Thank you. Your name, please.
>
> Aksakal: [gives his name]—I am a war veteran.

This performance can be understood as an ideal-typical example of "doing 'being aksakal'"—the old man used a formalized mode of communication, linking Nurlan Baike to other well-known historical figures from the village, citing proverbs and emphasizing that Nurlan Baike acts according to *salt* by paying respect to the aksakals and war veterans like himself. While the journalist had also inquired about the opening ceremony of the museum, the aksakal did not even mention Suiunbai Ata, in whose honor everyone had officially gathered. It was clear, then, that the event was mainly about Nurlan Baike.

After the tour through the museum, the aksakals were invited to join Nurlan Baike and the other state officials outside for tea in the two yurts that had been set up. A red carpet had been laid out leading from the museum to the right yurt. The aksakals and Nurlan Baike vanished inside the right yurt, while we were escorted to the left yurt, along with the visiting journalists. While we were being served tea, fruit, and bread, old women squatted outside in the shade, taking shelter from the burning sun, waiting for everybody to come back out. Fifteen minutes later we all gathered in front of the museum again to listen to speeches. The old women now joined the crowd, albeit sitting separately from the men, forming a second row behind them. The journalists stood close to the officials, positioning their cameras and microphones. The mayor of Engels, Altai Baike, was ordered by Nurlan Baike to start with "the distribution."

First, the names of all aksakals who were about to receive an envelope full of money were read out. Instead of giving an envelope to each old man directly, Nurlan Baike handed all of them over to Kozhoke Ata, whom he called *taiakem* (my mother's oldest brother), to distribute them at a later point. Everyone applauded. "Do not tell anyone how much you got," he reminded the elders. "It's a secret." Then, turning to the mayor, he asked, "Where is the school director? Children are next." Talking to the school director, who had come forward, he ordered, "Let's do it like this. There are too many children. In order to save time, why don't you distribute it [the money] yourself? According to this list, there are 107 children. I divided everything according to categories. Here!" And he handed over a list and envelopes. The schoolchildren hardly found time to present him with the flowers they were still holding in their hands as Nurlan Baike continued his tour de force of distributing envelopes filled with money for aksakals, schoolchildren, and poor families. Every time he handed over envelopes, people applauded. After twenty minutes he had distributed all the envelopes he had brought.

Nurlan Baike's performance in Engels was an effort to present himself as an honorable villager, influential patron, and caring relative. He invested in the symbolic construction of the village's history by erecting a museum devoted to one of the village's most famous members. He thereby also erected his own monument, as the museum is now associated with his name. While handing out money to different groups from Aral and Engels ("the poor," schoolchildren, old people), he singled out the aksakals in particular as his audience. He always gave the envelopes to a head: to Kozhoke Ata (his relative, and the senior elder of Kaimazar uruu), to the mayor, and to the school director.

Next, the district governor took the microphone and gave a long speech, praising Nurlan Baike for his generosity. By calling the latter by his first name only, he indicated that he was older than the businessman. "May your authority grow," he said. He then listed all the good deeds "Nurlan" had done in recent years, always mentioning the exact amount of money given by him: money for electricity; money for the water project Taza Suu, which was set up by an international organization; money for maintenance of the water project; and money for the school. And just as the governor of Talas had done during the anti-meeting, the governor also took the opportunity to address current political problems in the province, such as the unwillingness of some villagers to contribute to the water project (which, he noted, required another 150,000 som to be completed), and the ongoing protests further down the valley in another village where people had taken to the streets to protest the current plans of the government and an international company to extend gold mining activities throughout Talas. He reminded people to stay at home and not to engage in demonstrations. They should take care of their potatoes and rye instead. Winding up his speech, he wished for "more sons like Nurlan" for the village, and unity and peace among the people.

The next speech was delivered by the head of the provincial council of elders (*aksakaldar kengesh töragasy*).[13] He portrayed Nurlan Baike as someone spending sleepless nights thinking about his people and his village. Even the Kazakhs across the border, he said, know him as a "big person" (Kaz./Kyrg. *ülken adam*). He continued: "Isn't there a Kyrgyz saying, 'A son better than his father, a son as good as his father, a son not as good as his father'?[14] I think we can all agree that Nurlan will be better than his father—he left no one out, from the schoolchildren to the aksakals." He then referred to certain unnamed people of the village who were wealthy but would not share their wealth, not even slaughter a lamb for their ancestors.[15] He also touched upon current political issues related to the mining of gold in the area and then addressed the elders directly: "We, the aksakals, need to save our future generation. We need to save our sons and younger brothers like Nurlan. We need to save the best men. We need to increase their authority [Russ. *avtoritet*]. Then we will be free from our duty. The money he gives is not forever, but this person's [Nurlan Baike's] respect toward you is."

The district governor had indicated that "Nurlan" was a "boy" to him by addressing him by his first name only. The head of the aksakal council in Talas, however, praised his qualities and his role as the village's "best son," a son "better than his father." By addressing the businessman in these terms, state officials not only portrayed themselves as Nurlan Baike's older "fathers," they also downplayed the fact that it had been mainly his money that encouraged them to pay respect. By framing their praise in terms of descent, they invoked *salt*, according to which "children," such as Nurlan Baike, have to take care of their "parents," such as them. Likewise, Nurlan Baike had stressed through his appearance and behavior that he was not to be linked with politicians: he was not wearing a suit, as politicians usually do, and when handing out the envelopes he told the aksakals not to talk about the amount of money he was about to give them. The last point in particular stands in contradistinction to the common practice whereby politicians always publicly announce how much they give (as happened on Veterans' Day). The district governor, however, with Nurlan Baike standing next to him, meticulously listed how much money Nurlan Baike had spent for the village.

Appadurai (1990) has suggested that praise entails the public negotiation of gestures and responses, creating a "community of sentiment" that involves the emotional participation of the praiser, the one who is praised, and an audience. While in this way respect circulated between Nurlan Baike, the aksakals, state officials, and the audience, the situation remained firmly hierarchical in the sense that each party involved in the exchange made sure to always point out that Nurlan Baike was a "child" and a "son," and that the way he paid "respect" to them was according to *salt*, thus upholding their own status as aksakals or *bash*es.

After the head of the council of elders had spoken, the deputy of the provincial administration awarded Nurlan Baike the highest title a person in Talas can receive from the state: "The best person of Talas province." The state official then handed over a legal document (*toktom*) to Nurlan Baike, which he read out to everyone: "About awarding the title 'The best person of Talas province' to Nurlan [full name here]. The awards committee of the state administration of Talas province, having reviewed decision #2 on May 12, 2006, makes the following decision: For his contribution to Talas province's social and economic development and for his fruitful efforts, [full name here] is to receive the title 'The best person of Talas province,' and a medal to go along with it. This *toktom* is to be circulated among the mass media and the people." While still in line with previous ascriptions as "best son," the fact that state officials conferred this spectacular title on Nurlan Baike constituted a public acknowledgment of his position as *bash*. No wonder that the journalists he had brought along made sure to have the presentation of the document on film and tape. Whenever a speaker had finished talking, he would give Nurlan Baike a present. However, the businessman immediately redistributed it to an aksakal sitting in the audience, in a way refusing to indebt himself. What he was seeking in return for his generous donation was the audience's attention—acknowledgment that he was indeed a *bash*. He took the microphone out of the mayor's hand and started talking straight away about the political situation in the country:[16]

Aksakals! Within a single year we had two thousand seven hundred demonstrations. Two thousand seven hundred! A newborn baby also requires time to be cared for. My request to you is this: we need to give the current government time, am I right? And it is not good to tell lies, to go to demonstrations. . . . Are you less smart than [he mentions two opposition candidates' names]? Please be careful. I did not come here to make two sides hate each other. Those who want to can continue to go to demonstrations. If they have money, they can continue to go to the square [in Bishkek where the president's office is]. There is one true thing: he who cannot do anything is closest to conflicts, demonstrations, and meetings. . . . It's high time to distinguish between black and white. There are fourteen veterans sitting here who have reached even Berlin. Could you [talking to the aksakals] please tell them to stop this? Why do we need such a mess? . . . This is my request to you. I come here every quarter. I will come here every month. I will bring here money that I have earned, if it is needed. But stop going to demonstrations. . . . Two people out of ten in this country are rich. You started making each other work, you started hiring people to herd your animals [like *manaps* did]. Maybe it is the call of this time, but we need to go back a bit. Whenever we start to get full [i.e., to get rich] we need to go back. My dear friends, I am a person who grew up here. If you believe me, sometimes at nights I cannot sleep. . . . I have been talking with the heads of the provincial and the district administration. I decided to take all the rich people from Konezavod to Sulu Mai [from one end of the province to the other], saying, "Let's go. Let's help people. Let's give them three cows, five cows." Politics should be like this. Then the government will get better. It is really difficult to rule the district, the province. There is no fuel, there are no seeds, and there are no tractors. No state support, no state plan. When the first secretary of the district committee [during Soviet times] banged his fist on the table, everything was done in the kolkhoz because they brought fuel and seeds with them. And then the government could ask, "What are you doing? I have brought you everything." Now this thing came to us, which is the market. It is called "wild capitalism." Let's stop politics. Let's forget about deputies. Today we need to think about potatoes, beans, food, cows, and animals. This kolkhoz used to have forty-five thousand animals. These two villages [Aral and Engels] had forty-five thousand animals, right? Let's move on, and not do politics. We need to make this call from Konezavod and further. I cannot do this thing alone.

And when we come, we should not only speak nicely and eat a sheep, but we need to bring money. . . . We need to make politics around this topic. Different politics. Let's agree that we won't go to demonstrations. Nothing will come of it.

In reply, the audience—aksakals, old women, and some others who had listened attentively while he was speaking—clapped their hands and affirmed that they would not attend antigovernment demonstrations. Nurlan Baike wound up his speech by saying that he would like to honor those people who, just like him, also helped others: so he gave certificates to the journalists whom he had brought to Engels. While schoolchildren handed over flowers to the guests, the mayor of the village presented a traditional gold-embroidered coat (*chapan*) and a traditional Kyrgyz felt hat (*kalpak*) in the name of the village school to Nurlan Baike, who took the presents and immediately passed them on to Kozhoke Ata and to Abaskan Ata—the two senior elders of Kaimazar and Zhetigen uruu. He did the same with a vase and a painting that another official, who did not give a speech, handed over to him.

In his speech, Nurlan Baike presented himself as just and benevolent, as someone who cherishes *salt* and knows how to respect the elders, but who also has understood what it takes to rule the country. While he was talking as a businessman who is not involved in politics himself, the contemporary political situation had been the main point in his speech. However, he performed with a wider audience in mind than just the aksakals in front of whom he was speaking, since quite clearly none of these old people had taken part in any of the demonstrations he criticized so harshly. His own entourage of journalists, to whom he handed over certificates as part of the ceremony, would, through their coverage, further his own interests. These interests, it turned out, were utterly political, which became clear when he started to actively engage in Bishkek politics a couple of months later. This, however, happened only after the newspaper articles about his good deeds had been published both in the capital and in Talas.

After this last round of gift giving, the mayor's to-do list was finished. There were no more speeches scheduled for that day, and he wanted to proceed to the next part of the program: introducing the musicians Nurlan Baike had brought from Bishkek, who were supposed to entertain the audience. However, since Nurlan Baike's performance had been so overwhelming in terms of the amount of

FIGURE 5.3. Abaskan Ata and Nurlan "Ake" after the aksakal had bestowed "the ancient title" on the young businessman. The mayor (center), journalists, and state officials (in the background) took notice of the aksakal's creative performance (2006).

envelopes he had distributed, he had created an imbalance: he had indebted the aksakals in particular, who had accepted his money and listened to his words, but none of whom had been given an opportunity to speak in front of the audience so far. Nurlan Baike had underestimated the impact his performance would have on the aksakals. By forgetting to give them the floor, a chance to actively and creatively engage in "doing 'being aksakals,'" he casually disrespected them. He also forgot, as Mauss ([1925] 1990) observed so many years ago, that accepting a return gift is necessary in social relations. So before the musicians were called up, Abaskan Ata got up uninvited, went over to Nurlan Baike and the state officials, and said the following:

> I will speak briefly. I wanted to say that since ancient times people give nominations and titles like you just did [addressing the state officials who were standing by]. For instance, there were Kydyr Ake, Sart Ake, Turdu Ake. There were such people called *ake*.[17] What did they do? They helped needy people. This person [Nurlan Baike] is also like them. Even if he is young, he always helps veterans. He helps the needy. I am from Zhetigen. You [Nurlan Baike] are from Kaimazar. Why don't we [addressing the aksakals] give this boy the ancient

name? Why don't we call him Nurlan Ake? From now on we will call you Nurlan Ake. Even if we are older than you, you will be our *ake*.

The aksakals clapped their hands and mumbled words of agreement while Nurlan Baike looked puzzled and did not know quite how to react. Then, however, he raised his hands in acceptance and thanked Abaskan Ata (see figure 5.3).

The mayor finally declared the meeting closed, and Nurlan Baike introduced the musicians. While two famous female *komuz* players started to sing love songs for their elderly audience, Nurlan Baike invited his "guests from far away" to eat the traditional *besh barmak* food that the women from the village served them inside the yurt.[18] As soon as the guests had eaten, they left the yurt—and the event—without any further parting words. Now the aksakals were invited inside. The tablecloth was cleaned of bones and breadcrumbs and a second round of sheep meat and noodles with broth was served to the elders, who exchanged opinions about the musicians over their food. Sitting next to the imam of Engels and together with the other aksakals, I found out that there had not been enough time to treat the aksakals from Aral with food in their own village, which is why they had been brought to Engels. Before the elders departed, the envelopes that Kozhoke Ata had received for the others were distributed among the war veterans, who were then driven back home. We packed our belongings and headed toward the house of Kasym Ata, whom I had planned to visit that day. He was the only aksakal from Engels who had refused to attend the event.[19]

The aksakals respected Nurlan Baike's efforts by conferring a kinship title on him, which raised him in status even above them. He was no longer merely their kinsman, but a kinsman of superior status. This was necessary because, as Baiyz Apa once remarked, elders risk not being respected when they listen to young people speak out in public. In the case of Nurlan Baike, the elders avoided this danger of losing face by making their generous and attention-grabbing kinsman "older" and thus worthy of being listened to. Raising his hands in acceptance, Nurlan Baike then performed adequately according to his new title by immediately having meat served to him and his guests, and letting the aksakals wait outside. While the elders did not seem to mind, as attending to one's guest is according to *salt*, Nurlan Baike had also given preferential treatment to himself by eating before the elderly men. Eating together—in Kyrgyz culture as well as in other cultures—signifies amity, and Nurlan Baike decided to pursue such amicable relations with the state officials and the journalists, and not with the aksakals. Appadurai's "community of sentiment," which had been jointly evoked by harmonious speech acts, the exchange of symbolic objects, and the performance of (love) songs, turned out to sustain hierarchical relations by raising the status of Nurlan Baike as *bash*.[20]

Personal relations in Talas are perceived as orderly when they are hierarchical. Thus, amity is successfully established when hierarchical relations between individuals are created according to *salt*. Amity therefore does not entail closeness and equality between people. People do befriend each other, but the first thing they will want to find out is whether they are older or younger than their counterpart, because otherwise they will not even know how to address one another. Seniority entitles an actor (whether male or female) to privileged behavior and requires the junior to pay respect. The elderly men could have given Nurlan Baike the title of aksakal, which would have put him on a par with them and still would have raised his status significantly. However, they went even further and chose to put themselves in an inferior position by making Nurlan Baike their "older brother."

What Abaskan Ata's performance during the opening of the museum in Engels achieved was that he, speaking for all aksakals present that day, turned Nurlan Baike into their *bash*. While this act had no official political implications and was therefore belittled by some of the state officials who could not help but smile at Abaskan Ata's performance, the message was clear: if you act like a *bash*, you have to be acknowledged as a *bash*. Financial wealth allowed Nurlan Baike to be generous and host lavish events, thereby keeping others in a position of indebtedness. That he spent his wealth in this way also called for a symbolic acknowledgment of his status, a paying of respect and an attribution of authority. Sandra Barnes (1986) describes how titles acknowledge the excellence of people, validate their claims to leadership, convert actors into public servants, and provide symbolic capital that can be converted into further political and economic benefits and vice versa.[21] Nurlan Baike's new title, however, not only suggested future rights and privileges but—more importantly in the eyes of the aksakals—demanded appropriate behavior and entailed obligations that might also restrict some of his actions. Barnes has further argued that conferring high status on someone who has gained wealth or high office is unparalleled in its capacity to forge a bond between those who give and those who receive. The aksakals now expected Nurlan "Ake" to continue his good deeds and to take care of his kinsmen. They also made it easier for themselves to listen to his speeches and accept his presents without losing face.

In his own view, though, Nurlan "Ake" had obviously performed his role adequately enough to become a successful politician in Bishkek. In the spring of 2008, my research assistant Eliza told me she had seen a banner with his portrait spanning Chui Prospekt—the main street in downtown Bishkek—advertising his candidacy for political office.

CONCLUSION

Salt does not seem to fall out of favor in noncustomary institutional settings. It remains an important performative idiom through which actors order their relations with one another. The fact that these performances of elders today are literally being "bought" could at first sight be interpreted as a threat to their authority: by being "on duty" for younger people, they might lose face. However, aksakals react to these donations in ways that proclaim that their performance cannot be "bought" easily. In the cases presented here, they either remained strictly in the formalized mode of communication by focusing on yntymak (instead of explicitly endorsing a political candidate), or they symbolically passed on the money to younger people, thereby continuing to "do 'being aksakal'" with new means. In the last case, they made sure that the hierarchical relationship remained orderly by turning the young and "resourceful" businessman into their *bash*.

When I returned to my fieldsite in summer 2008, the imam of Engels told me that Nurlan "Ake" had not come back to the village since the day he opened the museum. Instead, he had become the sponsor of a youth organization in the capital. Even worse, he had refused to receive a delegation of aksakals who came to visit him in Bishkek to ask him for money. This behavior stands in stark contrast to his treatment of the aksakals in 2006 in Engels as well as in Bishkek, where he had invited village elders to a meeting in the Museum of National History to discuss—under the eyes of important politicians and the media and in the presence of some two hundred guests—how to support the elderly. But since he has consolidated his political standing in Bishkek, he does not have to return to Engels, where people are disappointed in him for "not taking care" of them, as the imam put it. Like many other aspiring politicians, Nurlan Baike deemed it necessary to invest in relationships with aksakals through *salt*. But once he succeeded as a politician, the obligations and duties that would have come with his new position as *bash* would have constrained his actions. Even as he was not expected to be physically present in villagers' lives and on festive or ritual occasions as the aksakals have to be, the villagers had expected him to continue giving money. Also, the aksakals had accommodated his way of "buying respect" by incorporating it into their way of "doing 'being aksakal'"; but according to *salt*, once is not enough. Nurlan Baike was expected to continually "buy respect" as long as he still had money. By remaining in Bishkek instead, he tried to dissociate himself from the obligations and expectations that tied him to the villagers. Most politicians in the capital are in a similar position: while *salt* can help actors get into politics, politicians then have to alienate themselves from some of the bothersome obligations that the position of *bash* foists upon them. This has proved difficult, as relatives expect politicians to take care of them financially. While rank-and-file citizens accuse politicians in general of doing "family business," they also consider it wrong if a wealthy relative of theirs refuses to offer such "help" to them.

The only way to cut loose from these obligations is not to return to the village, as Nurlan Baike has done. This last case, then, shows that if alternatives are more appealing, people might try to escape from the obligations *salt* imposes on them and seek their status privileges elsewhere. Just as Kasym Ata had the means to conform to *salt* only when he wanted to, young politicians and businessmen are financially independent. They nevertheless invest time and money in their relationships with respected elders and in presenting themselves as benevolent actors. In this sense, Nurlan Baike's behavior presents an extreme case: most politicians try to remain on good terms with their villages because they might need their support in the next election campaign or—more likely these days in Kyrgyzstan—a place to return to once their career has failed.

As of now, Nurlan Baike might be operating as a successful politician in Bishkek. However, he is expected to show up eventually in Engels. "People return to their home when they are dead at the latest," said the imam. "To not respect the aksakals is not good. They are the ones who will bury you in the end." This final comment shows that these young players are also under a considerable amount of pressure. Many of them acknowledge that their position obliges them to "give" in ways deemed appropriate for a *bash*. The Kyrgyz economy is suffering in part because of politicians' obligations to share the benefits of their state office with family, relatives, friends, uruu members, and fellow villagers. Recalling the statement of Kozhoke Ata about how officials of the Russian empire taxed people twice because "Moscow" (i.e., the tsarist administration) took their "fruit," we can see that in present-day Kyrgyzstan it is the other way around: in order to get something from villagers (e.g., their votes), *bash* have to "take care" of them by handing money down to them. This principle applies even if a politician that villagers supported during elections did not make it into office, as was revealed to me during a village meeting in Aral. Aksakals told the visiting district governor to put some pressure on a man who had run for parliament the year before. Even though he was not elected in the end, they were still expecting him to finish the construction work on the main street that he had begun as part of his election campaign. "He should finish what he has started," they said. "We supported him. It is not our problem that he did not get the job."

Chapter 6

TAKING AND GIVING CARPETS

"Taking and giving is a sign of respect; going and coming is a sign of harmony,"[1] a male Kyrgyz elder told me as we walked through the darkness to the house of a covillager and fellow lineage member who had died that day. On the way to the memorial service we talked about what kind of person the deceased had been, and the old man praised his kindness. When my Kyrgyz grandmother, Baiyz Apa, had heard the news only an hour earlier, she covered her mouth with her right hand. "Oi, Allah!" she murmured, while two of her grown-up children shook their heads in disbelief. "Bad news, bad news . . ." they said quietly, and the grandchildren stared at everyone with wide eyes, wondering what had spoiled the joyful mood everyone had been in just moments ago. Arriving at the house of the deceased, the old man and I went over to other village elders who, together with the village imam, were standing near the yurt in which the body had already been laid out. I had joined the elders that night; they are always among the first people to arrive at such a "bad feast" (*zhamanchylyk toi*),[2] and I wanted to see what people would be "taking and giving" and who would be "going and coming" on this woeful day.

In this chapter I draw on Beatty's (2005) concept of emotional practice for my investigation of Kyrgyz mortuary gift exchanges. Anthropologists often encounter people's affective responses in the context of social situations where they are not bracketed off from the flow of other kinds of interactions. Still, there remains a danger of reducing emotions to words and meanings, thereby failing to engage with the fact that they are also "under the skin" (Leavitt 1996, 523). The problem of how to grasp methodologically, analyze theoretically, and write convincingly about emotions in a way that takes both social and subjective dimensions into account has remained a difficult one. In an effort to move forward methodologically, Beatty (2005, 30) urges us to "look closer at varying pragmatic contexts" (2005, 34). Identifying the preoccupation with emotions as primarily internal feelings as "the standard Western view," he emphasizes that people in fact name and display emotions through what he calls "emotional practices," which are used "to excuse, persuade, evade, and manipulate rather than to describe feelings" (2005, 31).[3] This view does not so much focus on how people talk about their internal states (if they do at all); rather, it tries to assess how people deal with the public manifestations of affect. This links up to the force of custom, as in no other situation have I encountered the working of *salt* as forcefully as in mortuary rituals.[4]

During mortuary rituals, women and men engage in different performances and subject themselves and others to specific expected behavior, including emotional displays. While death unleashes emotional forces of bereavement in those individuals left behind, the two emotion concepts—*yntymak* (harmony) and *uiat* (shame-anxiety)—and their associated practices are central to the social organization of these rituals. They are locally conceptualized as belonging to different emotional states of being, and they are performed and (re)produced along gender lines. The short-term exchanges people undertake during these rituals, such as the giving and receiving of food, are locally interpreted as contributing to yntymak. Long-term exchanges, however, which involve the giving of more valuable and durable objects, are said to be motivated by uiat, a complex emotion that I gloss as shame-anxiety.

A FUNERAL WITHIN THE LINEAGE OF BÜRGÖ

After independence, Kyrgyzstan was subjected to decentralization, privatization, and far-reaching development initiatives, realized through the intense involvement of international organizations in local state affairs. While rural citizens in Kyrgyzstan never experienced the kind of "social collapse" that was reported in Eastern Europe (see, e.g., Heady and Miller 2006), political instability, unemployment, and the overall deterioration of living conditions have had a continuing impact on all areas of people's everyday lives, including the ritual economy. I became aware of the role of emotional practices in relation to ritualized exchange while living among members of the Bürgö lineage in Aral. In the following, I describe how mortuary rites were organized within this lineage around 2007, and how this practice linked up to a wider social context.

When a person from the Bürgö uruu dies, all male household members gather the same day to distribute among themselves the manifold tasks lying ahead. First, invitations (*kabar*; lit. "news") are written and distributed. If relatives or friends live far away, the invitation note is sent by post.[5] Then an *aksakal* or the oldest male person of the bereaved family picks out a leader (Russ. *brigadir*) from among the younger men of their uruu, who assembles twelve to fifteen men to dig the grave. These men, though, come from several different uruus in the village. Each household donates a certain amount of money: two rubles during Soviet times, and fifty som since independence. As the village population has grown significantly over the last three decades (roughly four thousand people live in the village today), the members of Bürgö decided at one point to deal with deaths separately within the two minor uruus of the greater lineage, Torutai and Sarytai. Both have since developed different rules for how to proceed when one of their members dies. Raia Apa, my neighbor and a member of Torutai, showed me a document from 1997 that recorded the decision of her uruu members to continue donating the same amount of money for funerals that they had donated since the 1970s. Kudaibergen Ata, a member of Sarytai, told me that no such written document existed for Sarytai, but that members had verbally decided to give twenty som to fellow households that had experienced a death. When a relative of the respective other minor uruu dies, ten som is given by each household. This money is called *yntymak akcha* (lit. "harmony money"). This money is used to purchase food such as fruit, candy, and cookies to help entertain guests.

Following the invitations and the collection of the yntymak akcha, another task is to wash the body of the deceased. This is done either by uruu members or, if the deceased is a woman, by relatives from her natal village. Four people are needed: one pours the water, one washes the head, one the torso, and one the feet. For their efforts these people are given clothing that accords to the body parts they have washed: a hat or a headscarf is given for washing the head, an outfit for washing the body, and shoes for washing the feet. The person who pours the water also receives clothing. Depending on the family, even more valuable items such as jewelry might be given.[6] After the body has been washed, it gets wrapped in a forty-meter-long piece of white cloth and is laid out inside a yurt that has been erected in front of the deceased person's house.[7]

The night I arrived with the elder, the body had already been prepared and wrapped by male relatives of the deceased and was obscured from sight by a curtain. I followed the elders and the imam to a room in the deceased person's house where food was going to be served. While there is little segregation of the sexes in everyday life, during rituals men and women are often seated in separate rooms. The rituals themselves are noticeably gendered. For example, at the funeral ritual in question, other young women of my age would not enter the room where men were seated except to serve tea and food, but I was taken along by the aksakal, with whom I interacted on a daily basis. While old and respected women such as Baiyz Apa were able to traverse gender boundaries and sit with the aksakals, for the most part they preferred the company of other women. A much more strict segregation was kept when the body was brought to the grave-yard. When Baiyz Apa told me that "women don't go to the graveyard to bury people," I decided that it would be inappropriate for me as well to accompany the men there.

For about four hours, until late into the night, we sat and listened to the elders talking about village politics and the rising prices of agricultural products and reminiscing about times gone by. Every time another elder entered the room, the imam or another person be-gan to lead a prayer (*namaz okuu*). When the leading elder ended the prayer by saying "*Oomin*," everyone repeated the word and stroked their faces with the palms of their hands from forehead to chin. The chit-chatting would stop and the men would talk about the deceased: "He was a good person." "He was a skilled horseman. Remember how he used to chase us in the mountains?" Everyone would smile and agree, and from there the conversation would return to topics of everyday life. Occasionally everyone would fall silent and the only sound to be heard was the stirring of spoons in teacups. Someone would then break the silence by reciting a sura from the Qur'an in Arabic, followed by a blessing in Kyrgyz, while all the others held their cupped hands in front of their faces.

At some point I joined the women in the kitchen and helped them prepare salads for the upcoming days, while the younger men cut up fresh horsemeat in the courtyard. The mostly younger and middle-aged women were busy allocating the tasks that lay ahead, worrying about the arrival of an estimated two hundred guests. One daughter-in-law expressed her anxiety: "I hope there will be enough food. I hope they will come well [i.e., bearing adequate gifts]. What if we cannot host them properly? It will be uiat in front of my mother-in-law." The other women calculated the amount of food necessary and reassured her, saying that everything would work out fine. Her invocation of uiat spoke of the social pressure to be hospitable to one's guests and expressed an anxiety about not being able to comply with the expectations of others.

That same night, men from the Torutai households gathered and discussed who would host those guests coming from farther away who would need to stay the night. In the past, the uruu members would arrange for two households to host up to fifteen guests each. If more guests arrived, more hosts would need to be found on an ad hoc basis. To make this duty more appealing, the chosen hosts were to receive five kilograms of meat from the house of the deceased, where a horse or cow was slaughtered for this occasion. In the year before I carried out fieldwork, however, Torutai members decided to contribute 200 som per household for the maintenance of overnight guests rather than having to host them. Thus, this responsibility has recently been delegated back to the household of the deceased. On the day in question, the daughter-in-law was worried, as her household still needed to secure overnight stays for a number of expected guests. Late at night, horsemeat was given to the elders, who ate with pleasure. Immediately after they had finished their meal, the men got up to leave. They would dutifully come back early the next morning to spend more time with the mourning family. Male elders characterize their own position during mortuary rituals in terms of their role as aksakals, the expectations of which they gradually learn to comply with as they grow older. As the aksakal Shailoobek Ata said to me the morning after we had been at the deceased person's house, "Society is a sphere in which people interact.[8] Yesterday a relative of ours died. I went to his funeral. There I am an aksakal. The dead person had sons and daughters. What do I do there? I don't work there—I just sit there. This is the position of an aksakal. The immediate family expressed their gratitude because I was there for a night. This is yntymak."

GIVING AND RECEIVING FOOD

While yntymak becomes manifest particularly through the presence of aksakals, each lineage household, as well as neighbors and other villagers close to the family, can contribute to yntymak by sending at least one or two members to pay their respects to the deceased. They are expected to bring food but are under no obligation to contribute to the larger expenses of the funeral.[9] Since bringing food for the ritual is women's business, wives often represent their absent husbands,

FIGURE 6.1. Baiyz Apa and Elmira Ezhe (2015).

delivering a plastic bag full of cookies, bread, and tea. This food is called *tasmal*. Women hand the bag over to one of the daughters-in-law, while another woman from the household carefully takes note of who has brought what. I became aware of the importance of each household bringing its own tasmal when my Kyrgyz grandmother Baiyz Apa insisted after a couple of months that I could no longer contribute to theirs when we went together to attend ceremonies. We did share the same yard, but as I had rented the house of her oldest son, where I lived with my partner, I had established my own household and could not simply attach myself to their gift-giving obligations. This was to the regret of Baiyz Apa's daughter-in-law Elmira Ezhe (see figure 6.1), who now had to pay for her household's tasmal again without my contribution. The only cash income this family had was the pension of Baiyz Apa and the meager childcare benefits Elmira Ezhe received for her five children. Going to a mortuary event, however, could easily eat up half the monthly income of the entire family. "I need to find money," Elmira Ezhe told me after it had turned out that Baiyz Apa would not let me contribute to their tasmal anymore. "It will be uiat to go to the shop lady and ask her again to put these things [cookies, bread, tea] on credit. I still have not paid her back for the previous times." Here we can see that not only the host but also the guests invoke uiat in the context of what is considered proper behavior. As she voiced her shame-anxiety, she touched her cheek with her index finger and moved it downward, thereby leaving a virtual stigma on her face. I saw this gesture frequently when women talked about uiat. These bodily expressions indicated to me that they seemed literally to pay a high price for their emotional well-being during these events, indebting themselves in order to avoid accusations of uiat.

After the funeral, when they have eaten together with the others, women are handed back their bags, filled anew with food from the ceremony plus an additional piece of meat from the main course. This food is called *keshik*. Upon returning home, it is shared among other relatives and neighbors who did not attend, thereby expanding the body of those who are mourning and remembering the deceased. The amount of keshik received should be roughly equal to the amount of tasmal the guests have brought. The additional meat, which is considered the most valuable food, is added to the bag for the sake of further redistribution. Taking keshik and giving tasmal—as voiced in the aksakal's proverb at the beginning of this chapter—is perceived as a sign of yntymak. While the obligation to bring tasmal to mortuary rituals might impose a financial burden on women and their households, this short-term exchange of food products maintains the mutuality between the giver and the host.[10]

While mortuary rituals in Talas lead people to engage in emotional practices such as yntymak, the rituals do not necessarily strengthen social bonds, as these events simultaneously intensify exchange practices, which in turn causes hardship and anxiety. Any simple picture of the situation is further challenged when we turn to the long-term exchanges of valuable objects accompanying mortuary rituals.

GIVING CARPETS

Whereas neighbors and distant relatives are expected to give tasmal on the occasion of funerals and other mortuary rituals such as the one-year commemoration of a person's death (*ash*),[11] it is obligatory for close relatives (*tuulgan*) of the deceased to give more valuable gifts. These gifts are collectively called *kiit* (lit. "textiles") and usually consist of valuable objects such as carpets and high-quality clothes and textiles, as well as a monetary gift known as *koshumcha*. While such money is expected from a particular circle of former schoolfriends, colleagues, and other male acquaintances of the household collectively known as *zhek zhaat* or *kattash*, it is the specific obligation of the in-laws (*kuda*) to deliver the more encompassing kiit to their affines.[12] Their connections are established first with a marriage and then stabilized throughout the years by "going and coming" and "taking and giving," as mentioned by the aksakal at the beginning of this chapter.

An acceptable kiit from kuda should consist of the following items: fifteen to twenty meters of cloth, a full outfit of men's or women's clothing (depending on the sex of the deceased), one large box filled with cookies, one large box filled with candy (two to three kilograms each), money (from one to five thousand som) or an animal (usually a sheep), and a carpet (usually worth between five hundred and five thousand som). The amount of koshumcha also varies, starting at one thousand som and going up to ten thousand som. There is an important difference between the "harmony money" (yntymak akcha) given by uruu members for funerals as outlined above and koshumcha (monetary gift) brought by zhek zhaat (male acquaintances). While the amount of the former is fixed and is collected on the day of the death, the latter depends on the relationship of the person to the male family member of the deceased, as well as on the gift giver's personal economic status. People expect the goods from close relatives, kuda, and zhek zhaat to be significantly more valuable and numerous than the tasmal brought by neighbors and distant relatives. The ranking of gifts thus objectifies the ranking of the relationships between individuals (see Werbner 1990, 33).

While similar regulations also exist in other parts of Kyrgyzstan (see Jacquesson 2008 for Naryn province and Hardenberg 2010 for Yssyk Köl province), giving carpets as a necessary part of kiit is specific to the Talas province only. These carpets are usually around two meters by three meters in size and are produced in China. One encounters them on the walls and the floors of people's homes, piled up in stacks in the bazaar, spread throughout the entire prayer hall in the mosque, and inside yurts during funerals. Baiyz Apa commented on the extravagant giving of carpets by referring to a well-known Kyrgyz stereotype: "Talas people are known for showing off and being proud."

Giving carpets as part of kiit and koshumcha has been practiced only since the mid-1980s. The elder Tülööberdi Ata recalled that when he was a child people used to cover the corpse with a coat on the way to the graveyard. The congregation of men would bring the coat back after the burial was over. Later, people started covering the body with blankets. Over the decades traders brought different materials to the region from Arab countries, China, and later from

Russia, and apparently people often switched to newly available materials for this purpose. Finally, they started using a carpet. The carpet, however, belonged to the mosque and would be brought back by the imam after the burial. The same carpet would be used for all funerals. People estimate that carpet exchange, as it exists today, began during the initial years of perestroika. "Since the Soviet Union collapsed," the village imam recalled, "things have escalated." Not only one, but several carpets would be put on top of the deceased. They were also given as presents to the imam who read the prayers at the grave and to the *brigadir* who organized the digging of the grave. In some cases, the family also put a sack of flour, a teapot, and teacups, as well as clothes for the imam, next to the open grave. Religious officials also started to receive money for reading the *zhanaza* prayer,[13] and especially for performing the cleansing ritual *zhanaza dooron*.[14]

In my fieldsite, as in most parts of Talas province, only women bring carpets and other goods to funerals and memorial rituals. When women deliver these gifts, they do so in their role as their father's daughter or as a daughter-in-law. In both of these roles they are the ones upon whom the obligation to bring is imposed. I became attentive to carpets early on during my fieldwork when I saw Baiyz Apa, along with her two daughters-in-law, Elmira Ezhe and Zhyldyz Ezhe, carrying a carpet to a funeral ceremony. The following day Elmira Ezhe told me that she had finally received her monthly childcare benefits, but that the money was gone already because they had to spend it on gifts for the funeral. I used this opportunity to ask her why they had bought a carpet for this occasion even as they struggled to make ends meet. She answered, "We had been given a carpet by this family not long ago during another funeral of a relative of ours." I found out that the carpet had cost them 500 som and that she had bought two boxes of cookies in addition, which meant that she had in fact spent more than their childcare benefits on gifts for this event. She then emphasized that it would be uiat for her not to be able to give back the money that I had lent her for a hospital check-up two months earlier, adding that she felt sick again but could not go and see a doctor because there was no money left. I did not dare continue asking why she carried on with this practice that caused them such financial hardship, as Elmira Ezhe's mood had deteriorated visibly from the moment I had begun asking. I also caught myself thinking that maybe my money had not been used for a check-up but, rather, to buy gifts, which might have been considered a more pressing issue at that time. I suddenly felt torn between wanting to tell her to use the money I give her only for "relevant things" and realizing that being able to comply with expected behavior during these rituals was a very relevant thing indeed. "Feeling sick," it seemed, could result as much from shame-anxiety as from a bad state of health. I had observed on several other occasions that people tended to sacrifice a lot in order to be able to present gifts during mortuary rituals. Kudaibergen Ata once had to choose between buying formula for the baby of his daughter-in-law, who suffered from anemia and could not breastfeed her child, and contributing money to buy a sheep for the funeral ceremony of a relative. The aksakal ordered that a sheep be bought first, and then he went looking for the baby formula.[15]

One day, when a close relative of Baiyz Apa had died in Engels, I accompanied the three women to the funeral to pay my respects. I perceived the scene outside the yurt, which had been erected in the courtyard of the person's house, as highly emotional. The sons of the deceased were standing next to the yurt with tears running down their cheeks. "Oh, my liver, my liver!" they cried out loud.[16] Other male relatives, friends, and neighbors approached them, gave their condolences, and handed over money to the youngest son of the deceased as part of koshumcha. Women carrying bags and rolled-up carpets bypassed the men and went directly into the yurt, out of which I heard the crying of female voices. There, the two daughters-in-law handed over their gifts to a woman who was seated close to the entrance. She was a relative of the family, but distant enough not to have to wear black clothes and a black headscarf (traur).[17] Her task was to take stock of the incoming gifts and list them along with the names of the gift givers. Next to her sat a daughter-in-law of the deceased man's family, who observed who was bringing what. Whenever a young woman entered with gifts, she called out the name of the visitor's husband. In the case of Baiyz Apa's daughters-in-law, she called out the names of Baiyz Apa's sons. Looking closely at who was handing over the gifts in the yurt, I noticed that it was always the daughter-in-law or the daughters of a family who did so, while the elder women went directly to the other elder women and joined them in singing songs of lamentation (koshok). In these songs, the good deeds of the deceased were praised in highly elaborate stanzas, and through their symphony an atmosphere of closeness and intimacy was created that immediately drew me in. My impression was that all the women, the elder ones singing as well as the younger ones, were genuinely emotionally affected. These were not hired professionals with no relation to the deceased. Occasionally, one of the women would suddenly weave a wail into the ongoing *koshok*.[18] I was moved by how the women's words transformed into crying sobs, and how melody and intonation created a deeply emotional yet soothing song that made everyone in the yurt, including myself, cry.[19] It conjured up in me feelings of helplessness and solitude in the face of death, while at the same time it strengthened my sense of belonging to the other women with whom I huddled. This experience, which I had on many occasions when observing mortuary rituals, led me to conceptualize ritualized wailing as a performance that creates a sense of isolation in each participant and listener, yet at the same time somewhat paradoxically grounds them in the shared experience of a common loss.[20] In addition to honoring the deceased and mourning together publicly, wailing also provides an opportunity for individuals to express and share their personal grief. Women and men are spatially segregated from one another during these events, with men standing outside and women inside the yurt.

After approximately thirty minutes I left the yurt and followed Baiyz Apa into the house of the deceased to a room where only women were sitting. The room was packed, so we had to squeeze in to be able to reach the *dastorkhon*—the cloth that is spread out on the floor and on which food is laid out. When the food arrived the atmosphere became more cheerful, with every group of four women sharing one large bowl of meat and noodles and people exchanging news and telling anecdotes. The spirit lifted even more, it seemed, when finally vodka was brought into the room by a young man who declared that "one has to fight bitterness with bitterness" and urged everyone to drink. As Baiyz Apa's family is known for not drinking, our glasses found happy customers in the women sitting next to us. In contrast to the crying just before in the yurt, inside this room nobody talked about the sad occasion anymore.

When we left about an hour later, the three women were handed a bag of food (*keshik*), as well as a small carpet, a blouse, and two scarves.[21] This was the gift deemed appropriate return for their kiit. These goods were taken directly from the incoming flow of items. In no way, though, did it equal in value the large carpet, the clothes, and the cookies they had brought.

THE EXPECTATIONS OF OTHERS

"We have to give because they gave to us," said Zhyldyz Ezhe on our way home from the funeral. "And because we gave to them today, they will continue giving to us in the future." Elmira Ezhe nodded. "Right, Apa?"

Zhyldyz Ezhe continued, addressing Baiyz Apa. "This is how it is."

Baiyz Apa replied as follows: "It is mandatory for us to participate. We have to do it, even if we cannot afford it. . . . We do not want to be left out from *salt*."[22]

In this as in many other instances I encountered during fieldwork, *salt* was presented as an agent in itself, forcing people to do certain things. To not follow it, beyond the sickness mentioned above, leads to the unbearable state of solitude, of exclusion from kin and community. The secretary of the village mayor, Kalipa Ezhe, explained her role as daughter during her father's funeral: "If we [women] go well [bring good things], then other women will say that I got married to a good place and that my husband respects my family. . . . If I go badly then it is uiat, because I have a good job here [at the mayor's office]. . . . If you bring things you can afford and even more, then it is good. I was both bankrupt and in grief after my father's death. It is bad when you are suffering emotionally and they make you suffer materially, too. Our *salt* is hard." The secretary's comment implies that women have no choice in the matter; they must adhere to these practices. Other younger women explain their feelings of being overwhelmed and pressured by employing bodily metaphors, saying that the gift-giving practice during funerals and one-year commemorations makes their "heads spin" (*bash alaman*). They are presenting themselves as "patients" of *salt*, according to which these emotional practices are obligatory and binding.[23] While all young women with whom I discussed the practice complained about their mothers-in-law or elder women in general and argued that the imams should do something about what was widely regarded as an un-Islamic practice, they equally emphasized that the imams were themselves husbands of wives and sons of mothers and therefore of no great help. Although young (and old) women often voiced their discontent with gift giving, I did not come across a single case in which individuals openly opposed the practice by refusing to give anything.[24]

Likewise, older women would rationalize their actions, saying, "We bring things in order not to make our daughters upset," thereby passing the burden of agency back to the daughters-in-law, who are the ones who are supposed to worry most about proper behavior. When I talked to older women about gift-giving practices, they would answer in the collective "we" form (all women), referring to the watching public as "they." Listening to conversations and observing what was going on during these rituals, however, it became clear to me that it was older women themselves who urged their daughters and daughters-in-law to provide the means but then removed themselves from the transactions and, therefore, partly from the obligation to give.

Older women supervise younger women as they carry out significant parts of mourning rituals with only one another as audience. In these events they perpetuate cultural templates that they themselves were subjected to as daughters and new brides, thereby ensuring conformity, exerting control, and reinforcing their role in society by motivating compliance with *salt* through shame-anxiety. "Whereas fear seems a poor basis on which to found a society or develop a system of law," Colson (1974, 45) reminds us, "we are unrealistic if we ignore the fear and concentrate solely on the advantages people see in their associations. A dynamic picture must include them both."

UIAT AS SHAME-ANXIETY

"Uiat!" might be one of the most frequent utterances a child will hear while growing up. Parents will comment on a child's behavior with the exclamation "Uiat!" or "Uiat *bolot*!" (It will be uiat!), accompanied by raised eyebrows, upset looks, and possibly even a light physical reprimand. Typical situations are, for example, when children drop a piece of bread on the floor, when they put their feet on the table, or when they scream while guests are around. Children are never given an explanation for why something is uiat, but they will learn how to behave in order to avoid these exclamations and the often associated punishment. Such "emotion work" (Hochschild 1979, 1983) is an important part of socialization. So-called feeling rules are present whenever children are reminded to evaluate the appropriateness of their behavior, as in "*Uialbaisynby?*" (Aren't you ashamed?).

But the socialization of children in terms of uiat (and other emotion words such as *urmat* [respect] and *namyz* [pride]) is not equivalent to the emotional practices of adults (see also Beatty 2005, 32). Grown-ups rarely accuse other adults of uiat in a confrontational manner. Uiat is talked about in public only in abstract ways, in the form of gossip or in order to prevent gossiping.[25] In the latter case, a person who has done something that might give others a cause for accusation might preemptively spread the news him- or herself. If a man misbehaves, often his wife will try to be the first to gossip about him to other women. What she is communicating is not her shame, but her awareness that his behavior was uiat—something that might also reflect back on her.

According to *salt*, women said, it was uiat not to listen to what elders say, to be drunk in public places, to talk negatively about the dead, and to address elder persons to whom they are related by their first names. For women it is also uiat not to be able to provide guests with adequate food and not to bring proper gifts to life-cycle rituals. Whereas the first examples are rather easy to adhere to, the danger of not being able to provide adequate food and bring proper gifts to each other's feasts seemed to loom constantly over many younger women's heads.

The concept of uiat is essentially tied to interactions such as listening, behaving, and being heard or seen, which always entail an observing and evaluating Other or presuppose an audience.[26] While talk about uiat has the outward social dimension described above, it is also indicative of reflexive processes on a subjective level, for it is through reflexivity that human actors conceive of their world as one that they themselves constantly produce (Heritage [1984] 1996, 109–10). Uiat is an emotional practice by means of which individuals are socialized into subjecting themselves to an awareness of others' expectations (see also Goffman 1959). Consider the following soliloquy of the secretary after she heard the news that, on an invitation to the funeral of a close relative, the district imam himself had expressly requested that guests not give carpets. Carpet giving is against shariat, the invitation explicitly stated. According to the secretary, this surprised most people, who proceeded to gossip about the invitation, wondering if perhaps the mayor was actually indirectly asking for carpets. She continued, as if talking to herself, "How can I distinguish between those who would have brought a carpet and those who never planned to do so? I mean, I do not want to be gossiped about by others. It would be uiat not to bring one."

In this example, the shame-anxiety was so strong that the funeral congregation continued the practice of gift giving, even though the actual recipient of these gifts had explicitly claimed he did not want to receive them. This example shows that the main recognition of the "taking and giving" and the "going and coming" lies not with the individual receiver of a gift but with the community. It is the self-reflection and self-evaluation of individuals more than external sanctioning by others that leads to performances judged to be "according to *salt*." When I pressed Baiyz Apa on the issue of whether people would really start gossiping about her or accuse her of inappropriate behavior if she stopped giving carpets at mourning rituals, or whether they might accept her new way of doing things as she is an authoritative person in the village, she thought about this question for a while. "Right," she answered, laughing. "Well, I do not know myself whether they would talk about it or whether they would leave me alone. I cannot be sure of it, actually."

The concept of uiat has thus far in the literature on Central Asia been translated as "shame" (see Bichsel 2008; Handrahan 2004; Werner 1997, 2009). But "shame" is usually understood as the result of an already broken bond and as becoming visible through acts of improper conduct (see Röttger-Rössler and Markowitsch 2009; Scheff 1988). In this sense, uiat is only used in children's socialization. For adults, uiat is a preventive emotional practice: it enforces conformist behavior and prevents people from breaking bonds. It also possesses an inherently positive aspect. The exclamation *"Uiat bolush kerek!"* (One must have uiat!) indicates that a sense of uiat is required in order to be able to act morally and properly, and to be able to recognize whether a given action or practice is in accordance with the social expectations of a group or contradictory to them. In contrast to "shame," which is usually used for the description of a short, negative emotional experience, uiat is a constant companion of women, who imagine themselves being talked about in a certain way by others.[27] While shame-anxiety is voiced in front of an audience, the consequences of an accusation lie predominantly in the imaginative realm. The differentiation between shame and shame-anxiety is therefore crucial, as the former is restricted to children's socialization, whereas the latter matters in the emotional practices of adults.

Having found that gift giving and shame-anxiety center on women's practices and perceptions, one wonders what the role of men is in all of this. As uiat is written into the bodies and consciences of individuals starting from early childhood, and as men are brought up in the same disciplining way as women, there is no reason to believe that men are not sensitive to uiat. After the first years of being taught about uiat, however, men are increasingly socialized in terms of urmat (respect).[28] They, too, have to guard their proper behavior; otherwise, they risk a drop in social status. Here as well the social context plays an important role: while being drunk in public is considered uiat for men, for example, being able to drink with others can in certain contexts be a part of showing that one deserves urmat.

In fact, offering a toast while drinking can even constitute an act of yntymak by wishing health and prosperity or by demonstrating that one knows how to "fight bitterness with bitterness."

While everybody should avoid uiat, the public discourse and the actions carried out in the name of uiat, such as the task of reminding others what might trigger this exclamation, lies exclusively with (older) women. This separation finds its spatial equivalent during mortuary rituals in the fact that men never enter the yurt. While knowing of gift giving and being involved in it in various indirect ways, men portray themselves as having nothing to do with these practices. Consider this statement of the driver who took me to my fieldsite for another visit in the summer of 2008: "Men just stay outside and are not allowed to enter the yurt. They just stay outside and do some work. We do not interfere in women's work. We have no business in what women do with carpets. We just stay outside."[29]

Younger men do not even enter the house of the deceased where the aksakals sit and pray. They gather outside, slaughter the animals, heat the samovar, and only come in briefly to pray (namaz). Kudaibergen Ata explained the gendered division of labor during mourning rituals in the following way:

> KA: Women give carpets, boxes [of candy and cookies], and other things. Men only give money.
>
> Judith: Why do women give these things?
>
> KA: Because it is the task of women. All of the properties and household items are women's. Men carry things, but then women give. Men buy these things. I buy things, because my wife doesn't have money. There must be only one head of the family who knows what to spend and where to spend it. Muslim people have one head for each family.

While Kudaibergen Ata was hinting at the fact that he is the breadwinner in the house, he is still buying "these things" for his wife and carries them to the yurt. This seems to align well with his Muslim identity to which he also referred—another example of how Islamic ideas are incorporated into salt. While men seem to have an interest in the continuation of gift giving during mourning rituals, they do not engage in these practices themselves but have their wives perform them.[30] However, as noted above, it is her husband's name that is called out when a woman gives gifts at a funeral. "One should give," continued the driver. "If my wife does not give, it will reflect back on me in a negative way—I will be an outcast." Thus, even if men publicly state that women waste the household's money, they give in to the women's demands because women's practices are considered appropriate and in accordance with *salt*. What the driver did not mention is that men also hand over money because their mothers, elder sisters, and wives exert pressure on them if they refuse to do so. "Women who do not work force their husbands to give money for koshumcha," said the mayor's secretary. Baiyz Apa explained that women manage the money even if the man is earning it: "Men deal only with outside tasks. Men do not know much about the details of bringing and giving. They only know how to earn the money. Men earn and women spend. Women know how to deliver and manage the money."[31]

There is an unspoken understanding at work here that is based on the assumption that women stand outside the formal demands of shariat. Aksakals talk in terms of shariat and thus formally uphold the primacy of Islamic law for communal affairs. Likewise, younger men engage in gift giving during "good feasts" without risking stigmatization but refrain from giving during mortuary rituals. However, all men close their eyes to the conditions that they also endorse— such as the demand for yntymak and the fear of uiat—both of which virtually force women to transgress against a widely shared understanding of what is or what ought to be proper according to shariat. But to say that women are "forced" to do these things obscures the complementary perspective: that they are also enabled and even expected to do the things men cannot do without losing respect. Thus men, even the aksakals, depend on women's practices to sustain relationships by "acting respectful," as the proverb at the beginning of the chapter suggests. By giving carpets, women may transgress the boundaries of shariat, but they also follow and uphold *salt*, according to which giving is a sign of respect. "I hate this part of *salt*," said Nurkyz, Baiyz Apa's eldest granddaughter, when we talked about the giving obligations associated with mortuary rituals. During our trip to her grandmother's village in 2008, she told me about the recent funeral of her paternal uncle, to which she brought a carpet, clothes, and money "as help," and from which she received a different carpet in return. "The woman writing down what I brought said half jokingly, 'All the carpets come from the last funeral.' She was probably right."

CASH FOR CARPETS

The fear of uiat sometimes causes people to overextend themselves financially. People in Talas have come up with a number of strategies to try to address this problem to some small degree. After a funeral is over, the family of the deceased will either split the profit made from the gifts or share the debt if they slaughtered many animals and provided large amounts of high-quality food. They also remain effectively indebted to all gift-giving women, who received less in return than they had brought. But those women know that there will be a countergift on the occasion of a mortuary feast held by their own family, which will continue the exchange but never complete it. The clothes and material given during such rituals are usually kept by the women of the deceased person's household, who will redistribute them to visiting in-laws or bring them as gifts to other life-cycle events. Cookies and candy are offered to frequent guests or brought as part of tasmal to other feasts. Some families also keep a couple of carpets for their own house or for further redistribution. However, most of the carpets do not stay with the bereaved. When I asked the mayor's secretary, Kalipa Ezhe, and the village librarian in 2005 about what people do with those carpets, they engaged in the following conversation:

> KE: They carry them back to the bazaar and try to sell them again. For 100 som or less. They will be carrying them from bazaar to bazaar like madmen [Russ/Kyrg. *sumasshedshiidei*].
>
> Lib: They sell them.
>
> KE: The bazaar vendors buy them back at lower prices. For instance, if people take the carpet back to the bazaar, they will get less. If the carpet was, let's say, 450, they . . .
>
> Lib: . . . the bazaar vendor will pay them only 300.
>
> KE: But when you ask why, they have many reasons. They say, "This part is dirty," or they say, "It smells strange." And then they sell it again to us. And we again buy from them for the next funeral. And they charge 500 som. It's all about wasting money.

Sometimes people do not even have to go to the trouble of carrying the carpets back to the bazaar in Talas because villagers who have to attend funerals or "good feasts" (*zhakshylyk toi*) such as weddings will ask to buy or borrow a carpet from them. The reciprocity in these

FIGURE 6.2. The carpet vendor with her book of *hadith* (2015).

transactions is often delayed until the lender demands the carpet back or the borrower is able to repay in money or in kind. This alternative also reduces the loss incurred by reselling to the bazaar vendors. In my fieldsite, this is the way carpets are usually redistributed, as both parties save the fuel costs and the effort that driving to town and negotiating with the bazaar vendors require. Knowing that their role in buying and selling carpets for mortuary rituals is controversial among the general population (see also Addo and Besnier 2008), the bazaar vendors eagerly emphasize that "we hope that people come on the occasion of good feasts." In fact, one of the women selling carpets was reading a book of the Prophet's sayings (*hadith*) while waiting for customers (see figure 6.2). When I asked her if she knew about the long-standing initiatives of officials to stop carpet exchange and, if yes, how she could reconcile her religious beliefs with her job, she replied, "I know that it is forbidden to bring carpets and material [to ritual events] and to slaughter animals. But we have *salt*. I would follow shariat, but they [her relatives] would not respect me. According to religion, we should not practice *salt* [*saltty karmabash kerek*]. But we are not listening. I do not know what to do. We try not to be excluded from the majority [*elden köpchülüktön chykpaily dep jüröbüz*]. We think of people, not God. But God is the one who created all of us."

In Talas, villagers have begun to set up a gift economy where prices are not dictated by outsiders but are negotiated between relatives and neighbors who are also often likely to lend rather than sell their carpets to one another, emphasizing that yntymak is kept this way. Despite these arrangements, people still feel that they are "destroying money" in these transactions. They possess, as Sloterdijk (1983, I, 37; II, 950) called it, an "enlightened false consciousness" in regard to this issue: they know very well what they are doing, but they still do it and are cynical about their own patterns of behavior.[32] When we talked about gift exchange in 2015, Ydyrys Baike phrased his thoughts in terms that are strikingly similar to Sloterdijk's argument: "People bring money [to a *toi*], and their money is gone in one day. The host of the toi, the one who takes that money, can go to other people's tois for the next ten to fifteen years. If Kyrgyz people would not go to tois for fifteen years, then we would be a lot better developed. They understand, but they still do not do it [*Any tüshünüp turup ele, zhazashpait*]."

Chapter 7

TAMING CUSTOM

In the early 1980s state officials, religious authorities, and the general public began debating the meaning, function, and proper application of *salt* and shariat in mourning rituals. Since then, there have been efforts to prevent certain practices, particularly that of presenting carpets to the deceased's family during mourning rituals, as state officials considered them to be a squandering of resources, and religious authorities declared them to be against shariat. However, the officials only managed to stop the practice for a short time when they were actually threatening people with imprisonment, and even then villagers continued to give carpets surreptitiously. For them, the giving and receiving of gifts, among them carpets, is an indispensable aspect of *yntymak*, which is integral to *salt*.

In January 2006, state officials tried their luck in taming custom yet again because they felt that "things have gotten out of hand," as the deputy governor of Talas district explained to me. The governor issued an official document (*toktom*) with the title "Concerning the elimination of squandering by certain individuals, which is not in accordance with *salt*," addressed to the regional heads of the four districts.[1] It carried the letterhead of the administration of Talas and the emblem of the Kyrgyz Republic and was stamped and signed by the governor. In this document, the governor ordered the formation of a working group called *Salt* for each village in the province. This working group was supposed to consist of the following people (in the following order): *aksakals*, women from the women's committee, the imam of the mosque, staff from the local village administration, and other knowledgeable persons. The document stipulated the following:

- that this working group should instruct the people in how to adhere to custom [*kaada salt*] in the correct way and how to keep social order [*nark nasil*]; this should be done in a public meeting;

- that the religious leader [*kazy*] of Talas province should instruct every imam of every village to intensify efforts to inform the people about those clauses of shariat that concern burial practices;

- that, according to the *kazyiat*, burial practices should be standardized throughout the province;

- that people are to be given two months to implement these new regulations, starting in January 2006;

- that the results of these reforms are to be assessed after the first quarter of 2006 [dates when each of the four districts in Talas province would be visited by state officials follow];

- that the responsibility to regulate the observance of this decree in the villages lies with the deputy of the governmental administration.

The following day, Bakai Azhy,[2] the religious official (kazy) of Talas province, issued a legal document (*buiruk*) titled "On establishing uniform conditions for the expenses of funerals in the province,"[3] addressed to all imams. This document resembles the governor's document in appearance, with the exceptions that the Kyrgyz state emblem is missing and the stamp of the kazyiat at the bottom of the page shows a mosque in the middle. In this document, the religious leader commands the following:

- that all imams should inform their communities about the proper way to conduct funerals;

- that the practice of tearing clothes or material into pieces for the purpose of remembrance [*zhyrtysh berüü*][4] should be stopped;

- that the distribution of money at the graveside should be abolished;

- that the imam should prepare the grave before the deceased is brought so that the body can be buried the day after the death;

- that every mosque has to provide a carpet to cover the body of the deceased, and that this carpet is to be returned to the mosque after the burial;

- that the practice of bringing carpets to the home of the deceased must be abolished;

- that at the place where a person died not more than one animal should be slaughtered;

- that the practice of slaughtering one animal per week [for a limited period following a person's death] must be abolished;

- that the ritual commemoration on the fifty-second day after a person's death, which involves the slaughtering of another animal, should also be stopped;
- that during the one-year anniversary [ash] not more than one animal should be slaughtered;
- that those who dig the grave should not be allowed to drink vodka;
- that the neighbors who live near the house where a person died should serve guests who come from afar;
- that in the house where the person died, only three days of mourning should be observed;
- that the practices of bringing carpets and other textiles and displaying clothes given to the deceased after his or her death should be stopped;
- that at the place where a person died, the practice of giving gold rings and earrings as gifts must be abolished;
- that the implementation of this particular order should be realized with the help of the working group *Salt* in each *aiyl ökmötü* of the province;
- that the head imam of each district should ensure the observance of this order.

These two legal documents show how state and religious officials collaborated, not only supplementing and supporting one another but also mutually reinforcing their very institutions: the provincial administration in Talas relied on the kazyiat to issue a document that directly related to the private realm of people's lives; the kazyiat, on the other hand, not only reacted to the state officials who issued the first document but also aligned the content of the religious document with state law by copying the style and language of the provincial administration. Both documents declare the practices revolving around mourning rituals "un-Islamic" and "not according to *salt.*" At the same time, they try to advise the general public on the right path in terms of both shariat and *salt.* The officials—state and religious alike—distinguish between a right and a wrong version of *salt.* Those who contributed to the production of these texts realized that the proscriptions they wanted to introduce would have to appeal to both *salt* and Islamic law, but the very fact that the working group to be formed is called *Salt* is interesting: it seems that even in order to constrain these "customary" practices, *salt* is needed as a frame of reference. By cross-referencing each other and by reproducing and combining elements of different normative domains into a new justification scheme, the governor and the kazy created "combined law" (Fitzpatrick 1983; Benda-Beckmann 1983). Thus, the two documents are reminiscent of tsarist and Soviet attempts to regulate religious life in Central Asia in format as well as content.

After the two documents reached Aral, the mayor wrote the name of the village imam on both of them, thereby transferring the issue to the religious official whom he must have deemed the most competent person to deal with this issue. I received copies of the documents from the mayor's secretary, Kalipa Ezhe, who explained how the documents were put into practice in Aral:

> We formed a working group headed by our imam. As part of the local administrative staff, I also became a member of this group. We had to go to funerals with the imam and aksakals and inform people to stop giving these gifts. However, people did not like us coming. They would say, "The body belongs to us. It is not your business what kind of respect I show toward my father, and you had better not interfere." It is hard to tell people to stop when they are grieving and want to slaughter a large animal. My husband's elder brother has nine sons. He invited all of them to the funeral of his wife, and I was counting the gifts: there were eighty-two carpets and forty-two blankets and one and a half rooms were filled with boxes.

Having said this, she then told me that she herself recently brought a carpet as part of her collective gift (*kiit*) to the funeral of a close relative. I was astonished:

> Judith: So you give carpets yourself, but tell others to stop?

> KE: It is not possible to do otherwise. . . . Why should people not bring them? And I am a little sister, a girl to them [meaning her relatives]. If I do not bring a carpet then they will be puzzled and say, "What is wrong with her? Is she okay? Why didn't she bring it?" because they have brought things to the funerals of my mother- and father-in-law. . . . If I do not bring it, then I will be gossiped about [*anda meni söz kylat*]. They will wonder why all the other people are bringing something but why I brought nothing. They will tell others that I have become snobbish [*togotpoi koidu*], or they will say that I have become arrogant [*kööp kalyptyr*].

She then reflected on the behavior of the religious officials: "Our *moldos* also take money when they perform *zhanaza dooron* for the dead. . . . They also receive money or carpets for this. It is the fault of the moldos, because they started taking money for *zhanaza dooron*. We have a proverb here: Do what the moldo tells you to do, but don't do what the moldo himself does."[5]

In Kalipa Ezhe's opinion, only the moldos could stop people from giving carpets because they perform several rituals for the deceased that ensure their smooth transition to the otherworld. Their important position, in Kalipa Ezhe's eyes, gives them leverage over a family and makes them potentially good arbiters. However, the religious officials also seemed reluctant to abandon the practice, as Kalipa Ezhe noted:

> They only talk about it [not giving carpets] during Friday mosque and at the graveyards. If they were giving speeches at public meetings to encourage people not to do these things, then it would work. This commission is not functional. The deputies [of the village parliament] also complain that they cannot go [to people's houses] and say, "I am the deputy and you have to stop practicing it." The moldo has to talk about it, whether at the graveyard or in public meetings, and say, "I will perform *zhanaza dooron* for free. Forty stones will be read for free."[6] If they said, "You should stop it. It is a sin [*künöö*] and creates difficulties for the deceased," then people would be reluctant to do it.

Kalipa Ezhe voiced her opinion that it would be up to the religious officials to stop people from practicing carpet exchange, but in fact imams cannot act independently even within what could be described as "their religious domain"; namely, the mosque and the graveyard: they still find themselves effectively subordinated to the aksakals. That this is not only an intergenerational issue (most imams in my fieldsite are young) was revealed to me when I talked to an older moldo who resides in a village about ninety kilometers from Aral and Engels. This moldo had been a little too eager to carry out mourning rituals according to what he considered the proper application of shariat, as we shall see below.

A FALLEN IMAM

In 2006 Nurdin Moldo was sixty years old, an age at which one is usually considered an aksakal.[7] He is one of the few people in Talas who received an Islamic education in Tajikistan in Soviet times and is able to read and write Arabic. He heads one of the two Islamic schools (Arab. *medrese*) in Talas province and is responsible for some twenty students from Kyrgyzstan and Kazakhstan, whom he houses and educates.

I went to visit Nurdin Moldo with my research assistant, Zemfira, because she considered him very knowledgeable "about Islam." When looking for him in the village, we asked for the imam, but people gave us a different name. When we asked for Nurdin Moldo, however, we were directed to the old Soviet kindergarten, which he had turned into his medrese a year earlier. He became religious after having a prophetic dream and so followed in the footsteps of his great-grandfather, who had been an imam as well. In 2005 he was granted permission by the Muslim Spiritual Board of Kyrgyzstan (*muftiyat*), located in Bishkek, to open this institution. As he was not salaried, he financed his medrese privately through joint labor on the twenty-five-hectare plot he rented from the mayor, where he and his students cultivated sunflowers and potatoes. Selling the harvest in autumn, he made just enough money to feed his students and his two teachers, who had received their education in Pakistan and from the Islamic University in Bishkek.

His wife, who served tea to us, described the institution as a "private medrese." Upon hearing this, I engaged him in a discussion on Islam and public life in Kyrgyzstan today. When I asked Nurdin Moldo what his relation to other religious and state officials was, he answered, "There is no relationship between the government and religion. Religion has no right to interfere with the work of the government. In a democratic country, every person can follow the religion of his or her choice. Likewise, if the government says, 'This religion is good and that one is bad,' it will stir conflict. The way they [the government] are handling it is right: at the present time no one is interfering with religion and the government acts independently." Later on, however, he explained that even in his "private" religious school he could not act independently of the muftiyat. He was in direct contact with the head of this institution (the mufti), who designs all religious programs and curricula and gives instructions about how to teach at the medrese. "They coordinate every activity we do," he explained. "We do not have the right to make independent decisions." In fact, the contemporary Muslim community (*ulama*) in Kyrgyzstan is structured exactly like the official religious leadership that existed in Soviet times (called SADUM). This means that the religious institutions are controlled by state institutions, as the two legal documents discussed above illustrate. Over the course of our conversation I noticed that, when it came to teaching Islam, Nurdin

Moldo emphasized his status as an aksakal more than his status as a religious official:

> I can never assume that I know more than others. Maybe there is a person who is of higher status, but who might respect me just as he would respect an aksakal. If they respect me as an aksakal, I will be happy for that, but I cannot put myself above them. Every person has to realize for oneself what is honest and what is just. One has to come to this conclusion by oneself. No one is allowed to tell you how to behave. We just talk about the things that are according to shariat, but whether people stick to it or not . . . is up to them.

This statement implies that knowledge about Islam and shariat can be best utilized by those who are capable of "doing 'being elder.'" Since he had emphasized the importance of being an aksakal, I assumed that he was a much respected individual in the village because he was both an elderly man and a religious head, and thus probably able to reconcile what often appeared to me to be the contradictory practices of *salt* and shariat. For this reason, I continued talking to him about my interest in the role of aksakals in society and the institution of the aksakal court. However, to my surprise, he hastened to distance himself from the aksakal court in his village. "I have nothing to do with them," he said. He told me that he was asked a couple of years ago to become a member of the local aksakal court and that he even went to some of their court meetings but soon dropped out. He said it was too difficult to combine the tasks of being a judge with the moral principles associated with being the imam of the village. "In court people become enemies of one another," he said. "And for me it would be difficult to bring all of their 'heads' together again. It is not right for an imam to take part in this kind of work. So I participated in the court sessions for a while, and then I understood that it was not the right thing to do." When I asked him if the current members of the aksakal court attend mosque services and pray, he said, "No, they don't."

Up to this point in our conversation I was still under the impression that I was talking to the current imam of the village. I continued asking about the differences between a moldo and an imam, and Nurdin Moldo told me that a moldo is someone who teaches and an imam is a religious official. When explaining the qualities of an imam, he said, "Actually, an imam has to be very educated; he has to have political knowledge and know the position of the government. Without this knowledge and without religious knowledge it is very difficult to become an imam. As for me, *Kudai* [God] forgive me, I was not appropriate for the position of imam." Somewhat surprised, Zemfira asked, "Excuse me, but aren't you the imam now?" Both the moldo and his wife acknowledged that he was no longer the imam. "I am the head of this medrese," he said. I asked him if he had given up his position as imam, or if something else had happened. His wife laughed very quietly as Nurdin Moldo answered, "In this case it does not matter how it happened. In this situation it is not necessary to say that someone did this or someone did that. It was the will of Allah. I have different work now. I educate the children, and I have to provide good conditions for them. I am in contact with the mufti. Allah is taking care of me."

As it turns out, he had stopped being the imam the year before, after having served the village in that capacity since the country's independence in 1991. Talking to other villagers later on, I found out that he had been discharged because of his efforts to alter the mortuary rituals in his village. With the help of Zemfira, I came across a document Nurdin Moldo had issued in conjunction with other religious officials and the head of the province in the summer of 2004, one and a half years before the combined law mentioned above reached Aral. The document contains all the points mentioned in the combined law but also includes additional ones such as the following:[8]

- that people should not slaughter a horse for the funeral ceremony;
- that the body should be buried within thirty-six hours;[9]
- that during the burial process the short version of the Qur'an should be read;
- that the amount of money that moldos get for *zhanaza dooron* should be reduced;
- that the residents of a village should not eat at the house where a person died;
- that the deceased should not be covered by an [expensive] carpet or other textiles;
- that when the family members send written information to their neighbors or relatives, they should indicate that guests should not bring carpets, textiles, or boxes of candy and cookies;
- that the amount of clothing a person receives for washing the body should be reduced;
- that the ritual of throwing money on the deceased should be abolished;

- that the face of the deceased should not be visible (during the funeral ceremony);

- that those who have changed their religion to a religion other than Islam should not be buried in Muslim cemeteries.

Interestingly, some of these additional rules contradict the combined law that was sent to Aral (e.g., to not cover the dead with a carpet on the way to the graveyard). This shows that it is not only *salt* that varies to a large extent throughout Talas province but also the interpretation of shariat. People's understanding of shariat is subject to negotiation, contestation, and reformulation. As soon as the two repertoires become mutually exclusive, as intended in Nurdin Moldo's order, people tend to act according to *salt*. The example also shows what happens to an imam if he deviates from what the aksakals consider appropriate.

Just as was the case with the two imams in Aral and Engels, Nurdin Moldo got his position as imam with the help of aksakals. And just as politicians need aksakals to carry out their campaigns and events according to *salt*, aksakals need imams not only to carry out certain formalized aspects of Islam such as conducting mosque services and leading prayers but also to do the administrative work that involves communication and cooperation between religious and state officials. They thereby delegate responsibility to the imams, who have to represent the community to the outside, and who will be held liable should noncustomary law clash with *salt*. It turned out that the aksakals and other villagers were not willing to support Nurdin Moldo in his endeavor to modify the mortuary rituals and bring them in line with what state officials considered *salt* and what Islamic officials—including himself—considered shariat.

Nurdin Moldo's story is remarkable, but it is by no means unique. People in my fieldsite knew of other places in the province where religious officials had also unsuccessfully tried to tame *salt* by enforcing shariat. Imams throughout the province have tried to set an example by not allowing the slaughtering of large animals, the hosting of guests, and the exchange of gifts during their own relatives' funerals, but people simply do not like this. As Kalipa Ezhe recalled, "There was one imam. When his father died, he buried him right away. There was a big fight afterwards [*chatak chykkan*]. His relatives were asking why he did this, not giving them a chance to show respect, not respecting them. 'We are hungry,' they said, 'and there was no *borsook* [fried bread].'"

But for the general population, *salt* and shariat are not exclusive, as Baiyz Apa made clear: "The imams say that wealth is the way to keep people together and united. If people did not give anything to one another, they would slowly drift apart. If we visit one another and bring something, it keeps us united. Shariat maintains people's relationships. Moldos do not stop *salt*. They cannot stop it. Shariat is being swallowed by people's *salt*. We bring something when the other person brings something." Baiyz Apa's comment combined *salt* and shariat by focusing on the obligatory aspect of "giving," which is an integral component of both legal repertoires. She then ordered the two hierarchically by describing shariat as a part of *salt*. While we can understand the phrase "shariat is being swallowed by people's *salt*" as a forceful act of custom, we can also interpret it as indicating a degree of flexibility that allows custom to merge with shariat.

Since 2006 state officials have carried out several more initiatives to control "excessive spending."[10] In June 2013, for example, the provincial administration sent an administrative ruling (*buiruk*) to Aral that states the following: "In recent years our people have mixed nationally treasured *salt* with family-based *ürp-adat*, ethnic *yrym zhyrym*, and newly established celebrations [*saltanat*]. The excessive spending during these celebrations has increased every year; it is the reason why our people cannot get out of the economic crisis and why our state cannot overcome its financial crisis. These celebrations have negatively affected our population." As a measure to battle this state of affairs, the administrative ruling referred to practices already established in 2006, including the formation of a working group in each village to educate people not to engage in excessive spending. In addition, this ruling postulates that all *aiyl ökmötü*s are obliged to publish an official document in *Manas Ordo*, the regional newspaper, reporting on the implementation of this reform.[11] Kalipa Ezhe, who provided me with this document, also showed me how the *aiyl ökmötü* from Aral complied with this order, namely, by writing an administrative ruling of its own that was then published in *Manas Ordo* a month later, in July 2013. This document reproduces the one from Talas almost verbatim. It states that a working group will be formed, what the task of this group will be, and that the *aiyl ökmötü* workers will be in charge of implementing this ruling. The text does not report any outcomes. When I asked Kalipa Ezhe about the implementation, she said quite simply, "We did not do it." But in October 2013, the village administration wrote an informational letter (*bildirüü*) to the provincial administration that lists the recent activities undertaken in regard to the issue:

- The working group has been formed.
- Instructors of the organization Adep Bashaty have visited the village and conducted lessons during which excessive spending at funerals was discussed.
- This year [2013], two new mosques were built in Aral. During the opening ceremonies, officials from the kazyiat came and warned people against excessive spending.
- On *Kurban Ait* holiday, the imams and the head of the *aiyl ökmötü* organized a joint meeting in the mosque. People slaughtered an animal and were again informed about the negative impact of excessive spending.
- We [the working group] wrote out parts of the *hadith* that concern excessive spending and distributed them among the people.

The village mayor signed the document. Two months later, in December 2013, another document was sent to the provincial administration, which again listed the above-mentioned five points and added another one:

- In November 2013 villagers voted to form a commission tasked with going to the homes of a deceased person's place and providing information on excessive spending. The issue of forming a commission, which was discussed with the head of the *aiyl ökmötü* and lineage elders, was postponed to the next people's meeting.

One and a half years later, this "next" meeting had still not taken place, Kalipa Ezhe admitted. This set of documents is remarkable not only for the repeated attempts of state personnel to contain certain aspects of *salt* but also for the willingness of state officials to cooperate with and make use of religious resources: meeting in mosques, engaging with new religious movements, and trying to locate relevant passages in Islamic texts that would support their endeavor. It is also remarkable because the state document distinguishes between *salt* as a "national" category, ürp-adat (located in the realm of the family), and *yrym-zhyrym* (located in "ethnic culture," *etnostuk*). *Salt* is thereby upgraded to a matter of national concern—failure to observe it properly is portrayed as the reason for people's economic hardship, and even the financial crisis of the state itself.

Whereas Kalipa Ezhe had mentioned in 2010 that it was the duty of the moldos to prevent excessive spending, in 2015 she emphasized the state's duty in taming custom: "The government gave an order, but it was not followed. If they monitored the situation and checked up on us like they are checking up on us right now in regard to the collection of biometric data [in the frame of the 2015 parliamentary elections], it would stop. But they have not taken control of this." The state may no longer be presented as "absent" in regard to these issues, but its activities are viewed as far from effective and even insincere.

Issuing documents, combining forces with the clergy, and emphasizing the detrimental economic impact of excessive spending are not enough to make people stop performing mortuary rituals "according to *salt*." However, although not much has happened thus far to curb excessive spending per se, the way people go about it has changed in recent years.

HALAL CELEBRATIONS IN TIMES OF "WILD CAPITALISM"

In 2007 people started to give money instead of carpets during mortuary rituals. When I returned to my fieldsite in 2008, Baiyz Apa, one of her daughters, Kakysh Ezhe, and her daughter-in-law Elmira Ezhe filled me in on the recent changes:

> EE: Now in the invitation note some people write to come without kiit. It means you just have to bring money with you.

> KE: During a *toi* [ritual celebration], they have recently started to announce the amount of money [each person gave] with a microphone.

> BA: It's like a competition [Russ. *konkurs*]. They all sit and observe what people bring. We go to these tois even if we have to borrow money. Sometimes we take out loans to be able to go to a toi.

> EE: We bring carpets, boxes [of candy and cookies], material, and *koshumcha* for funerals. We indebt ourselves. It would be better if we did not have such *salt*. But it is impossible to forbid this. People say it comes from ancient times. . . . We [Zhyldyz Ezhe and herself] are two *kelins* [daughters-in-law] in the family and we try to bring things. We really do face difficulties. Autumn is coming and we harvest our potatoes and just bring the money to the people. Then we sit without anything. We take the pension of [Baiyz] Apa and pay back the stores. Then we wait for the next pension. It is difficult for us but we have no other option. We will bring.

Judith: Has it [the obligation to give] increased in recent years?

EE: Yes.

BA: It is increasing. It is getting stronger.

It turned out that Baiyz Apa was now giving money instead of other items at "good feasts," but she continued to give carpets to close relatives, especially in-laws. When I returned in 2015, this development had not only intensified; people had also adapted their justifications to accord with the new monetary practice.

Kalipa Ezhe said, "Now the number of people who bring carpets is going down. Only very close relatives bring carpets. If I bring money, it is considered to be support [zhardam]."

Others drew on shariat to explain the new practice: "We are now having more halal tois," said a neighbor, using the Arabic word meaning "lawful," "in accordance with shariat." "When we give money, it is according to shariat, because money helps people directly."

"And if you bring a carpet?" I asked Kalipa Ezhe.

"This is no support," she explained. "Most of the time I bring money now, but if it is someone from my daughter's side [meaning her in-laws, kuda], I have no option because I am kudagyi. I will bring material, boxes, and a carpet in order not to put a mark on my daughter's face [kyzymdyn betine chirköö bolbosun dep]." She then mentioned that when her brother-in-law died, she asked her own relatives to bring money instead of other items: "We had to cover eighty-five thousand som because we slaughtered two cows. I explained to all of my relatives and friends [zhek zhaat] that we needed money. Most of them understood. But if it is our daughter, then we cannot go without a carpet. This would not be correct."

In general, the stories about spending money in the context of festivities and memorial rituals I encountered in my fieldsite were often combined with statements about how this new development is a step in the right direction. Talking to villagers in neighboring Engels, I encountered the same stories, but they were told with more bitterness. People seemed exhausted and desperate; their jokes were sarcastic and not funny anymore.[12] Syrgak Baike, the former village imam, and his wife, Dinar Ezhe, met me with stories of how, after last year's loss of the entire harvest due to heavy rains, "the whole village" went bankrupt and everyone took out loans to pay for the tois and memorial rituals. "We will bring carpets and cookies and chocolate, ten or twenty meters of material, and koshumcha no mat-

FIGURE 7.1. Some of Baiyz Apa's granddaughters with their small children relaxing at the end of a toi. The leftover meat has been packed into plastic bags to carry home (2015).

ter what," said Dinar Ezhe. "We will give a calf, a horse, and other animals for tois. The minimum amount is now three thousand som. We do this even if we have no flour at home. You have to go to a toi even if your child has no shoes."

When I asked her husband what happened to the initiatives of Yiman Nuru, the collective of elders he had established in 2005 that had been trying to change these customs during my earlier fieldwork (see Beyer 2013), he sighed. "We worked hard in the beginning," he said. "We made a law [*myziam kyldy*] and forced people to slaughter no more than one cow. We told them not to slaughter horses. We managed for two years, but it did not work out. It started again."

His wife added, "It is in our blood to slaughter animals and to see off the deceased person well. We cannot stop and go against it because this is our *salt*."

Kudaibergen Ata interpreted the recent changes as a sign of "prosperity" (*barchylyk*): "When I was a child, you can ask Baiyz [Apa], people did not bring anything. People use to read the Qur'an with what they had at the moment. Now people have a better life. They slaughter animals. . . . This is *salt*, not shariat. People enjoy prosperity. When people have, they give [*elde bar bolgondon kiyin bere beret*]." Rich people in particular are said to impose obligations on others, turning them into debtors by inviting them to their festivities. Kali-pa Ezhe said, "The rich make [the pressure] stronger. They pay ten thousand som to their zhek zhaat and they themselves treat people in cafés. Those who have money slaughter horses. Those who do not have enough feel bad. People are getting worse [about competing]. They cannot stop themselves." Her last sentence in particular shows that the "community of sentiment" (Appadurai 1990), which is manifested in mortuary rituals, is locally interpreted with ambivalence, the result of conspicuous consumption and the felt need to comply with the expectations and actions of others. It also reflects wider socioeconomic changes in the country, such as the increase in what people in Kyrgyzstan call "wild capitalism" (Russ. *dikii kapitalizm*). The term was originally coined in the early years of independence, when the post-Soviet states joined the global capitalist market. It stood for foreign influences that brought "shock therapies" to the Central Asian nations and threatened to overturn "social order" (see Nazpary 2002 for an ethnographic account from Kazakhstan). In my fieldsite, however, *dikii kapitalizm* is nowadays used in the context of prosperity. While the change from giving carpets and other items to giving money had officially been backed by the joint efforts of state officials and imams, villagers did not stop giving carpets because the authorities told them to but because money was suddenly available to almost everyone. The sudden influx of hard currency is the result of remittances from both men and women who have left the village to work in Kazakhstan, Russia, and Turkey. While only very few people from Aral and Engels had worked outside the country in 2005, just ten years later every household had at least one person temporarily working and living abroad. Recent research has shown that the money earned by migrant workers is used not only to build houses or buy cars at home but also to ensure continued participation in the ritual economy (see, for example, Isabaeva 2011; Reeves 2012; Ilkhamov 2013). Villagers approach the many microcredit institutions that have sprouted up like mushrooms all over the country in the last decade for the same reasons. While some indeed use the money to start a business, in a lot of cases the money is being directly fed into the ritual economy. Many households are heavily indebted now, my host family included.

Other innovations I encountered in 2015 were framed not in terms of prosperity but in terms of harmony and respect. Raia Apa, for example, told me that Bürgö uruu no longer practices the giving of *yn-tymak akcha*, as the number of households of both subgroups, Torutai and Sarytai, has increased in recent years. "However," she said, "there is something new: we now bring *tasmal*—candies and cookies." When I inquired about whom she was referring to when she said "we," she explained, "Starting from the little shop on our street down to here [effectively delineating Bürgö territory], neighbors bring tasmal when someone dies. If there is a toi, we bring 100 som each. Only women. It is out of respect [*syi*]. Now we do this. Before, we did not have this." In this case, the alteration of rituals is a direct response to a change in the demographic set-up of the village. While it no longer seems necessary for the subgroups to give small amounts of money to each other because they now have a sufficient number of relatives who can provide the necessary amount of cookies, sweets, and tea to host guests and neighbors, the women from both subgroups decided they needed to continue the practice nonetheless. Likewise, Kudaibergen Ata told me about a new practice within his family that he referred to as "our relatives' harmony" (*bizdin tuugandardyn yntymagy*): "We each collect five thousand som and go to one of my relatives twice a year. Then we drink at their place and give them the money. Each time it is forty thousand som. Then we tell them to buy a horse or anything they want. Now we will start [this practice] with the newly married couples and give forty thousand som to them. We will support them. I am last on the list. First of all we will give to those who have recently married, so they can buy something." As these recent innovations show, economic stratification, increasing inequality, and the monetization of the gift economy should not lead us to believe that this development is occurring at the expense of *salt* or emotional practices. Money as a form of value is always embedded in specific social worlds, despite its apparent capacity to transcend such grounds (Pedersen 2008, 6, referring to Keane 2008). Weiner (1976, 86) showed that amity and competition in fact both have their place in gift exchange: giving draws people together, whereas the ritualization of exchange emphasizes their separateness. In Talas even the competitive aspects of gift giving are publicly performed under the dominant paradigm of yntymak or other related moral concepts. Even the main restaurant in the provincial capital (also called Talas), where rich people celebrate their "good feasts," tellingly carries the name Yntymak. The fact that nowadays women have started to hand over money in the yurts with the words "This is my carpet" shows the compatibility of market behavior and kinship behavior, which were regarded as opposed in classic anthropological literature (Bohannan 1955, 60; Firth [1936] 1983; Fortes 1969). Most importantly, the emotional practices that are so central to these events have followed suit. Classic social theory assumed that the introduction of a monetized economy would lead to "affective neutrality" (Parsons and Shils 1951, 77–88), the "leveling of emotional life" (Simmel [1900] 1990, 432), or a "heightened degree of affect control" (Elias [1939] 2000, 477). This certainly does not hold true in present-day Talas. On the contrary, while the objects and the contexts continue to change, yntymak and *uiat* have remained at the core of mortuary rituals, as has the invocation of *salt* as the ultimate legitimation of why gift exchange needs to continue.

Conclusion

ORDERING EVERYDAY LIFE IN KYRGYZSTAN

Publications on the so-called postsocialist societies, among which Kyrgyzstan is usually counted, often begin in a similar way: "After the collapse of the Soviet Union . . . ," "After the break-up of the Soviet Union . . . ," or sometimes more lyrically: "Daylight broke on a group of newborn sovereign nations with the dissolution of the Soviet Union in 1991" (Svanberg 1999). Numerous scholars carrying out research on or in these countries often approach their topics of interest from what one might call a "change or continuity" perspective: they either emphasize what has remained the same after 1991, or they investigate the impact of "global" developments that are having an increasingly profound influence on these formerly "isolated" countries.[1] Change and continuity are further combined when "pre-Soviet," "Soviet," or "socialist" phenomena are identified and investigated with regard to how they are being "revitalized," "reinvented," or "re-appropriated" today.

In many ways, however, the year 1991 is not a good point of departure for an (ethnographic) exploration of Central Asia. The actual demise of the Soviet Union began several years earlier; namely, with Gorbachev's perestroika. Moreover, the positive connotations that the year 1991 carries for many Westerners do not necessarily ring true in these countries. What is known in the West as the period of "restructuring" is remembered in the East as the implosion of a powerful and pervasive social system and the undermining of the leading role of the Party (see Yurchak 2006). Rather than the "beginning," perestroika is perceived as "the beginning of the end" by many of those who were part of the Soviet Union. Whereas Gorbachev was celebrated in the West, he is remembered in the East as the one who "destroyed" the Soviet Union.

The events of 1991 are also not the only "transformation" that people in Central Asia have experienced. The years between 1928 and 1932—known as the years of the "Great Transformation"—are perceived by many of my elderly informants as having had a much more significant impact on their lives than the year 1991. Sedentarization, collectivization, the loss of livestock, starvation and hunger, the end of transhumance—all this posed greater challenges than the end of the Soviet Union and the subsequent privatization of the kolkhoz system (see chapter 2).

This perspective, though, has to be seen in conjunction with the particular location of my fieldsite. I have described the geographic distinctiveness of Talas province in the introduction, and my ethnographic chapters are intended to sustain the impression that life in a village in this particular part of the Soviet Union was fundamentally different from, for example, life in an industrial center in Eastern Europe. In an article on postsocialist nostalgia in Russia, Heady and Miller (2006, 47) argue that "feelings of nostalgia should be less in places where economic and social life has been less severely disrupted." This is the case not only for a rural setting compared to an urban setting but also for two rural settings, as Heady and Miller make clear. In the first of the two rural villages they describe, the kolkhoz had been the only context in which true village solidarity could develop (Heady and Miller 2006, 44). In the second village, feelings of nostalgia for the Soviet Union were noticeably weaker because there was a great deal of mutual aid and people could draw on their extensive kin networks (Heady and Miller 2006, 47).[2] There was also no sense of "social collapse," Heady and Miller state. This comparison already hints at the flaws in collapsing a geographic area as large and diverse as the former Soviet Bloc into a single category identified by the historicist term "postsocialist."

In the last two decades, some anthropologists have put a lot of effort into writing against the assumptions of political scientists and economists who "measure" degrees of social change in these countries or attribute the slow progress of the "transition" to the "communist mentality" or other "historical relics."[3] Many of them, though, have equally employed the notion of "postsocialism" and have oriented their research toward what has "continued" or what has "changed" since 1991. While acknowledging the important contributions made by this body of anthropological scholarship, I have the impression that many anthropologists cannot resist letting the fall of the Soviet Union overshadow their microstudies: even when they do not claim that a "transition" took place, they still refer back to the vocabulary of change and continuity. But the limits of the term "postsocialism" are well known among scholars today. Lemon (2006, 219) admits that

"many of us rack our brains for substitutes." She encourages scholars to "bracket the issue of general rubrics and terms (for now), and
to take up particular, counterintuitive intersections" (Lemon 2006,
219). Gurova (2015, 7) finds that "the current situation in Russia can
be characterized by a coexistence of traces of socialism, postsocialism, and a new post-postsocialist reality. . . . There is a need, therefore, to deconstruct this concept and allow other concepts and ex-
planatory models to appear." But in doing so, many scholars seem to
go in the opposite direction by coining even more "general rubrics"
such as the above-mentioned "post-postsocialism" (Sampson 2002),
"post-post-transition" (Buyandelgeriyn 2008), "global postsocialisms" (Rogers et al. 2009), or "post–cold war" (Chari and Verdery
2009). While trying to look "beyond post-socialism" (El-Ojeili 2015),
these terms present, to my mind, no solution to the problem; rather, they only shift the issue at stake to an even more abstract level.
I argue that what we need is not another way of categorizing these
societies if we want to understand how people in these countries
live today or have lived in previous decades. It is certainly valid for
scholars to link up their field studies with the comparative idiom of
postsocialism or any of the other new idioms if this helps them make
sense of their data. I have shown, however, that in Aral and Engels,
the year 1991 is not presented as a particularly dramatic event, nor do
people constantly emphasize aspects of "change" or "continuity" in
their reflections on the political economy. Instead, the most striking
phenomenon during my fieldwork was the extent to which people
emphasized *salt* and the various ways in which they ordered their
lives according to it. The force of custom resembles momentum; it
is a way of doing things and rationalizing them that moves through
time and accompanies its bearers wherever they are. It is only mini-
mally affected by seemingly major historical shifts such as "the time
of transition," and it is very difficult for politicians or religious institutions to steer—let alone control. Invoking *salt* to limit one's own
choices, and presenting oneself and one's community as beholden to
this repertoire, seems preferable to other options such as succumb-
ing to "shock therapies" or a new wave of "democracy."

I have noted that people from Talas are renowned throughout the
country for being proud and self-confident. They are the ones "who
never drown." That they are obviously successful in cultivating their
image is substantiated by the fact that "girls from Talas," for example, are widely recognized as "the best" and are, therefore, "more
expensive" in terms of bride price. Talas is also the province where

salt is considered to be "strongest." This had been my initial reason to conduct fieldwork in this area and not in another. Since two of my research assistants came from another province—Yssyk Köl—I could discuss with them what they considered to be "special Talas behavior": "excessive spending" during funerals and celebrations, the cultivation of stereotypical gender roles such as "tough" men and "beautiful" women, and the payment of a very high bride price in the case of arranged marriages being some of the most obvious ones. Does that mean that people from Talas have cultivated a distinct way of portraying themselves and their world that differs from how people in other parts of the country go about it? As I lack the ethnographic data for direct comparisons, I can only wonder whether my informants employ *salt* as an ideal model for "imagining the real" (Geertz [1983] 2000, 173) maybe more intensely than Kyrgyz in other parts of the country. In any case, it is striking that they often gloss over the tragic aspects of their history, such as the time of the Russian "invasion," the years of the Second World War, the forced collectivization, and the current difficulties of living a decent life in times of enduring economic hardship. Rather, they present these historical changes as deriving from their own choices—they were the ones who "threw Nikolai from the throne," the ones who decided to "privatize everything we had," and the ones "who will not go to the state" with their problems.

Invoking custom is a way to articulate togetherness. By performing what Herzfeld has called "cultural intimacy" (Herzfeld [2005] 2014), different sets of actors, ranging from the average villager to the political elite, resort to an imagined social order when legitimating their actions. The force of custom is, in Herzfeld's words, a "self-stereotype that insiders express ostensibly at their own collective expense" ([2005] 2014, 3). In doing so, however, they are far from being mere subjects to the will of the emerging nation-state. Criticizing Anderson's (1983) concept of imagined communities and Gellner's (1983) concept of nationalism for leaving no room for ordinary people to shape their own (nationalist) ideology, Herzfeld ([2005] 2014, 11) suggests that "the focus on cultural intimacy works against this static, elitist, and conflationary reading. Its data are ethnographic and are of a kind often summarily dismissed as mere anecdote." From the blood metaphor that anchors *salt* in the body to the invocation of shame-anxiety and the constant need for harmony, citizens employ essentializing strategies that are, in Herzfeld's words, a semiotic illusion: "By making sure that all the outward signs of identity are as consistent as possible, they literally create, or constitute, homogeneity" ([2005] 2014, 32). He reminds us that "*all* culture is in this sense invented" ([2005] 2014, 214, emphasis in original) and urges us to look at how and in what contexts such concepts are put to use.

Salt is one legal repertoire among others, but as my translation of *salt* as "custom" makes clear, it is far more than that. Beyond a small set of codified principles and rules, it is also perceived as an embodied, gendered, age-specific, and all-encompassing way of conduct. *Salt* is an ideal model of how my informants think their relations should be with one another. Throughout this book, my analysis of *salt* relied entirely on my informants' descriptions, which I have clothed in the analytical language of Western sociocultural anthropology. This approach shows that, when anthropologists attend to people's own models and how people use these models to reason about, reflect on, and justify their actions, they do not have to worry about whether the model fits the facts, a problem currently encountered by "transitologists" and anthropologists of "postsocialism." Thus, the inevitable discrepancy between reality and model is not an anthropological "problem" that I have to sort out or reconcile in order for my analysis to make sense or to be valid. It is part of the lived experience of my informants, who are so painfully aware of this tension that it can even make their "heads spin," as they themselves put it. The concept of reflexivity points exactly to this property of social action.[4]

But what do people in Talas achieve by invoking custom? Take, for example, Bektur Agai. In his position as village historian of Aral, he is the one who has set for himself the task of documenting *salt* in its idealized version. His writings and explanations are accounts not of real-life situations but of how life should be ordered according to *salt*. He is well aware of the fact that, for example, his descriptions of the uruu or the relations between old and young are not based on actual practice. The way he presents *salt* is analogous to how Evans-Pritchard presented the structure he abstracted from Nuer culture; namely, as his own "imaginative construct" (Evans-Pritchard 1962, 23; see Bailey 2003, 88–89). People acknowledged his ambition: at first, when I wanted to know about *salt* as such, I was usually referred to him or to the two senior elders of Kaimazar and Zhetigen uruus. Throughout this book I have closely attended especially to the performances of the elders, who are recognized as the "guardians of cultural knowledge" (Ellen 1993, 231) in Kyrgyzstan. Particular aspects of *salt* are specifically tied to them, such as the invocation of harmony (*yntymak*), the recitation of genealogies (*sanchyra*), the carrying out of certain tasks during rituals, and the settlement of disputes in the villages. These tasks themselves are hierarchically ordered in the sense that not all elders are able (or eligible) to perform all of them. In any case, the senior elder of the descent line (*eng uluu aksakal*) is regarded as worthy of the greatest respect. For example, when I started my field research, Kudaibergen Ata immediately began teaching me everything about the *aksakal* court. The other members, however, were reluctant to provide information, referring me back to him. At the same time, Kudaibergen Ata did not talk to me about *salt* and genealogies until he had introduced me to the senior elder of his descent line, Kozhoke Ata. Only after having shown respect to the elder by publicly acknowledging that he was the real expert on the issue of genealogy was Kudaibergen Ata able to start teaching me about *salt* and about the history of the village. In a similar manner, women generally did not talk about agriculture and animals because this was men's business. Men likewise were reluctant to give information on household routines. Whereas both have extensive knowledge of what is going on in these spheres, they defer to the authority of the proper "head" (*bash*) of the respective sphere, thereby demarcating not only others' spheres of competence but also their own.

The decisive element in the inevitably hierarchical relationship between young and old is the acknowledgment of the elders' authority. This is demonstrated through respectful behavior on the part of the young generation and the willingness to present themselves as wise and knowledgeable—that is, beyond individual ambition—on the part of the elders. The ideal relationship between the old and the young is locally understood as an inherent aspect of custom. It depends on the mutual acknowledgment of each other's positions in everyday life; for example, in the household, the mosque, the courts of elders, and the political arena. In the latter case, however, respect is not only paid to the elders; elders, too, have to respect younger politicians in their role as "head" (*bash*). When these two groups of actors meet, for example during political campaigns, they creatively adapt *salt* in order not to lose face in front of an immediate audience and in the presence of the media, who widely publicize the exchange of respect. I explored how young politicians and businessmen rely on *salt* as a way to "outsource" what they regard as necessary for achieving a certain status in politics, namely, the performance of yntymak. In the course of highly publicized events they "buy" respect from the male elders (by giving money and presents), while the elders in turn "pay" them respect by "doing 'being aksakal.'" The invocation of *salt* thus cannot be dispensed with in contemporary governance practices. It becomes even more relevant when state personnel and religious officials engage in the formalization of *salt*, often against what villagers consider proper. Life-cycle rituals such as funerals are of particular interest to all actors involved, as they encompass economic, religious, legal, social, and political aspects. They are also among the most visible occasions where ordering takes place according to *salt*, as assertions of various sets of actors, each claiming dominion over the interpretation of *salt*, are explicitly debated by villagers and judged against interpretations of Islamic law and state law.

But not even Bektur Agai himself is able to uphold the ideal he postulates at the beginning of his book on Aral genealogies. This became obvious in the way Baiyz Apa and Kudaibergen Ata commented on his account of the two major descent groups, in which they found that he had given predominance to his own uruu, Zhetigen, and downplayed the significance of Kaimazar uruu in the process. Thus, *salt* carries in itself the inevitable clash between what people do, what they say they do, and what they say they ought to do. Any study of it needs to take into account people's awareness of this predicament. Like all models, *salt* has only limited applicability—its abstract demands do not always guide people's practices. But even though as a model *salt* is idealized, it is linked to reality in the way people interact with one another by complying with it, invoking it, or complaining about it. I have also elaborated on how *salt* remains flexible; namely, through the process of customization. To look at customization means to reconstruct the means by which people try to deal with the fact that life is constantly changing. In Talas, customization is metaphorically exemplified when people state that *salt* is "swallowing" elements of noncustomary repertoires. Ideally, *salt* is flexible (while appearing stable), but it always needs to be seen in regard to a particular time and place and only in relation to its specific invocation in a given context. The cases reproduced and analyzed here, for example, represent a study of *salt* in Aral and Engels between 2005 and 2015.

In this book I have attempted to shed light on how my informants go about ordering their everyday lives "according to *salt*." Ordering is a practice and the invocation of *salt* is a particularly vivid and present mode of ordering that contributes to the shaping of selves and regulates one's interaction with others. Utterances invoking *salt* are always constructed in reference to how they will be heard: they are spoken and thought of with an audience in mind. In the claims-making situations I present in this book, these utterances can be understood as positioned diagnoses, where people present themselves either as agents or as patients. Talking and practicing *salt* is also a way of communicating to others that one is an expert in and of one's own culture, well versed in its routines and rituals, knowledgeable of its laws and sanctions. It furthermore provides rhetorical possibilities to appease outsiders like me who tend to question too much and not listen enough. "Our *salt* is like this" often serves as a final comment that indeed states "a different kind of social fact," as Gluckman (1955, 261) once remarked. But its main characteristic is neither the differences that distinguish it from "law," as the early legal anthropologists Llewellyn and Hoebel argued (1941), nor the reciprocal pressure it is seemingly able to exert within social relationships, as Malinowski said (1926). Rather, as a mode of ordering, it enables actors even as they claim to be constrained by it. Thus understood, it opens up possibilities to conceptualize, classify, and contextualize large- and mid-scale developments in an intimate idiom through which people force social and political change to assume the shape of custom.

NOTES

PREFACE

1. See also Haroche (1998, 218–19) on the role of posture, bearing, and movement in the work of Mauss, and her reference to d'Oncieu's account of 1593 on "the honours, forms of respect, arrangements for seating and precedence of the age, and the causes and reasons for them."

2. To translate *shariat* as "Islamic law" is an oversimplification. Law in the narrow sense of jurisprudence is *fiqh*, while shariat is the base fiqh draws upon to make judgments. *Shariat* is often translated as "a way of life" as it encompasses—just as custom does—a wide range of ethical norms that go far beyond our common understanding of "law" (see also Rosen 2006, 39).

3. Talas province (*oblast'*) is headed by a governor (*gubernator*), who has his offices in the "white house" (*ak üi*) in the provincial capital, also called Talas. The province comprises four districts (*raions*)—Bakai-Ata, Kara-Buura, Manas, and Talas—each headed by a government-appointed official (*akim*). Within the districts there are rural municipalities (*aiyl ökmötüs*), each headed by an elected mayor. If the villages are small, two or three may be grouped together to form one *aiyl ökmötü*; larger villages can constitute *aiyl ökmötüs* on their own. Aral and Engels, the villages where I carried out fieldwork, are located in Talas district (Talas *raion*), whose administrative center is Chat-Bazar.

4. Engels was officially renamed Üch Emchek in 1994. However, as most villagers continue to refer to it by its Soviet name, I have decided to do so as well.

INTRODUCTION: INVOKING CUSTOM

1. The official name of the country is "Kyrgyz Republic" (*Kyrgyz Respublikasy*), but people refer to it as Kyrgyzstan (that is, the titular ethnic group and the suffix *–stan*, which means "country"). Kyrgyzstan appeared first as a coherent territorial entity in 1924. It became a Soviet socialist republic in 1936 as part of the Soviet Union. At that time it was known as Kirgiziia. The country announced its independence from the Soviet Union in 1991.

2. *Alasangdan ulak al, ulak al da, tyna kal.*

3. The term *patiency* dates back to Lienhardt (1961), who talks of "passions" and "passiones" in the context of religious divination among the Dinka. The concept has been further discussed by Kramer (1984) and Schnepel (2008, 2009). Carrithers has recently argued that "'agency-cum-patiency' . . . recovers that fundamentally interactive character that makes rhetoric integral to human sociality" (2005, 578).

4. I agree with Karim, who suggests that anthropologists should regard their informants as "an observant people capable of their own reflexivity" (1993, 82). While I am taking my privileged position as an author into account as I interpret my ethnographic data (which I not only gathered but also helped to produce in the first place), I also pay close attention to people's reflexivity as they establish, maintain, and (re)produce *salt*. My aim is thus to describe "the procedures by which conversationalists produce their own behavior and understand and deal with the behavior of others" (Atkinson and Heritage 1984, 1). I try to come to terms with orderly phenomena as they are produced by "real-world people for the living of real-world lives" (Atkinson and Heritage 1984, 412).

5. *Salttan kalbailyk dep ele.*

6. As new elements are included in the repertoire of *salt*, without doubt many others disappear as they fall out of fashion, are forgotten, or are dropped in quiet agreement. Researching what is no longer part of *salt*, however, would be a different longitudinal study. Thus, this aspect of the dynamics of *salt* will throughout this book be hinted at only occasionally, as my focus lies more in the way people use *salt* to maintain their sense of something that is uniquely "ours."

7. F. von Benda-Beckmann (2003, 249) speaks of "adatisation," which can be loosely defined as the incorporation of Islamic legal concepts and Arabic terms into Minangkabau *adat*. This does not, however, signify a process of selective appropriation for them but, rather, a state of encompassment. Similarly, one could say that *salt* as a whole is more than the sum of its parts.

8. *Ata-enesine akarat kylgyndy tashbarang kylat, shariat dep zakonun tabat.* Whereas this particular proverb is well known in Talas, and I have heard grown-ups use it to admonish their misbehaving children, it would be wrong to assume that anyone takes it literally. It serves as a dramatic moral reminder that "one has to respect the elders."

9. According to the law *On Local Self-Governance*, a kurultai does not constitute a representative body of local self-governance, and its decisions are only advisory in nature, not legally binding. Therefore, the decisions would have been written down as if the village council had agreed upon them. See law *On Local Self-Governance*, No. 101, July 15, 2011, Art. 59.2.

10. See *Government Resolution of the Republic of Kyrgyzstan*, No. 117, February 26, 2010, Art. 1.2 (a).

11. About 255 US dollars at that time.

12. The muftiyat is the highest religious office in the country. It is located in the capital and coordinates as well as oversees all religious activities. It is, in turn, subordinate to state authorities.

13. On February 7, 2014, the declaration of the council was turned into a Presidential Decree (*ukaz*), which now has the full force of law: see *Decision of the Council of Defense on the State Policy in the Religious Sphere*, published February 7, 2014, in the national newspaper *Kabar*. Available online at the president's homepage: www.president.kg/ru/news/ukazy/3468_podpisan _ukaz_o_realizatsii_resheniya_soveta_oboronyi_kyirgyizskoy_respubliki _o_gosudarstvennoy_politike_v_religioznoy_sfere/ (accessed March 14, 2016).

14. See *Administrative Ruling: Talas Regional Administration*, No. 12, January 20, 2014.

15. From the Arabic *qadi* (Islamic judge). In contemporary Kyrgyzstan, the kazy is a clergyman who oversees the affairs of the imams on the provincial level. Each of the country's provinces has a kazyiat. Decisions coming from the highest religious office in Bishkek, the muftiyat, reach the village mosques via the kazyiat. The administrative structure of the religious institutions thus parallels that of state institutions. The roots of this setup can be traced back to Soviet times.

16. This position is also advocated in the article "Dinii sabatsyzdyktyn kesepetteri," which appeared in the journal *Kyrgyz Tuusu* 8 (February 3, 2015): 6.

CHAPTER 1. HISTORIES OF LEGAL PLURALITY

1. While a number of Russian scholars have touched upon the topic of Kyrgyz customary law, nobody has dealt with it specifically. When investigating historical sources in regard to how different legal repertoires were interrelated in the past, one needs to remember that most of these analyses by later scholars operate with an understanding of "customary law" that does not reflect my informants' perceptions of *salt*.

2. Until the 1930s Russians called the Kazakh "Kirgiz," "Kazakh-Kirgiz," "Kirgiz-Kazakh," or "Siberian Kirgiz," and the Kyrgyz "Kara-Kirgiz" (Black Kyrgyz) or "Dikokamennyi Kirgiz" (lit. Stone-Age Kyrgyz). In many cases they did not differentiate between the two at all. The question of the distinction between Kazakh and Kyrgyz became relevant to the colonizers only when national borders were about to be drawn in the early Soviet period, and national identities were required to go along with these demarcations. A number of important historical works have touched on the *obychie* (Russian for customs) and *obychnoe pravo* (Russian for customary law) of the Kazakh and Kyrgyz, including Barthold ([1922] 1956); Brodovskii (1913); Bukeikhanov ([1910] 1985); Dingelstedt (1891); Gins (1913); Grodekov (1889); Iakovlev (1912); Ivanov (1881); Izraztsov (1897); Korzhenevskii (1899); Kozhonaliev ([1963] 2000); Leontev (1890); Levchine (1840); Radloff (1870);

Sabataev (1900); Severtsov ([1873] 1947); Semenov (1998); and Zagriazhskii (1874).

3. These laws themselves were a heterogeneous set of legal norms and prescriptions that differed from region to region. They adopted and adapted many local elements. Legal unification not only remained partial until the end of imperial rule but also promoted and institutionalized cultural and legal diversity. For details see Jane Burbank (2006). I thank one of the anonymous reviewers for pointing this out.

4. Levchine (1840, 305, 391), for example, saw the Kazakhs as "savages" in need of "law and order." Other scholars were also convinced that they were part of a civilizing mission that brought enlightenment to the remotest areas of the tsarist empire. See Iğmen (2012a) for the example of Soviet culture clubs in Kyrgyzstan through which locals were exposed to Soviet notions of modernization.

5. See Martin (2001). In this sense, the "invention of customary law" in Central Asia can be compared to similar developments during the colonization of Africa and southeast Asia. I have discussed the arguments of Chanock (1992), Clammer (1973), and Hobsbawm and Ranger (1983) in regard to the Kyrgyz courts of elders in an earlier article (Beyer 2006).

6. Irons (1975, 55) speaks of an "irregular relationship between descent and residence" for the Turkmen. For a similar argument in the Mongolian case, see Humphrey and Sneath (1999).

7. Traditionally transmitted only orally, the Manas epic was recorded and written down by the Russian ethnographers Valikhanov and Barthold as part of the general codification process in the nineteenth century (see Van der Heide 2008).

8. For a list of taxes paid to manaps in the Yssyk Köl area, see Gullette (2010, 57).

9. The different rulers of the khanate were initially called *bek* (*bai, bii*) and only later called themselves khans (from Chinese/Manchu *han*; see Newby 2005, 32–33).

10. They thereby replicated what the Mongols had begun centuries earlier, setting Islamic law against their own code of law and ethics (the *yasa*) in an effort to undo "the hegemony of Islam in the political realm" (Khalid 2007, 26–27).

11. *Draft Statute on the Administration of Semireche and Syr-Dar'ia Provinces,* July 11, 1867.

12. See Kemper (2007) for the Caucasus and Sartori (2007) for the Fergana Valley.

13. See §§ 118 and 217 of the 1867 *Draft Statute for Elections of Aksakals;* Zimanov (1958, 196–97); Carrère d'Encausse (1967, 154).

14. From the Arabic *qadi* (Islamic judge). As kazy courts most probably did not exist among the nonsedentary Kyrgyz in the territory of contemporary Kyrygzstan, I do not consider the institution in further detail here. For

more on the kazy courts, see the work of Paolo Sartori (Sartori 2007, 2008, 2010a, 2010b, 2011).

15. The term *bolush* was frequently used by elders in my fieldsite to refer to the office of a local official during the time of Nikolai. However, this word only rarely appears in the scholarly literature. In the Kyrgyz language, Russian words are often adapted to fit Kyrgyz pronunciation rules, where labiodental fricatives (v and f) are turned into plosives (b and p), and "sh"-endings are common. I assume that the word comes from the Russian *volost'*, meaning "district," and that my informants are talking about a person who headed a *volost'*. See Aitpaeva (2007, 521) for a similar view. Kozhoke Ata used the word in a personifying way, conflating the person who headed the district with the district as such.

16. Here Kozhoke Ata refers to the newly formed office of "village elder" during "the time of Nikolai." See Kemper (2007) for examples from the Caucasus.

17. See Kozhonaliev ([1963] 2000) and Kachkeev (2007) for procedural details.

18. The difference between these aksakals and the aksakals that Newby describes could not be greater. Writing about Xinjiang in the nineteenth century, she notes that "the term aqsaqal was applied to the chief representative of any foreign (including western) trading community resident in Xinjiang," and that "the aqsaqal representing the British and the Russians were, of course, also functioning as political informants" (Newby 2005, 65n59, citing Skrine 1986, 108). According to Valikhanov, the head trader-aksakal in Kashgar (Xinjiang) even possessed his own police (1962, 333). Still, other variations existed. Within the khanate of Kokand, aksakals were appointed as irrigation officers, received salaries, and had assistants—the so-called canal aksakals (*aryk aksakal*; see Bichsel 2008, 72; Thurman 1999, 48–49, 93). In the Emirate of Bukhara, aksakals were appointed as local representatives and acted as intermediaries between the rural population and the commander in chief (*amir*). They were responsible for tax collection, irrigation issues, mediation, and protection (Wilde 2014). Wilde emphasizes that the institution of aksakals was fluid and constantly negotiated. He dismisses the analyses of Russian outside observers who had "the tendency to view the Central Asian Khanates through the lens of the nation-state," which accounts for translating the indigenous term *aqsaqali* as *aksakalstvo* in Russian (*aksakal*-ship) (Wilde 2014, 279–80).

19. Likewise, Douglas Northrop has shown that "Soviet authorities no less than their Central Asian subjects were reshaped through this protracted encounter, and it was the ongoing interactions between these groups— unstable, permeable, and interpenetrated as they were—that in the end defined what it meant to be both 'Bolshevik' and 'Uzbek'" (Northrop 2004, 7).

20. See Kuehnast (1997, 210). The following two quotes exemplify the Soviet propaganda prevalent at that time: "The national delimitation has

taken up the task of eliminating clan-based, tribal, and feudal forms of power, and consolidating in one state heterogeneous tribes, and educating the masses in this spirit" (Zelenskii n.d., cited in Haugen 2003, 100); "The real battle against harmful . . . tribal-patriarchal residues . . . against the survivals of the old order . . . blocking the path of Soviet development, must begin from the destruction of the old . . . family—of that primary cell of the conservative Central Asian village, a cell that refuses to surrender its position to the forces of the new . . . world" (a party analyst, cited in Massell [1968] 1980, 231–32; brackets removed for better readability).

21. In Central Asia, the year 1927 is generally remembered as the year of "the *hujum*"—casting off the veil. But in northern Kyrgyzstan this injunction was less incendiary as women veiled less there than in other parts of Central Asia. Soviet policies on "women's liberation" therefore concentrated on other issues such as blood feuds, bride abductions, bride price, underage marriage, and illiteracy (Northrop 2004, 77, 83).

22. For Soviet antireligious policy in Central Asia, see Kamp (2002, 2006), Keller (2001), Massell ([1968] 1980), and Northrop (2001, 2004).

23. The SADUM was a hierarchal organization with the head (mufti) based in Tashkent (Uzbekistan), one kazy for each of the five Soviet Central Asian Republics (Kyrgyzstan, Uzbekistan, Tajikistan, Kazakhstan, and Turkmenistan), and religious officials (imams) based in the provinces and towns that were subordinate to the kazys. The institution has remained intact to a great extent in contemporary Kyrgyzstan. On its homepage, the muftiyat in Bishkek mentions 1943 as the founding year of the institution (see www.muftiyat.kg, accessed March 14, 2016). Its recent initiative of paying the village imams enforces the top-down structure and ensures that the chain of command is being followed.

24. See Babadjanov (2004), Bellér-Hann (2004, 189), Bennigsen and Lemercier-Quelquejay (1979), and Poljakov (1992). This intertwinement is often oversimplified as "parallel" Islam in the literature (see Saroyan 1997). This approach, however, is rooted in positivist scholarship on religion as developed in the late nineteenth century, but which has its roots in the Enlightenment era. It fragments the life of Muslims into components that were labeled "real Islam" on the one hand, and "popular Islam," "folk Islam," or "non-official Islam" on the other (see DeWeese 2002, 310). While I do not question the "authenticity" of practices that my informants refer to as Islamic nor the "origin" of the rules they consider to be shariat, they themselves sometimes emphasize that, in comparison to (imagined) other believers, they know "little" about Islam or are "bad Muslims" because they do not adhere to scripture-oriented interpretations of the shari'a.

25. See Bobrovnikov (2005) and Kemper (2007) for the North Caucasus.

26. Massell ([1968] 1980, 231) uses the term *adat* to refer to customary law. The process he describes as "traditionalization" is similar to the empirical phenomenon I label "customization."

27. Teachings of the Prophet Mohammad.

28. See Decree of the Presidium of the Russian Soviet Federative Socialist Republic, *Ob utverzhdenii polozheniia o tovarishcheskikh sudakh i poloo-
zheniia ob obshchestvennykh sovetakh po rabote tovarishcheskikh sudov* (March 11,
1977); see also Alenkina (2015) for a comparison of the decree with the law
on the aksakal courts.

29. Vitebsky, for example, sees the current "rewriting of history" in the
so-called postsocialist countries as an attempt to "fill a vacuum" that people
created by forgetting their ancestors and by being forced to follow socialist
linear eschatology (2002, 282).

30. In just about any cultural context, state law is a mosaic of different
legal repertoires. This is even more the case with the post-Soviet republics.
For an in-depth analysis and critique of legal and judicial reforms in the
post-Soviet states since 1991, see Boulanger (2002), Knieper (2010).

31. *Zakon Kirgizskoi Respubliki: O sudakh aksakalov*, No. 158, Bishkek, July
30, 2003.

32. The Kyrgyz poet Kazybek was born in 1901. Being the son of a rich
man (manap), he was imprisoned during the Stalin era and died in 1936 (according to other sources, 1943). He is famous in Kyrgyzstan for his poems,
some of which he wrote during his imprisonment.

CHAPTER 2. SETTLING DESCENT

1. I thank Brian Donahoe for this insightful remark.

2. In the recent literature on Kazakhstan and Kyrgyzstan, descent has
come to be regarded first and foremost as a resource through which government officials construct the nation and politicians recruit their voters. Within this observable trend, two different developments can be distinguished:
while some scholars have emphasized descent and explore "tribalism" (Esenova 1998), "clan politics" (Collins 2002, 2006), "elite clans" (Kadyrov 2009),
and "the power of 'blood'" (Schatz 2004), others deny the importance of
descent and see territoriality as the decisive factor in these societies and thus
have pursued topics such as "the power of localism" (Radnitz 2005) and "the
rise of regional identities" (Jones Luong 2002). It is striking that throughout
the debate either one or the other phenomenon is identified as the key to
unlocking the complexities of the present-day Central Asian political landscape. Gullette has criticized these instrumentalist approaches, arguing that
it is misleading to understand descent and territoriality as the driving forces
behind the political or economic games of politicians. Gullette suggests that
political elites' description of this phenomenon as *traibalizm* (Russ.) "is an al-
legation of corruption; it is not primarily an identification of kinship" (2010,
3). In other words, politics is not necessarily based on, nor confined to, a
framework of kinship ties. He argues that genealogy, in contrast, is "a way to
examine relatedness through how it is established and maintained" (2010,
3). In his view, it is the people's genealogical imagination, which centers on
knowing one's patrilineal ancestors (*zheti ata*; lit. "seven fathers") and the

historical accounts of one's genealogy (*sanzhyra*) that "complements the government's nation-building project" (Gullette 2007, 384). I pick up from there.

3. Following Ingold (2000), I regard landscape as a lived phenomenon that is not "out there," but which people are a "part of" and which "is perpetually under construction": "The landscape tells—or rather is—a story. . . . It enfolds the lives and times of predecessors who, over the generations, have moved around in it and played their part in its formation. To perceive the landscape is therefore to carry out an act of remembrance, and remembering is not so much a matter of calling up an internal image, stored in the mind, as of engaging perceptually with an environment that is itself pregnant with the past" (Ingold 2000, 189).

4. My informants use the term *chong uruu* to refer to all the descendants of their ancestor Kaimazar, from which they are eight generations removed. As the adjective *chong* indicates that something is of greater significance, I translate *chong uruu* as "major descent line."

5. The term is from Mondragón (2009, 123).

6. See Iğmen (2012b) for details.

7. I borrowed the term "imperial landscape" from Mitchell (1994).

8. During the Second World War, many Talas men were sent to fight on the front lines, often spending up to five years abroad, both in service and as prisoners of war. From Aral alone, 222 men died in the war.

9. The three encampments that eventually came to make up the village of Engels were located further up in the mountains and were not consolidated as they have come to be in the present-day village setup. They were called Chöngör, Kuugandy, and Tegerek.

10. These pastures, in turn, are also divided along uruu membership, with each uruu having its own territory. The encampments consisted most probably not only of uruu members but also of cognates and other non-kin (see also Humphrey and Sneath 1999; Irons 1975; Jacquesson 2010; Sneath 2007).

11. In Engels this happened in 1939. When I asked Masalbek Ata, from Engels village, about this, he recalled: "I still know what my father said. He told me that in 1939 he had to give forty sheep and goats, and eleven cows and horses to the kolkhoz. That's how the kolkhoz got animals."

12. As in Aral, the three winter encampment sites of what is today Engels were first turned into artels and later into birikmes. In contrast to Aral, however, names changed only once: from Tegerek, Kuugandy, and Chöngör in "the time of Manas" to Örnök, Engels, and Özgörüsh in "the time of the kolkhozes." In 1950 the three birikmes were united to form Kolkhoz Engels.

13. Kolkhoz directors and leading personnel had to change their workplace frequently to avoid developing close ties to the local inhabitants. This strategy is also being applied in contemporary Kyrgyz politics, where governors are usually assigned to head those provinces they themselves do not come from.

14. The name Üch Emchek means "three breasts." Villagers typically explain this name by referring either to the striking mountain outside their village that reminds them of a body, or by pointing toward the three mountain streams—Chong-Aryk, Chöngör, and Tegerek—that flow through the village. Both explanations emphasize the nourishing aspect of the landscape for the village.

15. Kudaibergen Ata did not refer to "Zhetigen and Kaimazar" here because reference to Kaimazar would have included people from Engels who had already split off at that point.

16. *Sotik* is the Kyrgyz calque of the Russian word *sotok*, which is the genitive plural of *sotka*. One *sotka* is 0.01 ha (100 sq.m). The assigned land plots in the main valley and in other parts of the country were larger because they are less locked in by mountains than those in Aral. Engels received twenty-one sotik per person because they privatized a couple of years later, after a new land law had been passed.

17. According to the *Talas Entsiklopediasy* (Talas encyclopedia) of 1995, 3,824 people lived in Aral at that time, but Klijn (1998, 61) mentions that land was allocated to 4,500 individuals, a number that includes those who no longer resided in the village.

18. Villagers told me that the Kashka Zhol unit is the same as Pionir. It coincides with the westernmost encampment site. While I could never find out the history of this particular unit (which Klijn also does not mention in her work), it appears to have been fully merged into Aral birikme by the time I was in the field. For example, none of the younger men who worked in this unit mentioned that they were from Kashka Zhol. This divergence is common: the uruu names that Klijn's informants from the "lower" part of Aral gave her for the precolonial era (1998, 94–95) only partially overlap with the ones my informants gave me.

19. Klijn argues similarly when she asserts that, contrary to the perception propagated by many reports and articles on conditions in rural Kyrgyzstan, families in Aral were coping quite well with the economic crisis. She attributes this to the "organizational heritage [that] fitted quite well into the kolkhoz system" and which provided the Kyrgyz with the possibility "to overcome the short-term insecurity after independence" (Klijn 1998, 88).

CHAPTER 3. IMAGINING THE STATE

1. *Zakon Kirgizskoi Respubliki: O novoi redaktsii Konstitutsii Kyrgyzskoi Respubliki*, no. 410. See also the version of February 2003, *Konstitutsiia Kirgizskoi Respubliki*. Between 1993 and 2003, the constitution was completely revised once more (in February 1996), but no changes were introduced in regard to the aksakal courts. See Arts. 85 and 95 of the *Konstitutsiia Kirgizskoi Respubliki*, Bishkek (1996).

2. *Zakon Kirgizskoi Respubliki: O sudakh aksakalov*, no. 158, Bishkek, July 30, 2003.

3. For example, UNHCR 2000; the Convention on the Rights of the Child (2004, 65).

4. Decree *On the Registration of Aksakal Courts in Bishkek*, June 30, 2004. I did some comparative research on two aksakal courts in Bishkek. As it turns out, the courts are organized in fundamentally different ways from village aksakal courts: they have to report regularly to the district administration that coordinates the institutions of local self-governance. From there the judges also receive a small monthly salary and occasional "training" from state judges of the district courts. The most striking difference, however, is that the Bishkek aksakal courts are predominantly staffed with female members of non-Kyrgyz ethnic background (see Beyer 2015b).

5. In this regard, the institution resembles the Uzbek *mahalla* community. See Noori (2006, 138).

6. Giovarelli and Akmatova (2002, vii), in reference to the World Bank.

7. "Kyrgyzstan—a country of human rights" was also the president's slogan for the year 2003.

8. The cause of the people's discontent seems to have been the devastating results of the parliamentary elections in February and March 2005, in which only six of seventy-five seats went to the opposition. While the son and daughter of President Akaev won seats, well-known opposition politicians such as Kurmanbek Bakiev (who later became president) did not. The immediate cause of the uprising, however, was not election fraud but long-standing discontent with Akaev and his family among the Kyrgyz population (see Beyer 2005b).

9. This court case is one of ten full-fledged court cases that I observed in Aral and Engels in the course of fieldwork in 2005–2006. I obtained data on how the disputes evolved before they reached the court, took part in the court sessions, and stayed in touch with all parties involved after the court cases were over in order to assess the posttrial stage. In addition, I took part in about forty smaller and larger cases—presided over only by the head of the court—that never became official. When I returned to the field in 2008 and 2010 for brief periods of follow-up research, I participated in additional cases. While I have copies of all protocols and other written documents issued by the two courts since their very inception (in 1995 and 1996, respectively), these materials cannot be presented here. Moreover, as these documents were mostly written on the assumption that they at some point would be read by state officials in order to check on the work of the aksakals, they reveal more about how the aksakals want to present themselves "to the state" than about how the aksakal court in fact operates.

10. All of the names in this section with the exception of the aksakals are pseudonyms.

11. The villages simply could not afford to have a policeman, as there was no money for his housing and living expenses. People joked that he could live with the mayor and his family instead.

12. See Beyer (2006) for examples.

13. While this judge knew about my research interests in studying the aksakal courts, I had come to her to participate in state court sessions in order to be able to compare the two styles of what I call "court making." The judge not only summarized people's perceptions, which I had already gotten to know in both villages, but also related it to the aksakals, presenting them as a legitimate alternative to state legal adjudication.

14. It is no secret that the Kyrgyzstan judiciary is corrupt. These costs are also at play when villagers opt against officializing their documents in terms of landownership.

15. De facto interaction with state courts is thus minimal. The situation in the capital is quite different. There, aksakal court members are directly subordinate to the city administration. They get paid a small monthly salary and their work is regularly evaluated by state judges (see Beyer 2015b).

16. In contrast to how the aksakal presented it, this is not the divorce itself, but only the first step toward it. The actual divorce will have to take place in front of a state court. What is solved, however, is the question of how the property, the land, and the children will be divided between the couple. When I left in September 2006, the couple had not been to the state court. When I returned in 2008, the situation was still the same. In this case, people gave the same reasons they give in regard to why they do not officialize their documents: the costs are too high, the procedure is too time-consuming, and it is considered shameful (*uiat*) to bring one's disputes into the open.

17. This is done even though the mayor should not be part of the court procedure. Very often, however, the mayors act as if they are court members. In a few rare cases I was made a member of the court and my assistant was asked to take the minutes. As we were recording and writing down the sessions anyway, we simply made a copy and handed the original notes over to Kudaibergen Ata or Kasym Ata or the respective secretary, who filed them along with the other documents.

18. While these objects make aksakal court documents look more official, I found out that the village received them only in 2002. Each aiyl ökmötü was required to pay for the manufacture of these two symbols of state bureaucracy, but because there had been no money in the budget, they were only recently paid for by the mayor.

19. One som was approximately equal to US$0.025 (two and a half cents) in 2005 and US$0.015 (one and a half cents) in 2015.

20. This handling of written and oral legal evidence has quite interesting ramifications especially as it aligns very much with how my informants talk about another document: the Qur'an. In fact, I have come across a striking similarity between how the constitution (often invoked as "the law" by aksakal judges as well as villagers in general) and the Qur'an are talked about and rhetorically employed as part of legal reasoning: in both cases, it is not the actual document but invocations of "the book" that form the centerpiece of many speech acts and practices. See Beyer (2015a) for details.

21. This is even more the case if the aksakals use the money generated in court sessions to buy food for themselves when the court case is over (see below). In none of the cases I took part in was the money handed over to the state courts as prescribed in Art. 29 of the law on the aksakal courts.

22. I also attribute local knowledge of how state courts operate to television programs such as the American series *Law & Order* (Russ. *Zakon i poriadok*). In a seminar they attended in Bishkek, some city aksakals told the overseeing state judge that often they learn about "how judges behave" from watching TV shows in which court cases are staged in front of an actor playing a judge (see Beyer 2015b).

23. "The book" is a compilation of state laws about the aksakal courts and is in and of itself a symbol of bureaucracy. I checked it at a later point and found nothing written on the inside of the back cover.

24. The aksakals often complained about the fact that their work was not being adequately rewarded. They were of the opinion that their work either should be financially compensated or should at least entitle them to free transportation or discounts when buying certain products such as tea, sugar, and tobacco. That Akaev had planned to pay them a salary is well known to all aksakal judges in Talas.

25. I myself noticed how much the state is perceived as something "foreign" when occasionally people in my fieldsite who did not know me referred to me as being someone "from the district" (*raiondon*), that is, a state official.

26. In fact, the situation is quite the contrary: rather than giving villagers a stake in state-building processes themselves, new laws on local self-governance have significantly undermined villagers' participation in village politics. Since 2008, for example, the mayor can no longer be elected directly by the villagers but only by the members of the village council (*aiyl kengesh*), and only after the candidacy has been approved by the provincial administration. This led an informant of mine to comment that the current mayor was "elected by the governor."

CHAPTER 4. PERFORMING AUTHORITY

1. *Aksakaldardy syilash kerek.* While this proverb refers only to male elders, people say that elderly women should be equally respected, as is indicated by sayings that refer to both men and women, such as, "One must respect one's parents." I use the term *elder* when speaking of all elders, and the term *aksakal* when speaking of male elders only.

2. I adapt this construction from Harvey Sacks ([1970/1971] 1984, 414), who argued that even "being ordinary" needs to be actively pursued: "There is not 'an ordinary person' as some person, but as somebody having as one's job, as one's constant preoccupation, doing 'being ordinary'—it is not that somebody is ordinary; it is perhaps that that is what one's business is, and it takes work, as any other business does."

3. *Zhezde* is used to address the husband of an older sister.

4. The household head is either the oldest male person (the aksakal) or the widow of the aksakal. Only when both parents have died will the youngest son, who stays with his parents to take care of them, become the head of the household.

5. See Grodekov (1889, 8–9). However, as my assistant Eliza pointed out to me, this practice would be considered shameful (uiat) in her hometown in the Yssyk Köl province, where elders should never be given the head of an animal: "They say old people don't have teeth. Therefore, they should get meat and not bones. The head is all bones and skin."

6. This is especially the case when there is only one son in the family and he does not stay with his parents but lives, for example, in Bishkek. If he has a child, it is likely that this child will be raised in the house of the grandparents, who need a male relative to take care of them when they grow old. Likewise, grandparents can demand granddaughters from their sons if they feel they could use a helping hand in the house or simply because they enjoy being surrounded by their grandchildren.

7. My friend's grandmother, who lives in Bishkek, is a huge fan of Jackie Chan movies. When one of her daughters-in-law gave birth to a son, she decided to name the child in honor of the martial arts actor, who is a well-known figure in Kyrgyzstan. Everyone tried to talk her out of this decision, but she would not budge.

8. The literal translation of *aksakal* is "white beard." Although not all elders have beards, a long beard is the *pars pro toto* for the male elder. Elders can choose to have a beard or not, but it is not customary for young men to have them. However, those young men who want to publicly state that they follow Islam according to its new scripture-oriented interpretation can be recognized easily by their long beards. This, in turn, disturbs some aksakals, who consider it an illegitimate appropriation of "their" characteristic: "Only aksakals should wear beards," one old man told me once when we spotted a pious young man who had come to Aral from "outside" to teach about Islam (see below). Another visible feature associated with aksakals is the tall white felt hat (*kalpak*) that old men wear. While younger men may wear these hats during festivities, only old men wear them in everyday life. My assistant Zemfira pointed out to me that some young politicians in Bishkek wear kalpaks in public in order to show their patriotic mindset and to claim the positive attributes of the aksakals for themselves.

9. Art.13 stipulates that an aksakal judge who is directly related to a claimant or a defendant is not allowed to judge over the respective case.

10. See Noori (2006, 129) for a similar finding in the case of *mahalla* elders in Uzbekistan.

11. During the court session, villagers from Engels were present, too.

12. *Sakal toido kerek.* Here again, "beard" (*sakal*) is used as a *pars pro toto* for the male elder.

13. In other parts of Kyrgyzstan elderly women can also be addressed with the term *aksakal* (pers. comm. with Aksana Ismailbekova), but this is not customary in Talas.

14. See Lui (2012) for Uzbeks in Kyrgyzstan and van der Geest (1998) for the African context.

15. This fundamental ambivalence toward elders is known from other contexts as well. See van der Geest (2002, 458) for Ghana, where witchcraft accusations are put forward against elders as a hidden way of airing frustration and dislike.

16. *Karyiany syilabagan, karyganda syi korboit*, or: *Zhakalaba atangdy, zhakalasang, seni da balang bir künü zhakalait* (Do not beat up your father, or one day your son will beat you up).

17. While most girls finish high school, there were very few women over the age of twenty who were not already married and had a child. Marriages usually take place right after graduation from high school. Only in rare cases do married women work outside their own households. In Aral, for example, the secretary of the mayor, the librarian, the woman who works in the post office, and a handful of teachers are the only women in the village holding jobs.

18. The name Arstan Baike is a pseudonym.

19. He could not have known that I would participate in the case because the aksakal had decided spontaneously to take me along.

20. *Biz özübüz. Özübüz özübüzdö kalsyn.*

21. He also keeps the land of another son who lives in Bishkek, but he claims that, should the son want it, he would give it to him.

22. We know from many other ethnographic contexts that tensions between young and old are likely to arise over this issue (see, e.g., Fortes 1949; Parkin [1972] 1994).

23. See Dekker (2003) for details on the land reform in Kyrgyzstan.

24. When I was discussing village politics with a group of young men, for example, one of them told me that the mayor had told them to vote for a particular political candidate during the parliamentary elections in 2005. Commenting on this, the man said, "Power squeezes" (*Bülik kysat da*). "Power" in this case referred to the mayor, but equally to those state officials (in Talas) who were dictating their rules to the mayor, who was—on a provincial level—in the same position that his staff was in regard to him. These state officials in Talas, in turn, describe themselves as being the subjects of other officials "in the capital." This description is quite contrary to how power used to be described in official Soviet rhetoric, where it belonged to "the people" and authority to the Party (Mayer 1992, 412, quoting Brezhnev).

25. See, e.g., Abu-Lughod (1986, 92).

26. But see Rasanayagam (2002, 83) for a different treatment of (appointed) neighborhood *oqsoqols* (Uzbek for *aksakal*) in the Fergana Valley.

27. He stepped down from the position in 2014.

28. The name Bakai Moldo is a pseudonym.

29. I noticed that my informants would often refer to "the people" (*el*) when they in fact only meant aksakals. This hints at the perception that what aksakals decide is at the same time "the opinion of the people."

30. McBrien (2008) reports the same phenomenon for the imam in her fieldsite in southern Kyrgyzstan.

31. The name Nurdin Moldo is also a pseudonym.

32. From Arabic *namaz*, meaning the obligatory Islamic prayer.

33. *Aila zhok. Bailanyp kaldym.*

34. In one instance, an individual became a local moldo after having had a career as a policeman, a photographer, and a businessman selling vodka. He learned Arabic and started performing certain rituals at funerals because of the money he could earn. The other example is a man who became religious and was appointed imam of his own volition. However, as he continued drinking vodka, he was removed from his position and now lives a somewhat marginalized life in the village, albeit often showing up when aksakals gather, as if to restore his reputation by being close to elders.

35. Between 2010 and 2015 the number of mosques in Aral doubled, from two to four. There are now two mosques in the upper part, which were realized with "help from outside"—meaning with financial support from Saudi Arabian and Kuwaiti sponsors. In the lower part of the village where Bürgö uruu resides ("my" part of the village), the small mosque that had been located in the "house of culture" was closed, and in its place two mosques were built with money provided by two young male villagers, who named the mosques after their deceased fathers. By creating religious places of worship for all men and dedicating them to their fathers, these two men have thereby established a novel way of remembering the dead.

36. The certificate reads (in Russian): *Blagodarstvennaia Gramota. Prezidium Pravleniia Obshchestva Po Rasprostraneniu Politicheskikh i Nauchnykh Znanii KSSR Nagrazhdaet [Full Name] Za Aktivnoe Uchastie v Provedenii Ateisticheskoi Propagandy Sredi Naseleniia.*

37. This is known throughout Muslim countries. See Lambek (1990) and Mostowlansky (2007).

38. "In the name of Allah, the Beneficent, the Merciful."

39. People in my fieldsite use the terms *moldo* and *imam* interchangeably.

40. From *davat* (Arabic *da'wa*). See Mostowlansky (2007) and Toktogulova (2009).

41. *Köp okugan bilbeit, köptü körgön bilet.*

42. The term *mashbara* is borrowed from Arabic and refers to a communal decision made in a council. It also exists in other Muslim countries such as Indonesia, where it is called *musyawarah*. See F. von Benda-Beckmann (1977); K. von Benda-Beckmann (1984); Geertz ([1983] 2000, 213).

43. See also Waite (2006), who makes a similar point for the case of Xinjiang.

44. The organization was founded in Kyrgyzstan in 2003 and claims to receive no funding from foreign institutions. See De Cordier (2010) for a short overview of the organization's goals and activities.

CHAPTER 5. BUYING AND PAYING RESPECT

1. I found out that these were old Soviet banners that were being reused as the slogan was also appropriate for what the aksakals were performing—yntymak.

2. See van der Geest (2002, 440) for the African context.

3. The term *dezhurnyi* can also be used as a substantive, in which case it refers to the person on duty, such as a conductor on a train, a janitor in a housing complex, a warden, or a night watchman. The combination of the Russian adjective *dezhurnyi* (on duty) with the Kyrgyz word for old man (*chal*) hints at the origins of this concept in Soviet or even tsarist times, when elders were first approached in their roles as heads or mediators by Russian officials.

4. He voiced his fear that if aksakals continue working for politicians, then "an aksakal will just be a hat" (*aksakal degen al zhön ele shapke*), meaning that aksakals will be reducible to the traditional felt hats (*kalpak*) that they wear.

5. They used the Russian word themselves, which indicates that they did not consider this particular way of speaking as "theirs" but as being typical of the previous political era. See also Yurchak (2006).

6. It was hard to tell whether those who had answered with "Hurrah!" were also making fun of his misjudgment in terms of the time and the occasion, or whether they, being reminded of former times, genuinely approved of his performance.

7. I am using the term *elders* here because there are also female veterans in Talas. In Aral and Engels, however, all veterans are aksakals.

8. The elders' monthly pensions are calculated in proportion to the number of years they worked in the kolkhoz. Judging from what my elderly key informants received, the average pension was eight hundred som per month. In 2005–2006 a loaf of bread at the bazaar cost five som and a kilogram of potatoes twenty-five som.

9. Bloch suggests that formalized speech acts (such as talking about yntymak) severely restrict the possibility of conveying specific messages leading to particular action. He argues that as each event becomes like the other, the potential of language to be creative is thereby diminished. Not only does what is being said become detached from a particular time and a particular place, but the speech as such is also distanced from the actual speaker: the elder is transformed into an ancestor speaking eternal truth (Bloch [1989] 1997, 26, 44; see Mayer 1992, 403). Bloch has been criticized by Lambek (1990) for underestimating the creativity that can also be found in formalized speech acts, which are far more than mere repetitions with homeostatic

grounding and system-perpetuating effects. Actors can choose to ennoble a certain topic by presenting it in a novel context or style. Through such noticeable exertions of creativity these actors are also making a claim toward being recognized as individuals to be reckoned with.

10. During parliamentary elections the politician who had handed over the sealed envelopes to the veterans offered young families who were expecting a son five thousand som if they named their child after him.

11. In his analysis of the elevation ritual of the Central Asian khans, a ritual said to date back to the Mongol emperor Chingiz Khan, Sela (2003, 1) has emphasized that, while being elevated on a white felt rug by the most important dignitaries of the realm symbolized the superior position of the khan, "it at the same time made him dependent upon those who held him, probably wishing they would not let go."

12. *Ata ene ölsö, ölsün, tonu zherde kalbasyn.*

13. A state institution on the provincial level responsible for the distribution of money for veterans and the organization of festivities for aksakals.

14. *Atadan artyk uul, ataga teng uul, atadan kem uul.*

15. I was told later by the aksakal that he was referring to the head of the aksakal court, Kasym Ata, who was conspicuously absent that day.

16. Since I consider the content of his speech relevant for my following interpretation, I quote some passages at length here. The original speech lasted fifteen minutes.

17. *Ake* is used to refer respectfully to one's older brother. A Kyrgyz proverb exemplifies this: *Uluunu ake de, kichüünü ükö de* (Call an elder person *ake* and a younger one *ükö*).

18. The komuz is a stringed instrument.

19. The previous year Nurlan Baike had campaigned for the politician who had handed out envelopes to the aksakals on Veterans' Day in the district center a few days before the museum was opened (as described earlier in the chapter). Kasym Ata's favorite candidate, however, had lost, and not attending the opening ceremony was his way of refusing to pay respect to the businessman. Again, he was breaking with *salt*, according to which guests (*meiman*) are the most honored persons.

20. This case turns upside down some assumptions about membership by kinship in classical anthropological literature. It was Fortes (1969, 228) who argued that membership in the community was not marketable. It cannot be acquired by purchase, by right of occupational specialization, by property ownership, or even by residence.

21. See also Bourdieu (1977, 179).

CHAPTER 6. TAKING AND GIVING CARPETS

1. *Sylyktyktyn belgisi—alysh-berish; yntymaktyn belgisi—barysh-kelish.*
2. *Toi* means "feast" or "celebration."
3. In a different context, Biehl and Locke recently argued that "the hu-

man sciences are challenged to respect and incorporate, without reduction, the angst, uncertainty, and the passion for the possible that life holds through and beyond technical assessments." They concluded that "perhaps this task is what ethnography does best" (2010, 319). Drawing on Deleuze and Guattari, Biehl and Locke suggest that by "listening as readers and writers, rather than clinicians, our own sensibility and openness become instrumental in spurring social recognition of the ways ordinary people think through their conditions" (2010, 335). While reflecting on my own role as the experiencing Other, I remain committed to my informants' interpretations of their emotional practices and the ways they try to align their personal and social struggles in the face of death. I thus explore the role of emotional practices in relation to aspects of gender and ritualized exchange in the context of increasing social stratification and economic inequality.

4. This is with the exception of bride kidnapping (*ala kachuu*). I have decided to not elaborate on this controversial practice, which is common throughout this part of the country, as I did not focus on it during my research. While I gathered data from people's stories on this topic and have been witness to unsuccessful attempts, I have no data stemming from direct participant observation of an actual kidnapping (and I am happy about that). The difference between *ala kachuu* and the other "customary" practices I am concerned with in this book is that bride kidnapping involves actual force—violence and often rape. This makes it a topic that should be investigated on its own. Due to the ethical implications such research would trigger, there is still a lack of literature on it (but see Werner 2009; Kleinbach and Salimjanova 2007).

5. During the time of my fieldwork, there were only two telephones in the whole village: one in the mayor's office, the other in the post office. Since 2009, however, cell phone connections have been established, which makes the coordination of large-scale events such as funerals much easier.

6. In former times the belongings of the deceased were given, but nowadays new items have to be purchased and given to those who wash the body. Because of these gifts, the task of washing the deceased has become attractive to relatives who, as the imam of Aral told me, even argue over who has the right to do it. Whereas washing the dead is considered deeply impure in other parts of Central Asia (see Kehl-Bodrogi 2008), there seems to be no stigma attached to it in my fieldsite.

7. The erection of the yurt is organized by the patrilineal kin group and can be observed throughout Kyrgyzstan—even in the neighborhoods of Bishkek, where yurts are erected in the courtyards between multistory apartment buildings.

8. He used the Russian word *sfera*. Being a former teacher, his knowledge of Russian was very good, and he would demonstrate it by occasionally switching from Kyrgyz to Russian.

9. See also Fortes (1969, 242) for the Tallensi.

10. Since Mauss's *The Gift* ([1925] 1990), the social importance of exchange for relations between individuals and groups has been generally acknowledged. Lévi-Strauss has argued that "there is much more in the exchange itself than in the things exchanged" (Lévi-Strauss 1969, 59). According to Sahlins (1972, 186), it is by means of exchange that people underwrite or initiate social relations and thereby transcend Hobbesian chaos. Acts of reciprocity such as the sharing, redistribution, and eating of food create, sustain, and display social relations that are expressions of community (Gudeman 2001). The exchanges that occur during death rituals are often interpreted as a mechanism to strengthen social bonds. In the case of Uzbekistan, Kehl-Bodrogi noted that "death rituals effectively strengthen the solidarity and unity of kinship groups" (2008, 121; for the case of Xinjiang see also Bellér-Hann 2008, 158).

11. *Ash* is a major memorial ritual that takes place usually one year after the death of a person. According to *salt*, large animals (horses, cows) must be slaughtered, and in many cases a monument will be erected at the grave site. Gift exchange is a significant part of this ritual. The same ritual might be held again three years after the death.

12. See Werner (2000) for Kazakhstan.

13. *Zhanaza* is a prayer that is always performed by the imam or moldo to guide the deceased into the afterlife (*tigi düinö*).

14. After *zhanaza* has been performed, an elderly person of the family of the deceased can ask, "Is my relative indebted to anyone present?" I was told by my informants that people are usually reluctant to raise their voices, but if they do, they should have two witnesses standing there at the grave. The issue is then negotiated on the spot, and through another prayer reading by the imam or moldo, the debt is considered settled. The deceased is thereby declared free of all sins. The ritual is under strong criticism from the muftiyat in Bishkek because it is regarded as "un-Islamic," especially when imams or moldos charge money for their services. Cholponkul Ata compared *zhanaza dooron* to bribing a judge or a state attorney in order to escape a sentence. While people kept talking about this ritual in a general way, I did not encounter a concrete example of it while I was in the field. The two imams of Aral and Engels told me that they accept no money for it, and that they perform *zhanaza dooron* only for respected aksakals, as it is believed that the sins of the person get transferred to the one conducting the ritual. If Allah does not accept the request, the imam will be stuck with the sins of the deceased. To have a religious official perform *zhanaza dooron* for supposedly sinful younger persons is said to be extremely costly. This practice has a long tradition in Central Asia (see Babadjanov 2004; Bellér-Hann 2008, 153, for the case of Xinjiang, where the sins of the deceased were ritually disbursed to strangers by the graveside).

15. The situation is similar to that described by Werner for Kazakhstan (1997, 252), where the resources poor households expend on ritual exchange come at the expense of the families' basic nutritional needs.

16. In Kyrgyzstan, the liver is the organ that is said to "hurt" in times of grief and emotional distress.

17. The Russian word *traur* (itself a German loanword) refers to a state of mourning. While the Kyrgyz have appropriated the Russian term, here it refers to a woman's attire.

18. See Kuchumkulova (2007) for an analysis of a *koshok* in Yssyk Köl province, and Jacquesson (2014) for Naryn province.

19. See also Abu-Lughod (1986, 69), Briggs (1993), Gamliel (2010).

20. Ritualized wailing is often interpreted as a "mélange of affect and cognition" (Feld 1995, 96), as it bridges "the internal (subjective) and the external (social) worlds" (Gamliel 2010, 72). Gamliel (2010, 86) looks at ritualized wailing from the perspective of "emotion management" (Hochschild 1979, 1983) and shows how professional Yemenite wailers ritually manage distress (see also Abu-Lughod 1986, 69).

21. I had only brought tasmal and thus received approximately the same amount of food back. I also received a white headscarf.

22. *Salttan kalbailyk dep ele.*

23. On the concept of "patiency," see introduction note 3.

24. In the case of the material presented here, it would therefore be misguided to look for (young) women's power and resistance in and through these performances, as has been done, for example, by Hegland (1998a, 1998b, 2003) for Shi'a women's mortuary rituals.

25. I once witnessed how the imam of Engels reprimanded a drunken villager who was hanging out in front of his house by saying "*Uiat!*" The person simply answered "*Uiat emes!*" (It is not uiat!). In the case of grownups, the concept does not work as a direct form of accusation: if someone is behaving in a way that will lead others to exclaim "*Uiat!*," it is likely that this person has already transgressed societal expectations to such a degree that invoking custom has no effect any more.

26. G. H. Mead coined the term "generalized Other" (1962) to describe how actors align themselves in a social field; namely, by constantly imagining others' attitudes toward their behavior through internalized communication.

27. Casimir (2009, 283) argues that nobody can constantly feel shame over a long period of time.

28. *Urmat* is also a Kyrgyz male first name.

29. Note that I had not talked to this person about carpets before. He also did not know about my research. He himself associated the giving of carpets directly with women's work.

30. Exceptions are when a man is engaged to be married, the father of the bride, or the groom. Men also engage in gift-giving practices when, for

example, they celebrate their own birthdays or the twentieth anniversary of their graduation.

31. It would therefore be misleading to conceptualize the gendered dimension of gift giving only in terms of male dominance (cf. Kandiyoti 1988; Werner 2009; Hegland 1998a; Goluboff 2008).

32. Sloterdijk distinguished this term from the Marxist "false consciousness," often simplistically rendered as "they do not know it, but they are doing it" (see Torrance 1995, 4).

CHAPTER 7. TAMING CUSTOM

1. *Uluttuk kaada salttarga zhat, artyk bash ysyrap korchuluktu zhoiuu zhönündö, Toktom*, no. 2, January 19, 2006. Jacquesson (2008) cites several Russian-language Kyrgyz newspapers from the 2001–2005 period that report the drafting of similar laws by state officials. None of these laws, however, has ever been passed. She also reports that the Spiritual Administration of the Muslims of Kyrgyzstan issued several legal provisions that tried to curb customary law because it was considered against shariat.

2. Kalipa Ezhe referred to him as Bakai Moldo. *Azhy* indicates that this person has conducted the *hajj* to Mecca. The name is a pseudonym.

3. *Maiyt koiuuda zhumshaluuchu chygymdarga oblastta birdei sharttardy küiruu zhönündö, Buiruk*, no. 7, January 20, 2006. *Buiruk* can be translated as "order," but also as "fate." People often talk about *Kudaidyn buirugu* (God's will). It is a legal opinion issued by religious officials, but I initially felt reluctant to refer to this document as a fatwa (as was done during Soviet times), as this Arabic word was not used in Kyrgyz and because the document was closely modeled in content and format on the *toktom* issued the day before. In later stages of my fieldwork, however, the imams themselves referred to these documents as fatwas.

4. *Zhyrtysh berüü*, often also called *zhyrtysh zhyrtuu*, refers to the tearing of pieces of cloth and handing them out to guests as part of keshik. In former times, the clothes of the deceased were used for this, but nowadays new textiles are used. The piece of cloth handed out is supposed to be taken home and woven into a different fabric. This is to remind the mourners to continue praying for the deceased.

5. *Moldonun aitkanyn kyl birok kylganyn kylba.*

6. "Forty stones" is also known as *dalil*. Like *zhanaza*, but unlike *zhanaza dooron*, *dalil* is performed for every deceased person by the imam or moldo, who, along with the aksakals of the village, gather at the grave and start counting prayer beads while reciting the phrase *la illah ila Allah* (Arab. "There is no God but Allah"). They put a small stone onto the ground for every one hundred recitations (one round). But for the purpose of the ritual, each stone counts for one thousand. As soon as they reach forty thousand (having counted forty rounds), they take these stones and place them in the grave under the head of the deceased. When the deceased is asked questions

(*surak*) by the angels, these stones will provide evidence (the literal translation of *dalil*) that he or she has led a good life. They will also help the deceased to answer the questions correctly in order to go to paradise (*beiish*). When I asked Baiyz Apa and the imam of Engels, both described the ritual in the way that Kalipa Ezhe described it, but they called the ritual "seventy-two stones" instead of "forty stones"—another example of how varied *salt* is within these two villages.

7. The name is a pseudonym.

8. This document is not an official document but a typewritten list of the new rules, signed by Nurdin Moldo and other religious officials of the Kara Buura district of Talas province.

9. People in my fieldsite strongly oppose this regulation because they say preparing graves in advance is "calling for a bad thing to happen" (*zhaman-dykty chakyruu*).

10. See *Ukaz Presidenta KR*, no. 71, March 23, 2012; *Talas Raion Administra-tiön Buiruk*, no. 126, June 11, 2013; *Aral village Aiyl Ökmötü Buiruk*, no. 25, July 1, 2013; *Talas Raion Administration Buiruk*, no. 12, January 20, 2014.

11. This is the same procedure described in the introduction.

12. In this regard I encountered a big difference between the two villages. When I spoke to informants in both fieldsites, they all mentioned that Engels, in contrast to Aral, does not receive any support from "Taldy Bulak"—the name of a mountain area in the vicinity of the Aral *aiyl ökmötü* that villag-ers also used to refer to the mining company that had been looking for gold there since 2006. Apparently, the company gives different kinds of social and economic support to the village in both kind and cash. There were two new combines, for example, that were used by all villagers in common and which had been paid for by "Taldy Bulak." A daughter of Ydyrys Baike and Zhyldyz Ezhe is receiving a stipend, along with many other students, that allows her to study in Bishkek. The company also pays for renovation work in the village schools and gives a monthly sum directly to the *aiyl ökmötü* to be used for so-cial work. Engels does not receive any of this, as it is located in another valley higher up. Villagers identified the steady financial stream received in Aral as one of the major reasons why living in Aral is "better" than living in Engels.

CONCLUSION: ORDERING EVERYDAY LIFE IN KYRGYZSTAN

1. For recent examples see Bridger and Pine (1998), Davé (2007), Manning (2007), Nazpary (2001).

2. On postsocialist nostalgia and its relation to identity, see also Hann (2012).

3. See, for example, Verdery (1996). For examples of "transitology," see the literature discussion in Beyer (2005a). See Carothers (2002) for a critical ap-proach toward "transitology" from a political science perspective, and Stiglitz (1994) for criticism from an institutional economics perspective.

4. This is certainly not a novel suggestion. It was put forward as early as the 1950s by Edmund Leach ([1954] 1997), who made a similar observation in regard to the Kachin of Highland Burma.

GLOSSARY

adat: custom; customary law (from the Arabic *'ada*)

airan: beverage made from diluted yoghurt

ak üi: lit. "white house"; administrative building of the governorate in Talas

ake: respectful form of address to an older brother

aksakal: lit. "whitebeard"; a male elder (cf. Uzb. *oqsoqol*)

aksakaldar sotu: court of elders

amir: commander in chief; despotic monarch in nineteenth-century Bukhara

anti-meeting: gathering organized by the government against the opposition

apa: mother

artel': (Russ.) sedentary work unit (during Soviet times)

aryk aksakal: lit. "canal elder"; appointed irrigation officers during tsarist/ Soviet times

aryz: letter of complaint addressed to the aksakal court

ash: memorial ritual conducted one year after a person's death

ata: father

aul: the Russian version of the Kyrgyz word for village (cf. *aiyl*)

avtoritet: (Russ.) authority, usually referring to a person

aiyl: village

aiyl kengesh: village council

aiyl ökmötü: rural municipality; also used to refer to the mayor

bai: rich (person)

baike: older brother

bailyk: wealth

bala: child

bash alaman: spinning of one's head

bash: lit. "head"; the head of a family or a person in a position of leadership

bata: blessing

beiish: paradise

bek: see *bai*

besh-barmak: lit. "five fingers"; traditional Kyrgyz food served during celebrations, consisting of boiled meat and homemade noodles

bii: see *bai*; leader; judge during tsarist times

biilik: power

bir atanyn baldary: lit. "children of one father"

birikme: the Kyrgyz word for sedentary work unit (see *artel'*)

bismilla ir-rakhman-ir-rakhim: "In the name of Allah, the Beneficent, the Merciful" (from the Arabic)

bizdiki: ours

bolush: appointed district head during tsarist times (from the Russian *volost'*)

brigadir: (Russ.) head of a work unit in the kolkhoz; head of a group of men digging the grave

buiruk: decree; fate (e.g., *Kudaidyn buirugu*, "God's will")

chapan: embroidered coat for men

chong: big

chong-apa: grandmother

chong-ata: grandfather

dalil: (Arab.) evidence; ritual performed by the imam at the grave, also known as "forty stones"

davaatchys: proselytizers (from the Arabic *da'wa*)

dezhurnyi chal: (Russ./Kyrg.) lit. "old man on duty"; derogative term referring to an elder engaging in political affairs

dikii kapitalizm: (Russ.) lit. "wild capitalism"; used to refer to the present-day economic situation in Kyrgyzstan

dyikan charba: farmers' association, formed after 1991

el: people

eng uluu aksakal: the oldest aksakal of a descent line

erezhe: custom; customary law

etnograf: (Russ.) ethnographer

ezhe: older sister

fatwa: legal opinion (from the Arabic)

genealogiia: (Russ.) genealogy

hadith: (Arab.) teachings of the Prophet Mohammad

ideologiia: (Russ.) ideology

imam: (Arab.) head of a mosque congregation

iuridicheskii byt': (Russ.) juridical everyday life

kaada-salt: custom; customary law

kainene: mother-in-law

kalpak: white felt hat worn by aksakals

kanybyzda: lit. "in our blood"

kazy: judge (from the Arab. *qadi*)

kelin: daughter-in-law

kengesh: council

keshik: bag filled with food and meat given back to a guest at the end of a ritual

khan: sovereign; military ruler; see *bai* (from the Chinese/Manchu *han*)

kiit: lit. "cloth/clothes"; gifts and/or money brought by relatives of a deceased to memorial rituals

kilem: carpet

klub: name for the former house of culture

kolkhoz: collective farm during Soviet times

komuz: Kyrgyz stringed instrument

konstitutsiia: (Russ.) constitution

kontora: (Russ.) office; the central building in a kolkhoz

koshumcha: money brought by former schoolfriends, colleagues, and other male acquaintances to a "good" or a "bad feast"

kuda: in-laws

kul: slave

kulak: (Russ.) lit. "fist"; rich peasants during late tsarist and early Soviet times

künöö: sin

Kuran okuu: lit. "reading the Qur'an"; praying

kurultai: large political gathering

kurut: dried milk curds rolled into small balls

kymyz: drink made of fermented mare's milk

kyrgyzcha: lit. "in a Kyrgyz way"; also, the Kyrgyz language

kyrky: memorial ritual, conducted forty days after a person's death

kyshtak: winter encampment

kyz aluu: lit. "to take a girl"; to marry

kyzym: lit. "my daughter"

mahalla: Uzbek neighborhood community

manap: sovereign ruler, see *bai*

manty: steamed dumpling filled with meat

mashbara: council (from the Arabic *mushawara*)

medrese: (Arab.) Islamic school

meiman: guest

meniki: mine (poss. pron.)

mentalitet ichinde: "in the mentality"

moldo: Islamic teacher; a person well versed in Islamic law (from the Arabic *mulla*)

müchösü: member

murap: (Arab.) distributor of water

myizam: law

naarazy: sick

namaz: prayer

nark: customary law, order

nark nasil: social order

nemis: German (from the Russian *nemets*)

nike: marriage

obychie: (Russ.) customs

obychnoe pravo: (Russ.) customary law

ökül-ata: godfather

ökül-ene: godmother

ökürüü: wailing

oomin: amen

öpkösü: lungs

orden: (Russ.) medal

orozo: fasting during Ramadan

otmai: tax for the use of pasture

palas: thin carpet; blanket

piket: (Russ.) demonstration

plemia: (Russ.) tribe

plof: rice dish

po sovetski: (Russ.) lit. "in the Soviet style"

raiondon: (someone) from the district (from the Russian *raion*, "district")

reklama: (Russ.) advertisement

rod: (Russ.) clan

salt: custom; customary law

salt boiuncha: according to *salt*

sandalet: sandal; fig. "slave"

sanzhyra: Kyrygz genealogy

sanzhyrachy: teller of genealogy

shariat: lit. "the path"; Islamic law (from the Arabic *shari'a*)

som: Kyrgyz currency; one US dollar was approximately forty som in 2005 and sixty som in 2015

sotik: a unit of measurement; 1 *sotik* = 1/100 hectare or 100 sq.m (from the Russian *sotok*)

sovetskii chelovek: (Russ.) a Soviet person

starshina: (Russ.) appointed elder on the village level during tsarist times

surak: (Arab.) question

tartip: order (in the disciplining sense)

tasmal: bag filled with food brought to any kind of festivity

tigi düinö: the afterlife

toi: feast

toktom: decree

tör: place of honor in a room or a yurt facing the door

traibalizm: (Russ.) form of corruption expressed through regional and kin-ship ties

traur: (Russ.) black clothes symbolizing a state of mourning

tülöö: spring ritual, praying for rain

tütün: lit. "smoke"; household

tuugandardyn yntymagy: lit. "relatives' harmony"; money given within an extended family during gatherings

tynchtyk: peace

ubagynda: (historical) time

uiat: shame-anxiety; shame

ulama: (Arab.) Muslim community

ülken adam: (Kaz./Kyrg.) lit. "big man"

ürp-adat: custom; customary law

uruu; chong uruu: descent line; major descent line

vlast': (Russ.) power, see *bülik*

yntymak: harmony

yntymak akcha: lit. "harmony money"; money given within an uruu during funerals

yntymak kerek!: Harmony is needed!

yrym-zhyrym: custom; customary law

zakon: (Russ.) law

zasedatel': (Russ.) deputy

zhailoo: mountain pasture

zhakshylyk toi: lit. "good feast" (e.g., marriage, birthday, jubilee)

zhamanchylyk toi: lit. "bad feast" (e.g., mourning rituals)

zhanaza: prayer performed by a religious official to guide the deceased to the afterlife

zhanaza dooron: cleansing ritual after a person has died, sometimes performed for money

zhek zhaat: former schoolfriends, colleagues, and other male acquaintances

zheti ata: seven fathers; one's ancestors

zhetilik: ritual on the seventh day after a person's death

zhezde: husband of an older sister

zhutuu: to swallow

zhyrtysh berüü: piece of cloth added to a bag of keshik; also: *zhyrtysh zhyrtuu*

zindan: historical Central Asian prison

BIBLIOGRAPHY

Abrams, Philip. 1988. "Notes on the Difficulty of Studying the State." *Journal of Historical Sociology* 1 (1): 58–89.

Abramzon, Saul M. 1971. *Kirgizy i ikh etnogeneticheskie i istoriko-kulturnye sviazi*. Leningrad: Izdatel'stvo "Nauka."

Abu-Lughod, Lila. 1986. *Veiled Sentiments: Honor and Poetry in a Bedouin Society*. Berkeley: University of California Press.

Addo, Ping-Anne, and Niko Besnier. 2008. "When Gifts Become Commodities: Pawnshops, Valuables, and Shame in Tonga and the Tongan Diaspora." *Journal of the Royal Anthropological Institute* (n.s.) 14 (1): 39–59.

Aitpaeva, Gulnara. 2007. *Mazar Worship in Kyrgyzstan: Rituals and Practitioners in Talas*. Bishkek: Maxprint.

Akaev, Askar. 2005. Unpublished speech from the third republican meeting of aksakal courts, Bishkek, February.

Alenkina, Natalia. 2015. "Sud aksakalov: Vne (ne)gosudarstvennyi organ po rassmotreniiu sporov: Vozmozhny li paralleli s treteiskim i tovarishcheskim sudom?" *Sravnitel'noe Konstitutsionnoe Obozrenie* 1: 11–28.

Amnesty International. 1996. *Kyrgyzstan: A Tarnished Human Rights Record*. At https://www.amnesty.org/en/documents/eur58/001/1996/en/ (accessed March 14, 2016).

Anderson, Benedict. 1983. *Imagined Communities: Reflections on the Origin and Spread of Nationalism*. London: Verso.

Anonymous. 1996. "The Aksakal Court in Kyrgyzstan: An Instrument of Barbarianism and a Violation of Human Rights." [In Russian.] *Nezavisimaia Gazeta* (Moscow), 30 January.

Appadurai, Arjun. 1990. "Disjuncture and Difference in the Global Cultural Economy." In *Global Culture, Nationalism, Globalization, and Modernity*, edited by Mike Featherstone, 295–310. London: Sage.

Arno, Andrew. 1993. *The World of Talk on a Fijian Island: An Ethnography of Law and Communicative Causation*. Norwood, NJ: Ablex.

Atkinson, J. Maxwell, and John Heritage. 1984. *Structures of Social Action: Studies in Conversation Analysis*. Cambridge: Cambridge University Press.

Babadjanov, Babken. 2004. "From Colonization to Bolshevization: Some Political and Legislative Aspects of Molding a 'Soviet Islam' in Central

Asia." In *Central Asian Law: A Historical Overview. Festschrift for the Nine-tieth Birthday of Herbert Franke*, edited by W. Johnson and I. F. Popova, 153–72. Topeka: Society for Asian Legal History, University of Kansas.

Bacon, Francis. 1740. *The Works of Francis Bacon: Baron of Verulam, Viscount St. Alban, and Lord High Chancellor of England*. Vol. 3. London: J. Walthoe (etc.)

Bailey, F. G. [1969] 1996. *Stratagems and Spoils: A Social Anthropology of Politics*. Boulder, CO: Westview Press.

Bailey, F. G. 2001. *Treasons, Stratagems and Spoils: How Leaders Make Practical Use of Values and Beliefs*. Boulder, CO: Westview Press.

Bailey, F. G. 2003. *The Saving Lie: Truth and Method in the Social Sciences*. Philadelphia: University of Pennsylvania Press.

Barnes, Barry. 1986. "On Authority and Its Relationship to Power." In *Power, Action and Belief: A New Sociology of Knowledge?*, edited by John Law, 180–95. London: Routledge & Kegan Paul.

Barnes, Sandra T. 1986. *Patrons and Power: Creating a Political Community in Metropolitan Lagos*. Manchester: Manchester University Press.

Barthold, Vasilii. V. [1922] 1956. "A Short History of Turkestan." In *Four Studies on the History of Central Asia*, translated by V. Minorsky and T. Minorsky, 1–68. Leiden: Brill.

Baumann, Richard, and Charles L. Briggs. 1990. "Poetics and Performance as Critical Perspectives on Language and Social Life." *Annual Review of Anthropology* 19: 59–88.

Beatty, Andrew. 2005. "Emotions in the Field: What Are We Talking About?" *Journal of the Royal Anthropological Institute* (n.s.) 11 (1): 17–37.

Beatty, Andrew. 2010. "How Did It Feel for You? Emotion, Narrative and the Limits of Ethnography." *American Ethnologist* 112 (3): 430–43.

Bellér-Hann, Ildikó. 2004. "Law and Custom among the Uyghur in Xinjiang." In *Central Asian Law: A Historical Overview. Festschrift for the Ninetieth Birthday of Herbert Franke*, edited by W. J. and Irina F. Popova, 173–94. Topeka: Society for Asian Legal History, University of Kansas.

Bellér-Hann, Ildikó. 2008. *Community Matters in Xinjiang 1880–1949: Towards a Historical Anthropology of the Uyghur*. Leiden: Brill.

Benda-Beckmann, Franz von. 1977. "Entscheidungsvorgänge in vorindustriellen Gesellschaften." In *Gesellschaftliche Entscheidungsvorgänge*, edited by Andreas Müller, 45–62. Basel: Birkhäuser Verlag.

Benda-Beckmann, Franz von. 1979. *Property in Social Continuity: Continuity and Change in the Maintenance of Property Relationships through Time in Minangkabau, West Sumatra*. The Hague: Martinus Nijhoff.

Benda-Beckmann, Franz von. 1983. "Why Law Does Not Behave: Critical and Constructive Reflections on the Social Scientific Perception of the Social Significance of Law." In *Proceedings of the Symposium on Folk Law and Legal Pluralism, 11th IUAES Congress, 1983, Vancouver*, edited by Harald Finkler, 232–62. Ottawa: Commission on Legal Pluralism.

Benda-Beckmann, Franz von. 1984. "Law out of Context: A Comment on the Creation of Traditional Law Discussion." *Journal of African Studies* 28: 28–33.

Benda-Beckmann, Franz von. 2003. "Legal Anthropology, Legal Pluralism and Islamic Law." In *The Dynamics of Power and the Rule of Law*, edited by Wim van Binsbergen, 247–62. Münster: Lit.

Benda-Beckmann, Franz von. 2005. "Pak Dusa's Law: Thoughts on Law, Legal Knowledge and Power." *Journal of Transdisciplinary Environmental Studies* 4 (2): 1–12.

Benda-Beckmann, Keebet von. 1984. *The Broken Stairways to Consensus: Village Justice and State Courts in Minangkabau. Verhandelingen Van Het Koninklijk Instituut Voor Taal-, Land- En Volkenkunde* 106. Dordrecht: Foris Publications, KITLV Press.

Bennigsen, Alexandre, and Chantal Lemercier-Quelquejay. 1979. "Official Islam in the Soviet Union." *Religion in Communist Lands* 7 (3): 148–59.

Beyer, Judith. 2004. "Recht in 'Transformation': Zur Rhetorik der Verfassungsreform in Kirgistan." Master's thesis, Eberhard-Karls University, Tübingen.

Beyer, Judith. 2005a. "Rhetoric of 'Transformation': The Case of the Kyrgyz Constitutional Reform." In *Realities of Transformation: Democratization Policies in Central Asia Revisited*, edited by Andrea Berg and Anna Kreikemeyer, 43–62. Baden-Baden: Nomos.

Beyer, Judith. 2005b. "'It Has to Start from Above': Making Politics before and after the March Revolution in Kyrgyzstan." *Danish Society for Central Asia's Electronic Quarterly* 1: 7–16.

Beyer, Judith. 2006. "Revitalisation, Invention and Continued Existence of the Kyrgyz Aksakal Courts: Listening to Pluralistic Accounts of History." In *Dynamics of Plural Legal Orders.* Special double issue, *Journal of Legal Pluralism and Unofficial Law* nos. 53–54 (2006), edited by Franz von Benda-Beckmann and Keebet von Benda-Beckmann, 141–76. Berlin: Lit.

Beyer, Judith. 2013. "Ordering Ideals: Accomplishing Well-Being in a Kyrgyz Cooperative of Elders." Special issue, *Central Asian Survey* 32 (4): 432–47.

Beyer, Judith. 2015a. "Constitutional Faith: Law and Hope in Revolutionary Kyrgyzstan." *Ethnos: Journal of Anthropology* 80 (3): 320–45.

Beyer, Judith. 2015b. "Customizations of Law: Courts of Elders (Aksakal Courts) in Rural and Urban Kyrgyzstan." *PoLAR* 38 (1): 53–71.

Beyer, Judith, and Roman Knee. 2007. *Kirgistan: Ein ethnografischer Bildband über Talas/Kirgistan—A Photoethnography of Talas.* Munich: Hirmer.

Beyer, Judith, and Zemfira Inogamova. 2010. *Baiyz Apanyn zhashoo tarzhymaly.* Bishkek: Gulchynar.

Beyer, Judith, and Felix Girke. 2015. "Practicing Harmony Ideology: Ethnographic Reflections on Community and Coercion." *Common Knowledge.* Special issue: Peace by other means. Symposium on the role of ethnography and the humanities in the understanding, prevention, and resolution of enmity. Part 3, edited by Jeffrey Perl. 21 (2): 196–235.

Bichsel, Christine. 2008. *Conflict Transformation in Central Asia: Irrigation Disputes in the Ferghana Valley.* Central Asian Studies Series. London: Routledge.

Biehl, Joao, and Peter Locke. 2010. "Deleuze and the Anthropology of Becoming." *Current Anthropology* 50 (3): 317–51.

Bloch, Maurice. [1989] 1997. *Ritual, History and Power: Selected Papers in Anthropology.* Monographs on Social Anthropology 58. London: Athlone Press.

Bloch, Maurice, and Jonathan Parry. 1989. "Introduction: Money and the Morality of Exchange." In *Money and the Morality of Exchange*, edited by Jonathan Parry and Maurice Bloch, 1–32. Cambridge: Cambridge University Press.

Bobrovnikov, Vladimir O. 2005. "Verbrechen und Brauchtum zwischen islamischem und imperialem Recht: Zur Entzauberung des iskil im Daghestan des 17. und 19. Jahrhunderts." In *Rechtspluralismus in der Islamischen Welt: Gewohnheitsrecht zwischen Staat und Gesellschaft*, edited by Michael Kemper and Maurus Reinkowski, 297–315. Berlin: De Gruyter.

Bohannan, Paul. 1955. "Some Principles of Exchange and Investment among the Tiv." *American Anthropologist* 57: 60–70.

Bohannan, Paul. 1967. *Law and Warfare: Studies in the Anthropology of Conflict.* Garden City, NY: Natural History Press.

Boulanger, Christian, ed. 2002. *Recht in der Transformation: Rechts- und Verfassungswandel in Mittel- und Osteuropa.* Berlin: Berliner Debatte Wiss-Verlag.

Bourdieu, Pierre. 1977. *Outline of a Theory of Practice.* Cambridge: Cambridge University Press.

Bridger, Sue, and Francis Pine, eds. 1998. *Surviving Post-Socialism: Local Strategies and Regional Responses in Eastern Europe and the Former Soviet Union.* London: Routledge.

Briggs, Charles L. 1993. "Personal Sentiments and Polyphonic Voices in Warao Women's Ritual Wailing: Music and Poetics in a Critical and Collective Discourse." *American Anthropologist* 95 (4): 929–57.

Brodovskii, Mark. 1913. "Ocherk kirgizskoi stepi: Proiskhozhdenie Kirgiz i ikh prezhnee i nyneshnee upravlenie." *Zemlevedeni* 3.

Brower, Daniel. 2003. *Turkestan and the Fate of the Russian Empire.* London: Routledge Curzon.

Brusina, Olga. 2000. "Folk Law in the System of Power of Central Asian States and the Legal Status of the Russian-Speaking Population." *Journal of Legal Pluralism and Unofficial Law* 45: 71–76.

Brusina, Olga. 2005. "Die Transformation der Adat-Gerichte bei den Nomaden Turkestans in der zweiten Hälfte des 19. Jahrhunderts." In *Rechtspluralismus in der Islamischen Welt: Gewohnheitsrecht zwischen Staat und*

Gesellschaft, edited by Michael Kemper and Maurus Reinkowski, 227–53. Berlin: De Gruyter.

Bukeikhanov, Alikhan. [1910] 1985. *Kirgizy.* Reprint. Oxford: Society for Central Asian Studies 5:19–58.

Burbank, Jane. 2006. "An Imperial Rights Regime: Law and Citizenship in the Russian Empire." *Kritika* 7 (3): 397–431.

Burbank, Jane, and Frederick Cooper. 2010. *Empires in World History.* Princeton, NJ: Princeton University Press.

Buyandelgeriyn, Manduhai. 2008. "Post-Post-Transition Theories: Walking on Multiple Paths." *Annual Review of Anthropology* 37: 235–50.

Carothers, Thomas. 2002. "The End of the Transition Paradigm." *Journal of Democracy* 13 (1): 5–21.

Carrère d'Encausse, Hélène. 1967. "Organizing and Colonizing the Conquered Territories." In *Central Asia: A Century of Russian Rule*, edited by Edward Allworth, 151–71. New York: Columbia University Press.

Carrithers, Michael. 2005. "Comments: Why Anthropologists Should Study Rhetoric." *Journal of the Royal Anthropological Institute* 11: 577–83.

Casimir, Michael J. 2009. "'Honor and Dishonor' and the Quest for Emotional Equivalents." In *Emotions as Bio-Cultural Processes*, edited by Birgitt Röttger-Rössler and Hans J. Markowitsch, 281–316. New York: Springer.

Chanock, Martin. 1985. *Law, Custom and Social Order: The Colonial Experience in Malawi and Zambia.* Cambridge: Cambridge University Press.

Chanock, Martin. 1992. "The Law Market: The Legal Encounter in British East and Central Africa." In *European Expansion and Law: The Encounter of European and Indigenous Law in 19th- and 20th-Century Africa and Asia*, edited by Wolfgang J. Mommsen and Jaap A. de Moor, 279–305. New York: Oxford University Press.

Chari, Sharad, and Catherine Verdery. 2009. "Thinking between the Posts: Postcolonialism, Postsocialism and Ethnography after the Cold War." *Comparative Studies in Society and History* 51 (1): 6–34.

Clammer, John. 1973. "Colonialism and the Perception of Tradition in Fiji." In *Anthropology and the Colonial Encounter*, edited by Talal Asad, 199–220. Atlantic Highlands, NJ: Humanities Press.

Collins, Kathleen. 2002. "Clan, Pacts, and Politics in Central Asia." *Journal of Democracy* 13 (3): 137–52.

Collins, Kathleen. 2006. *Clan Politics and Regime Transition in Central Asia.* Cambridge: Cambridge University Press.

Colson, Elizabeth. 1974. *Tradition and Contract: The Problem of Social Order.* Lewis Henry Morgan Lectures Series. Chicago: Aldine.

Conley, John M., and William M. O'Barr. 1998. *Just Words: Law, Language, and Power.* Chicago: University of Chicago Press.

Das, Veena. 2004. "The Signature of the State: The Paradox of Illegibility." In *Anthropology in the Margins of the State*, edited by Veena Das and Deborah Poole, 225–52. Santa Fe, NM: School of American Research.

Das, Veena, and Deborah Poole. 2004. "State and Its Margins: Comparative Ethnographies." In *Anthropology in the Margins of the State*, edited by Veena Das and Deborah Poole, 3–33. Santa Fe, NM: School of American Research.

Davé, Bhavna. 2007. *Kazakhstan: Ethnicity, Language and Power*. London: Routledge.

De Cordier, Bruno. 2010. "Kyrgyzstan: Fledgling Islamic Charity Reflects Growing Role for Religion." *Eurasianet.org*, December 8, 2010. At http://www.eurasianet.org/node/62529 (accessed March 14, 2016).

Dekker, Henri. 2003. *Property Regimes in Transition: Land Reform, Food Security, and Economic Development: A Case Study in the Kyrgyz Republic*. Aldershot, UK: Ashgate.

DeWeese, Devin. 2002. "Islam and the Legacy of Sovietology: A Review Essay on Yaacov Ro'i's 'Islam in the Soviet Union.'" *Journal of Islamic Studies* 13: 298–330.

Dingelstedt, Victor. 1891. *Le régime patriarcal et le droit coutumier des Kirghiz*. Paris: Thorin.

Elias, Norbert. [1939] 2000. *The Civilizing Process: Sociogenetic and Psychogenetic Investigations*. Oxford: Blackwell.

Ellen, Roy. 1993. *The Cultural Relations of Classification: An Analysis of Nuaulu Animal Categories from Central Seram*. Cambridge: Cambridge University Press.

El-Ojeili, Chamsy. 2015. *Beyond Post-socialism: Dialogues with the Far Left*. Basingstoke, UK: Palgrave Macmillan.

Esenova, Saulesh. 1998. "'Tribalism' and Identity in Contemporary Circumstances: The Case of Kazakhstan." *Central Asian Survey* 17 (3): 443–62.

Evans-Pritchard, Edward E. 1962. *Essays in Social Anthropology*. London: Faber.

Evans-Pritchard, Edward E. [1940] 1963. *The Nuer: A Description of the Modes of Livelihood and Political Institutions of a Nilotic People*. Oxford: Clarendon Press.

Feld, Steven. 1995. "Wept Thoughts: The Voicing of Kaluli Memories." In *South Pacific Oral Traditions*, edited by Ruth H. Finnegan and Margaret Orbell, 85–108. Bloomington: Indiana University Press.

Firth, Raymond. [1936] 1983. *We, the Tikopia: A Sociological Study of Kinship in Primitive Polynesia*. Stanford, CA: Stanford University Press.

Fitzpatrick, Peter. 1983. "Law, Plurality and Underdevelopment." In *Legality, Ideology and the State*, edited by David Sugarman, 159–82. London: Academic Press.

Fortes, Meyer. 1949. *The Web of Kinship among the Tallensi*. London: Oxford University Press.

Fortes, Meyer. 1969. *Kinship and the Social Order: The Legacy of Lewis Henry Morgan*. London: Routledge.

Francis, Paul, and Robert James. 2003. "Balancing Rural Poverty Reduction and Citizen Participation: The Contradictions of Uganda's Decentralization Program." *World Development* 31 (2): 325–37.

Frank, Allen. 2014. "A Month among the Qazaqs in the Emirate of Bukhara: Observations on Islamic Knowledge in a Nomadic Environment." In *Explorations in the Social History of Modern Central Asia (19th–Early 20th Century)*, edited by Paolo Sartori, 247–66. Leiden: Brill.

Friedman, Thomas. 2003. "Imagining the Post-Apartheid State: An Ethnographic Account of Namibia." PhD diss., University of Cambridge, UK.

Fuller, Chris, and Bénéi Harriss. 2001. *The Everyday Society and State in Modern India*. London: Hurst.

Gamliel, Tova. 2010. "Performed Weeping: Drama and Emotional Management in Women's Wailing." *Drama Review* 54 (2): 70–90.

Geertz, Clifford. [1983] 2000. "Local Knowledge: Fact and Law in Comparative Perspective." In *Local Knowledge: Further Essays in Interpretive Anthropology*, edited by Clifford Geertz, 167–234. New York: Basic Books.

Geest, Sjaak van der. 1998. "Opanyin: The Ideal of Elder in the Akan Culture of Ghana." *Canadian Journal of African Studies/Revue Canadienne des Études Africaines* 32 (3): 449–93.

Geest, Sjaak van der. 2002. "From Wisdom to Witchcraft: Ambivalence towards Old Age in Rural Ghana." *Africa: Journal of the International African Institute* 72 (3): 437–63.

Geiss, Paul Georg. 2001. "Legal Culture and Political Reforms in Central Asia." *Central Asia and the Caucasus: Journal of Social and Political Studies* 6 (12): 114–25.

Gellner, Ernest 1983. *Nations and Nationalism*. Ithaca, NY: Cornell University Press.

Gins, G. K. 1913. "V kirgizskikh aulakh (ocherki iz poezdki po semirech'iu)." *Istoricheskii Vestnik* 10: 285–332.

Giordano, Christian. 1996. "The Past in the Present: Actualized History in the Social Construction of Reality." *Focaal* 26/27: 97–107.

Giovarelli, Renée, and Cholpon Akmatova. 2002. "Local Institutions that Enforce Customary Law in the Kyrgyz Republic and Their Impact on Women's Rights." In *Agriculture & Rural Development e-paper*, edited by World Bank. Washington, DC: World Bank. At http://www.unece.org/fileadmin/DAM/hlm/prgm/cph/experts/kyrgyzstan/documents/WB.customary.law.kg.pdf (accessed March 14, 2016).

Gluckman, Max. 1955. *The Judicial Process among the Barotse of Northern Rhodesia*. Manchester: Manchester University Press.

Goffman, Erving. 1959. *The Presentation of Self in Everyday Life*. Garden City, NY: Doubleday, Anchor Books.

Goffman, Erving. 1983. "The Interaction Order (1982 American Sociological Association presidential address)." *American Sociological Review* 48: 1–17.

Goluboff, Sasha. 2008. "Patriarchy through Lamentation in Azerbaijan." *American Ethnologist* 35 (1): 81–94.

Graeber, David. 2004. *Fragments of an Anarchist Anthropology*. Chicago: University of Chicago Press.

Grodekov, Nikolai. 1889. *Kirgizy i Karakirgizy Syr-Dariinskoi Oblasti: Iuridicheskii byt*. Vol. 1. Tashkent: Tipo-Litografiia S. I. Laxtina.

Gudeman, Stephen. 2001. *The Anthropology of Economy*. Malden, MA: Blackwell Publishers.

Gudeman, Stephen, and Alberto Rivera. 1990. *Conversations in Columbia: The Domestic Economy in Life and Text*. Cambridge: Cambridge University Press.

Gullette, David. 2007. "Theories on Central Asian Factionalism: The Debate in Political Science and Its Wider Implications." *Central Asian Survey* 26 (3): 373–87.

Gullette, David. 2010. *The Genealogical Construction of the Kyrgyz Republic: Kinship, State and "Tribalism."* Leiden: Global Oriental.

Gurova, Olga. 2015. *Fashion and the Consumer Revolution in Contemporary Russia*. Milton Park: Routledge.

Handrahan, Lori. 2004. "Hunting for Women: Bride-Kidnapping in Kyrgyzstan." *International Feminist Journal of Politics* 6 (2): 207–33.

Hann, Chris. 2012. "Transition, Tradition, and Nostalgia: Postsocialist Transformations in a Comparative Framework." *Collegium Antropologicum* 36 (4): 1119–28.

Hansen, Thomas Blom. 2001. *Wages of Violence: Naming and Identity in Postcolonial Bombay*. Princeton, NJ: Princeton University Press.

Hansen, Thomas Blom, and Finn Stepputat. 2001. *States of Imagination: Ethnographic Explorations of the Postcolonial State*. Durham, NC: Duke University Press.

Hardenberg, Roland. 2010. "How to Overcome Death? The Efficacy of Funeral Rituals in Kyrgyzstan." *Journal of Ritual Studies* 24 (1): 29–43.

Haroche, Claudine. 1998. "Form, Movement and Posture in Mauss: Themes for Today's Anthropology." In *Marcel Mauss: A Centenary Tribute; Methodology and History in Anthropology*, vol. 1, edited by Wendy James and N. J. Allen, 213–25. New York: Berghahn Books.

Haugen, Arne. 2003. *The Establishment of National Republics in Soviet Central Asia*. London: Palgrave Macmillan.

Heady, Patrick, and Liesl L. Gambold Miller. 2006. "Nostalgia and the Emotional Economy: A Comparative Look at Rural Russia." In *Postsocialism: Politics and Emotions in Central and Eastern Europe*, edited by Maruska Svasek, 34–52. New York: Berghahn Books.

Hegland, Mary Elaine. 1998a. "The Power Paradox in Muslim Women's *Majales*: North-West Pakistani Mourning Rituals as Sites of Contestation over Religious Politics, Ethnicity, and Gender." *Signs* 23 (2): 391–428.

Hegland, Mary Elaine. 1998b. "Flagellation and Fundamentalism: (Trans)-Forming Meaning, Identity, and Gender through Pakistani Women's Rituals of Mourning." *American Ethnologist* 25 (2): 240–66.

Hegland, Mary Elaine. 2003. "Shi'a Women's Rituals in Northwest Pakistan: The Shortcomings and Significance of Resistance." *Anthropological Quarterly* 76 (3): 411–42.

Heritage, John. [1984] 1996. *Garfinkel and Ethnomethodology.* Cambridge: Polity Press.

Hertz, Robert. [1907] 2004. "A Contribution to the Study of the Collective Representation of Death." In *Death, Mourning, and Burial: A Cross-Cultural Reader*, edited by Antonius C. G. M. Robben, 197–212. Oxford: Blackwell.

Herzfeld, Michael. 1992. *The Social Production of Indifference: Exploring the Symbolic Roots of Western Bureaucracy.* Chicago: University of Chicago Press.

Herzfeld, Michael [2005] 2014. *Cultural Intimacy: Social Poetics in the Nation-State.* London: Routledge.

Hirsch, Francine. 2005. *Empire of Nations: Ethnographic Knowledge and the Making of the Soviet Union.* Ithaca, NY: Cornell University Press.

Hobsbawm, Eric J., and Terence O. Ranger. 1983. *The Invention of Tradition.* Cambridge: Cambridge University Press.

Hochschild, Arlie R. 1979. "Emotion Work, Feeling Rules, and Social Structure." *American Journal of Sociology* 85 (3): 551–75.

Hochschild, Arlie R. 1983. *The Managed Heart: Commercialization of Human Feeling.* Berkeley: University of California Press.

Humphrey, Caroline. 2002. *The Unmaking of Soviet Life: Everyday Economies after Socialism.* Ithaca, NY: Cornell University Press.

Humphrey, Caroline, and David Sneath. 1999. *The End of Nomadism? Society, State and the Environment in Inner Asia.* Central Asia Book Series. Durham, NC: Duke University Press.

Huskey, Eugene, and Gulnara Iskakova. 2002. "Kyrgyzstan." In *Legal Systems of the World: A Political, Social, and Cultural Encyclopedia*, edited by Herbert Kritzer, C. Neal Tate, and Jose Juan Toharia, 837–42. Santa Barbara, CA: ABC-CLIO.

Iakovlev, M. 1912. *Spravochnaia knizhka dlia aulnykh starshin, volostnykh upravitelei narodnykh sudei inorodcheskogo upravleniia.* Omsk.

Ibraeva, Gulnara. 2007. "Iz opyta poiskov natsional'noi identichnosti i legitimnykh struktur upravleniia v Kyrgyzstane." In *Federal'nyi Obrazovatel'nyi Portal ESM.* At http://www.ecsocman.hse.ru/data/515/626/1219/ibraeva.pdf (accessed March 14, 2016).

Iğmen, Ali. 2012a. "The Emergence of Soviet Houses of Culture in Kyrgyzstan." In *Reconstructing the House of Culture: Community, Self, and the Makings of Culture in Russia and Beyond*, edited by Brian Donahoe and Joachim Otto Habeck, 163–87. New York: Berghahn Books.

Iğmen, Ali. 2012b. *Speaking Soviet with an Accent: Culture and Power in Kyrgyzstan.* Pittsburgh, PA: University of Pittsburgh Press.

Ilkhamov, Alisher. 2013. "Labour Migration and the Ritual Economy of the Uzbek Extended Family." *Zeitschrift für Ethnologie* 138 (2): 259–84.

Inda, Jonathan, and Renato Rosaldo. 2002. *The Anthropology of Globalization: A Reader.* Malden, MA: Blackwell.

Ingold, Tim. 2000. *The Perception of the Environment: Essays in Livelihood, Dwelling and Skill.* London: Routledge.

Ingold, Tim. 2009. "Against Space: Place, Movement, Knowledge." In *Boundless Worlds: An Anthropological Approach to Movement*, edited by Peter Wynn Kirby, 29–44. New York: Berghahn Books.

Irons, William. 1975. *The Yomut Turkmen: A Study of Social Organization among a Central Asian Turkic Speaking Population.* Anthropological Paper Number 58. Museum of Anthropology, University of Michigan.

Isabaeva, Eliza. 2011. "Leaving to Enable Others to Remain: Remittances and New Moral Economies of Migration in Southern Kyrgyzstan." *Central Asian Survey* 30 (3–4): 541–54.

Isakov, Bektur. 2001. *Aral sanzhyrasy.* Talas.

Ivanov, D. 1881. "Verkhov'ia sistemy Talasskogo Ala-Tau." *Izvestiia Imperatorskogo Russkogo Geograficheskogo Obshchestva* 17: 193–98.

Izraztsov, N. 1897. "Obychnoe pravo ('adat') kirgizov Semirechenskoi oblasti." *Etnograficheskoe Obozrenie* 3: 67–94.

Jacquesson, Svetlana. 2008. "The Sore Zones of Identity: Past and Present Debates on Funerals in Kyrgyzstan." *Inner Asia* 10: 281–303.

Jacquesson, Svetlana. 2010. *Pastoréalismes: Anthropologie historique des processus d'intégration chez les Kirghiz du Tian Shan intérieur.* Wiesbaden: Reichert Verlag.

Jacquesson, Svetlana. 2014. "Performance and Poetics among the Northern Kirghiz: Terms and Their Problems, 1845–1864." In *Explorations in the Social History of Modern Central Asia (19th–Early 20th Century)*, edited by Paolo Sartori, 181–206. Leiden: Brill.

Jenkins, Janis. 1991. "The State Construction of Affect: Political Ethos and Mental Health among Salvadoran Refugees." *Culture, Medicine, Psychiatry* 15: 139–65.

Jones Luong, Pauline. 2002. *Institutional Change and Political Continuity in Post-Soviet Central Asia: Power, Perceptions, and Pacts.* Cambridge: Cambridge University Press.

Just, Peter. 2007. "Law, Ritual and Order." In *Order and Disorder: Anthropological Perspectives*, edited by Keebet von Benda-Beckmann and Fernanda Pirie, 112–31. New York: Berghahn Books.

Kachkeev, Maksat. 2007. *Stellung der Richter in Kirgistan und Kasachstan: Eine Analyse vor dem Hintergrund der allgemein anerkannten rechtsstaatlichen Prinzipien und der historischen Entwicklung der Justiz in diesen Ländern. Schriftenreihe zum Osteuropäischen Recht.* Vol. 6. Berlin: Berliner Wissenschafts-Verlag.

Kadyrov, Shohrat. 2009. *Elitnye klany: Shtrikhi k portretam.* Oslo: University of Oslo Press.

Kamp, Marianne. 2002. "Pilgrimage and Performance: Uzbek Women and the Imagining of Uzbekistan in the 1920s." *International Journal of Middle East Studies* 34: 263–78.

Kamp, Marianne. 2006. *The New Woman in Uzbekistan: Islam, Modernity and Unveiling under Communism*. Seattle, WA: University of Washington Press.

Kandiyoti, Deniz. 1988. "Bargaining with Patriarchy." *Gender and Society* 2 (3): 274–90.

Kandiyoti, Deniz, and Nadira Azimova. 2004. "The Communal and the Sacred: Women's Worlds of Ritual in Rural Uzbekistan." *Journal of the Royal Anthropological Institute* 10 (2): 327–49.

Karataev, Olzhobai, and Salaidin Eraliev. 2005. *Kyrgyz etnografiiasy boiuncha sözdük*. Bishkek: Biiktik.

Karim, Wazir Jahan. 1993. "With *moyang melur* in Carey Island: More Endangered, More Engendered." In *Gendered Fields: Women, Men and Ethnography*, edited by Diane Bell, Pat Caplan, and Wazir Jahan Karim, 78–92. London: Routledge.

Keane, Webb. 2008. "Market, Materiality and Moral Metalanguage." *Anthropological Theory* 8 (1): 27–42.

Kehl-Bodrogi, Kristina. 2008. *"Religion Is Not So Strong Here": Muslim Religious Life in Khorezm after Socialism*. Münster: Lit.

Keller, Shoshana. 1992. "Islam in Soviet Central Asia, 1917–1930: Soviet Policy and the Struggle for Control." *Central Asian Survey* 11 (1): 25–50.

Keller, Shoshana. 2001. *To Moscow, Not Mecca: The Soviet Campaign against Islam in Central Asia, 1917–1941*. Westport, CT: Praeger.

Kemper, Michael. 2007. "Adat against Shari'a: Russian Approaches towards Daghestani 'Customary Law' in the 19th Century." In *Religion et politique dans le Caucase post-Soviétique*, edited by Bairam Balci and Raoul Motika, 74–95. Paris: Maisonneuve & Larose.

Kenzhaliev, Zaylagi. 2005. "Das kasachische Gewohnheitsrecht in sowjetischer und postsowjetischer Zeit." In *Rechtspluralismus in der Islamischen Welt: Gewohnheitsrecht zwischen Staat und Gesellschaft*, edited by Michael Kemper and Maurus Reinkowski, 331–41. Berlin: De Gruyter.

Khalid, Adeeb. 2007. *Islam after Communism: Religion and Politics in Central Asia*. Berkeley: University of California Press.

Khazanov, Anatoly. 1983. *Nomads and the Outside World*. Cambridge: Cambridge University Press.

Kleinbach, Russ, and Lilly Salimjanova. 2007. "Kyz ala kachuu and adat: Non-consensual Bride Kidnapping and Tradition in Kyrgyzstan." *Central Asian Survey* 26 (2): 217–33.

Klijn, Floor. 1998. *An Island in Time: Continuities and Changes in a Kyrghyz Mountain Community*. Master's thesis, University of Amsterdam.

Knieper, Rolf. 2010. "Pulls and Pushes of Legal Reform in Post-Communist States." *Hague Journal on the Rule of Law* 2 (1): 111–26.

Korzhenevskii, Nikolai L. 1899. "Ob uporiadochenii kirgizskikh brakov." *Turkestanskie Vedomosti* 8. Tashkent.

Kozhonaliev, Sabyrbek. [1963] 2000. *Obychnoe pravo Kyrgyzov*. Bishkek: Fond Soros.

Kramer, Fritz W. 1984. "Notizen zur Ethnologie der Passiones." In *Ethnologie als Sozialwissenschaft. Sonderheft 26. Kölner Zeitschrift für Sozialpsychologie*, edited by Ernst Wilhelm Müller, René König, Klaus-Peter Koepping, and Paul Drechsel, 297–313. Opladen: Westdeutscher Verlag.

Kuchumkulova, Elmira M. 2007. "Kyrgyz Nomadic Customs and the Impact of Re-Islamization after Independence." PhD diss., University of Washington.

Kuehnast, Kathleen Rae. 1997. "Let the Stone Lie Where It Has Fallen: Dilemmas of Gender and Generation in Post-Soviet Kyrgyzstan." PhD diss., University of Michigan.

Lambek, Michael. 1990. "Certain Knowledge, Contestable Authority: Power and Practice on the Islamic Periphery." *American Ethnologist* 17 (1): 23–40.

Law, John. 1994. *Organizing Modernity*. Oxford: Blackwell.

Leach, Edmund R. [1954] 1997. *Political Systems of Highland Burma: A Study of Kachin Social Structure*. London: Athlone Press.

Leavitt, John. 1996. "Meaning and Feeling in the Anthropology of Emotions." *American Ethnologist* 23 (3): 514–39.

Lemon, Alaina. 2006. "Afterword." In *Postsocialism: Politics and Emotions in Central and Eastern Europe*, edited by Bruce Kapferer and Maruska Svasek, 214–20. New York: Berghahn Books.

Leontev, A. 1890. "Obychnoe pravo Kirgiz: Sudoustroistvo i sudoproizvodstvo." *Iuridicheskii Vestnik* 5: 114–39.

Levchine, Alexis de. 1840. *Description des hordes et des steppes des Kirghiz-Kazaks ou Kirghiz-Kaissaks*. Paris: Imprimerie Royale.

Lévi-Strauss, Claude. 1969. *The Elementary Structures of Kinship*. Revised edition. Translated by James Harle Bell and John Richard von Sturmer. Boston: Beacon Press.

Lienhardt, Godfrey. 1961. *Divinity and Experience: The Religion of the Dinka*. Oxford: Oxford University Press.

Liu, Morgan. 2012. *Under Solomon's Throne: Uzbek Visions of Renewal in Osh*. Pittsburgh, PA: University of Pittsburgh Press.

Llewellyn, Karl, and E. Adamson Hoebel. 1941. *The Cheyenne Way: Conflict and Case Law in Primitive Jurisprudence*. Norman: University of Oklahoma Press.

Malinowksi, Bronislaw. 1926. *Crime and Custom in Savage Society*. London: Kegan Paul.

Manning, Paul. 2007. "Rose-Colored Glasses? Color Revolutions and Cartoon Chaos in Postsocialist Georgia." *Cultural Anthropology* 22 (2): 171–213.

Martin, Virginia. 2001. *Law and Custom in the Steppe: The Kazakhs of the Middle Horde and Russian Colonialism in the Nineteenth Century*. Richmond: Curzon.

Massell, Gregory. [1968] 1980. "Revolutionary Law in Soviet Central Asia." In *The Social Organization of Law*, edited by Donald Black and Maureen Mileski, 226–61. New York: Academic Press.

Mauss, Marcel. [1925] 1990. *The Gift: The Form and Reason for Exchange in Archaic Societies*. New York: Norton.

Mayer, Robert C. 1992. "Hannah Arendt, Leninism and the Disappearance of Authority." *Polity* 24 (3): 399–416.

Maynard, Douglas W., and Steven E. Clayman. 2003. "Ethnomethodology and Conversation Analysis." In *The Handbook of Symbolic Interactionism*, edited by Larry T. Reynolds and Nancy J. Herman-Kinney, 173–202. Walnut Creek, CA: Altamira Press.

McBrien, Julie. 2008. "The Fruit of Devotion: Islam and Modernity in Kyrgyzstan." PhD diss., Martin-Luther-University Halle-Wittenberg.

Mead, George H. 1962. *Mind, Self and Society*. Chicago: University of Chicago Press.

Mitchell, Timothy. 1994. *Colonising Egypt*. Berkeley: University of California Press.

Mondragón, Carlos. 2009. "A Weft of Nexus: Changing Notions of Space and Geographical Identity in Vanuatu, Oceania." In *Boundless Worlds: An Anthropological Approach to Movement*, edited by Peter Wynn Kirby, 115–33. New York: Berghahn Books.

Moore, Sally Falk, ed. 2005. *Law and Anthropology: A Reader*. Oxford: Blackwell.

Mostowlansky, Till. 2007. *Islam und Kirgisen "on Tour."* Wiesbaden: Harrasowitz.

Nader, Laura. 1990. *Harmony Ideology: Justice and Control in a Zapotec Mountain Village*. Stanford: Stanford University Press.

Nalivkin, Vladimir P. 1886. *Kratkaia istoriia Kokandskogo Khanstva*. Kazan.

National Academy of Sciences of the Kyrgyz Republic, ed. 1995. *Talas Entsiklopediasy*. Bishkek.

Nazpary, Joma. 2002. *Post-Soviet Chaos: Violence and Dispossession in Kazakhstan*. London: Pluto Press.

Newby, Laura. 2005. *The Empire and the Khanate: A Political History of Qing Relations with Khoqand c. 1760–1860*. Leiden: Brill.

Noori, Neema. 2006. "Delegating Coercion: Linking Decentralization to State Formation in Uzbekistan." PhD diss., Columbia University.

Northrop, Douglas. 2001. "Languages of Loyalty: Gender, Politics and Party Supervision in Uzbekistan, 1927–41." *Russian Review* 59 (2): 179–200.

Northrop, Douglas. 2004. *Veiled Empire: Gender and Power in Stalinist Central Asia*. Ithaca, NY: Cornell University Press.

Nurbekov, Kubanychbek. 1981. *Gosudarstvenno-pravovoe stroitelstvo Sovetskogo Kirgistana*. Frunze.

Örücü, Esin. 2006. "A Miscellany from a Comparative Lawyer." In *Festschrift Liber Amicorum Tugrul Ansay. Zum 75. Geburtstag/In Honour of His 75th Birthday*, edited by Sabih Arkan and Aynur Yongalik, 267–81. Alphen aan den Rijn: Kluwer Law International.

Parkin, David J. [1972] 1994. *Palms, Wine and Witnesses: Public Spirit and Private Gain in an African Farming Community*. Prospect Heights, IL: Waveland Press.

Parkin, David J. 1996. "Introduction: The Power of the Bizarre." In *The Politics of Cultural Performance*, edited by David Parkin, Lionel Caplan, and Humphrey Fisher, xv–xl. New York: Berghahn Books.

Parry, Jonathan, and Maurice Bloch, eds. 1989. *Money and the Morality of Exchange*. Cambridge: Cambridge University Press.

Parsons, Talcott, and Edward A. Shils. 1951. *Toward a General Theory of Social Action*. Cambridge, MA: Harvard University Press.

Pedersen, David. 2008. "Introduction: Toward a Value Theory of Anthropology." *Anthropological Theory* 8 (1): 5–8.

Poljakov, Sergei P. 1992. *Everyday Islam: Religion and Tradition in Rural Central Asia*. New York: Sharpe.

Prior, Daniel. 2014. "High Rank and Power among the Northern Kirghiz: Terms and Their Problems, 1845–1864." In *Explorations in the Social History of Modern Central Asia (19th–Early 20th Century)*, edited by Paolo Sartori, 137–79. Leiden: Brill.

Radloff, Wasilii. 1870. *Aus Sibirien: Lose Blätter aus meinem Tagebuch*. Leipzig: Weigel.

Radnitz, Scott. 2005. "Networks, Localism and Mobilization in Aksy, Kyrgyzstan." *Central Asian Survey* 24 (4): 405–24.

Ranger, Terence O. 1983. "The Invention of Tradition in Colonial Africa." In *The Invention of Tradition*, edited by Eric Hobsbawm and Terence O. Ranger, 211–62. Cambridge: Cambridge University Press.

Rapport, Nigel, and Joanna Overing. 2000. *Social and Cultural Anthropology: The Key Concepts*. London: Routledge.

Rasanayagam, Johan. 2002. "The Moral Construction of the State in Uzbekistan: Its Construction within Concepts of Community and Interaction at the Local Level." PhD diss., University of Cambridge.

Redfield, Robert. 1956. *Peasant Society and Culture: An Anthropological Approach to Civilization*. Chicago: University of Chicago Press.

Reeves, Madeleine. 2012. "Black Work, Green Money: Remittances, Ritual, and Domestic Economies in Southern Kyrgyzstan." *Slavic Review* 71 (1): 108–34.

Reeves, Madeleine. 2014. *Border Work: Spatial Lives of the State in Central Asia*. Ithaca, NY: Cornell University Press.

Rogers, Doug, Mike McGovern, Sean Brotherton, Erik Harms, and Susanna Fioratta. 2009. *Gobal Socialisms and Postsocialisms*. Call for papers for the annual SOYUZ Symposium at Yale University, April 24–26, 2009.

Rosen, Lawrence. 2006. *Law as Culture: An Invitation*. Princeton, NJ: Princeton University Press.

Röttger-Rössler, Birgitt, and Hans Markowitsch, eds. 2009. *Emotions as Biocultural Processes*. New York: Springer.

Sabataev, S. 1900. "Sud aksakalov i sud treteiskii u kirgizov Kustanaiskogo uezda, Turgaiskoi oblasti." *Etnograficheskoe Obozrenie* 3: 66–72.

Sacks, Harvey. [1970/1971] 1984. "On Doing 'Being Ordinary.'" In *Structures of Social Action: Studies in Conversation Analysis*, edited by J. Maxwell Atkinson and John Heritage, 413–29. Cambridge: Cambridge University Press.

Sahlins, Marshall. 1972. "On the Sociology of Primitive Exchange." In *Stone Age Economics*, edited by Marshall Sahlins, 185–230. Hawthorne, NY: Aldine de Gruyter.

Sahlins, Marshall. 1999. "Two or Three Things That I Know about Culture." Huxley Lecture 1998. *Journal of the Royal Anthropological Institute* 5: 399–421.

Sampson, Steven. 2002. "Jenseits der Transition: Elitekonfigurationen auf dem Balkan neu gedacht." In *Postsozialismus: Transformationsprozesse in Europa und Asien aus ethnologischer Perspektive*, edited by Chris Hann, 425–52. Frankfurt am Main: Campus Verlag.

Saroyan, Marc. 1997. *Minorities, Mullahs, and Modernity: Reshaping Community in the Late Soviet Union.* Berkeley: University of California Press.

Sartori, Paolo. 2007. "When a Mufti Turned Islamism into Political Pragmatism: Sadreddin-Khan and the Struggle for an Independent Turkestan." *Cahiers d'Asie Centrale* 15/16: 118–39.

Sartori, Paolo. 2008. "Judicial Elections as a Colonial Reform: The Qadis and Biys in Tashkent, 1868–1883." *Cahiers du Monde Russe* 49 (1): 79–100.

Sartori, Paolo. 2010a. "Colonial Legislation Meets Shari'a: Muslims' Land Rights in Russian Turkestan." *Central Asian Survey* 29 (1): 43–60.

Sartori, Paolo. 2010b. "What Went Wrong? The Failure of Soviet Policy on Shari'a Courts in Turkestan, 1917–1923." *Die Welt des Islam*, 50: 397–434.

Sartori, Paolo. 2011. "The Birth of a Custom: Nomads, Shari'a Courts and Established Practices in the Tashkent Province, ca 1868–1919." *Islamic Law and Society* 18: 293–326.

Sartori, Paolo, ed. 2014. *Explorations in the Social History of Modern Central Asia (19th–Early 20th Century).* Leiden: Brill.

Sartori, Paolo, and Pavel Shablei. 2015. "Sud'ba imperskikh kodifikatsionnykh proektov: Adat i shariat v Kazakhskoi stepi" (The imperial codification project and its own undoing: Custom and sharia in the Qazaq steppe). *Ab Imperio* 2: 63–105.

Schacht, Joseph. [1964] 1982. *An Introduction to Islamic Law.* Oxford: Clarendon Press.

Schatz, Edward. 2004. *Modern Clan Politics: The Power of "Blood" in Kazakhstan and Beyond.* Seattle, WA: University of Washington Press.

Scheele, Judith. 2010. "Councils without Custom, Qadis without State: Property and Community in the Algerian Touat." *Islamic Law and Society* 17: 350–74.

Scheff, Thomas. 1988. "Shame and Conformity: The Deference-Emotion System." *American Sociological Review* 53: 395–406.

Schmitz, Andrea. 1990. "Zur Frage einer Dualorganisation bei den Kirgisen." In *Münchner Beiträge zur Völkerkunde*, edited by Jörg Helbig and Thomas O. Höllmann, 69–104. Munich: Staatliches Museum für Völkerkunde.

Schnepel, Burkhard. 2008. *Tanzen für Kali: Ethnographie eines ostindischen Ritualtheaters*. Berlin: Reimer.

Schnepel, Burkhard. 2009. "Zur Dialektik von agency und patiency." *Paragrana* 20: 1–8.

Schoeberlein, John. 2007. "Talas und seine kulturellen Kontexte in Zentralasien/Talas's Central Asian cultural contexts." In *Kirgistan: Ein ethnografischer Bildband über Talas/Kirgistan — A Photoethnography of Talas*, by Judith Beyer and Roman Knee, 19–35. Munich: Hirmer.

Schuyler, E. 1885. *Turkestan: Notes of a Journey in Russian Turkestan, Khokand, Bukhara, and Kuldja*. New York: Charles Scribner's Sons.

Sela, Ron. 2003. *Ritual and Authority in Central Asia: The Khan's Inauguration Ceremony*. Bloomington: Indiana University Press.

Semenov, Petr Petrovich. 1998. *Travels in the Tian'-Shan 1856–1857*. London: Hakluyt Society.

Severtsov, Nikolai A. [1873] 1947. *Puteshestviia po turkestanskomu kraiu*. Moscow: Ogiz.

Shahrani, Nazif. 1984. "'From Tribe to Umma': Comments on the Dynamics of Identity in Muslim Soviet Central Asia." *Central Asian Survey* 3 (3): 27–38.

Shahrani, Nazif. 1986. "The Kirghiz Khans: Styles and Substance of Traditional Local Leadership in Central Asia." *Central Asian Survey* 5 (3/4): 255–71.

Simmel, Georg. [1900] 1990. *The Philosophy of Money*. Edited by David Frisby. London: Routledge.

Simpson, Meghan. 2003. "Whose Rules? Customs and Governance in the Kyrgyz Republic." *Local Government Brief*, June. At http://www.lgi .osi.hu/publications/2003/241/1.doc (accessed October 24, 2012; link no longer active).

Skrine, Clarmont P. 1986. *Chinese Central Asia: An Account of Travels in Northern Kashmir and Chinese Turkestan*. Hong Kong: Oxford University Press.

Sloterdijk, Peter. 1983. *Die Kritik der zynischen Vernunft*. Berlin: Suhrkamp.

Sneath, David. 2007. *The Headless State: Aristocratic Orders, Kinship Society and Misrepresentations of Nomadic Inner Asia*. New York: Columbia University Press.

Spencer, Jonathan. 2007. "Anthropological Order and Political Disorder." In *Order and Disorder: Anthropological Perspectives*, edited by Keebet von Benda-Beckmann and Fernanda Pirie, 150–65. New York: Berghahn Books.

Ssorin-Chaikov, Nikolai. 2003. *The Social Life of the State in Subarctic Siberia*. Stanford, CA: Stanford University Press.

Stiglitz, Joseph E. 1994. *Whither Socialism?* Cambridge, MA: MIT Press.

Stoler, Ann Laura. 2004. "Affective States." In *A Companion to the Anthropology of Politics*, edited by David Nugent and Joan Vincent, 4–20. Oxford: Blackwell.

Strathern, Andrew. 1973. "Kinship, Descent and Locality: Some New Guinea Examples." In *The Character of Kinship*, edited by Jack Goody, 21–34. Cambridge: Cambridge University Press.

Svanberg, Ingvar. 1999. "Preface." In *The Kazak Nation*, edited by Ingvar Svanberg, vii–viii. Richmond: Curzon.

Thurman, J. M. 1999. "Modes of Organizations in Central Asian Irrigation: The Ferghana Valley, 1876 to Present." PhD diss., Indiana University.

Toktogulova, Mukaram. 2009. "Le rôle de la da'wa dans la réislamisation au Kirghizistan." *Cahier d'Asie Centrale* 15/16: 83–102.

Torrance, John. 1995. *Karl Marx's Theory of Ideas*. Cambridge: Cambridge University Press.

UNFPA, UNICEF, WHO/ILO and Institute of Equal Rights and Opportunities. 2003. *Improving the Quality of Sexual and Reproductive Health Care through Empowering Users. Report of Baseline Study in Pilot Villages.*

UNHCR (CRS/C/Q/KYR/1). 2000. *Implementation of the Convention on the Rights of the Child: List of Issues to Be Taken Up in Connection with the Consideration of the Initial Report of Kyrgyzstan* (CRC/C/41/Add.6). Geneva: Office of the United Nations High Commissioner for Human Rights.

Valikhanov, Chokan Ch. 1962. "O sostoianii Altyshara ili shesti vostochnykh gorodov Kitaiskoi provintsii Nan-lu (Maloi Bukharii) v 1858–9 godakh." *Sobranie Sochinenii* 2: 265–412.

Van der Heide, Nienke. 2008. "Spirited Performance: The Manas Epic and Society in Kyrgyzstan." PhD diss., Universiteit van Tilburg.

Verdery, Katherine. 1996. *What Was Socialism and What Comes Next?* Princeton, NJ: Princeton University Press.

Vite, Oleg. 1996. "Izbirateli—vragi naroda? (Razmyshleniia ob adekvatnosti elektroal'nogo povedeniia i faktorakh, na ee uroven' vliiaiushchikh)." *Etika Uspekha* 9: 58–71.

Vitebsky, Piers. 2002. "Rückzug vom Land: Die soziale und spirituelle Krise der indigenen Bevölkerung der russischen Arktis." In *Postsozialismus: Transformationsprozesse in Europa und Asien aus ethnologischer Perspektive*, edited by Chris Hann, 265–86. Frankfurt: Campus Verlag.

Vladimirtsov, Boris Ia. 2002. *Raboty po istorii i etnografii mongol'skikh narodov*. Moscow: "Vostochnaia Literatura" Rossiskaia Akademiia Nauk.

Waite, Edmund. 2006. "The Impact of the State on Islam amongst the Uyghurs: Religious Knowledge and Authority in the Kashgar Oasis." *Central Asian Survey* 25 (3): 251–65.

Watson, James L. 1996. "Fighting with Operas: Processionals, Politics, and the Spectre of Violence in Rural Hong Kong." In *The Politics of Cultural Performance*, edited by David Parkin, Lionel Caplan, and Humphrey Fisher, 145–59. Providence, RI: Berghahn Books.

Weiner, Annette B. 1976. *Women of Value, Men of Renown: New Perspectives in Trobriand Exchange*. Austin: University of Texas Press.

Werbner, Pnina. 1990. *The Migration Process: Capital, Gifts and Offerings among British Pakistanis*. New York: Berg Publishers.

Werner, Cynthia A. 1997. "Household Networks, Ritual Exchange and Economic Change in Rural Kazakstan." PhD diss., Indiana University.

Werner, Cynthia A. 2000. "Gifts, Bribes and Development in Post-Soviet Kazakstan." *Human Organization* 59 (1): 11–22.

Werner, Cynthia A. 2009. "Bride Abduction in Post-Soviet Central Asia: Marking a Shift towards Patriarchy through Local Discourses of Shame and Tradition." *Journal of the Royal Anthropological Institute* 15: 314–31.

Wilde, Andreas. 2014. "Creating the Facade of a Despotic State: On Aqsaqals in Late 19th-Century Bukhara." In *Explorations in the Social History of Modern Central Asia (19th–Early 20th Century)*, edited by Paolo Sartori, 267–98. Leiden: Brill.

Yurchak, Alexei. 2006. *Everything Was Forever, Until It Was No More: The Last Soviet Generation*. Princeton, NJ: Princeton University Press.

Zagriazhskii, G. 1874. "Zametki o narodnom samoupravlenii u kara-kirgiz." In *Materialy dlia statistiki Turkestanskogo kraia*, vol. 3, 362–71. St. Petersburg: Turkestan Statistical Committee.

Zimanov, Salyk Z. 1958. *Obshchestvennyi stroi Kazakhov pervoi poloviny XIX veka*. Alma-Ata: Izdatelstvo Akademii Nauk Kazakhskoi SSR.

INDEX

Note: Page references in *italics* refer to illustrations.

animals, xxiv, 4, 11–12, 14, 46–47, 49, 51–54, 56, 68, 85, 88, 127, 168, 177, 188n11; slaughtering, 6, *38*, 39–41, 58, 150–53, 156–57, 163, 165, 168, 199n11; theft of, 12, 68. *See also* livestock

animism, 24

anthropologists, 173, 176, 182n4; role of in Central Asia, 76. *See also* ethnographers

anthropology, xvi, 20, 176

anti-meeting, 112–13, 125. *See also* demonstrations

Appadurai, Arjun, 126, 131, 169

Arabic, xxi–xxii, 6, 101, 104–6, 138, 159, 167, 195n34, 201n3

Aral: encampment, 46, 48, 50–51, 188n12; kolkhoz, 51, 52; village, xvi–xvii, *xvi*, xxiv, *xxvii*, 3–4, 10–15, 41–58, *42*, 82–86, 110, 158, 162–65, 181n3, 188n8, 189nn16–17, 189n19, 194n17, 195n35, 202n12; work unit, (*birikme*), 53–56, 189n18

artel' (small work unit), xxii, 29, 48–49, 51, 188n12

ash (memorial service one year after a person's death), 141, 157, 199n11

Atambaev, Almaz, 15–17, 108

atheism, 29, 97, 104

audience, 88, 97, 99, 112–15, 118–21, 124, 126, 128–30, 147–49, 177–78

authority, 14, 22, 121–22, 177, 194n24; of *aksakal*s, 61, 71, 82–111, 115–116, 121–34; as interaction, 121–124, 131; performing, 82–111; religious, 15, 102–111; state, 61

azhy, 156, 201n2

Bakiev, Kurmanbek, 64–65, 113, 117, 190

Barnes, Sandra, 131

Barthold, Vasilii, 184n7

bash (head of family, descent line, community, business, etc.), 35, 50, 60, 84–85, 90–97, 119–21, 131–34, 177; female, 90–92, 119; politicians as, 112, 114, 126–32, 177. *See also* head

beard: Islamic, 105, 108; as *pars pro toto* for male elder, 87, 89, 92, 193n8; "whitebeard," xxii, 193n8. See also *aksakal*

Beatty, Andrew, 135, 147

behavior, 120, 170, 182; appropriate, 131, 136, 140, 144–47, 149, 177; of children, 147; embodied, 89; emotional, 89, 95, 136, 147, 149; "foreign," 16; inappropriate, 69, 98, 132–33, 149; kinship, 170; market, 170; of others, 89, 182; reflecting on, xviii, 6, 8–9, 20, 154, 158, 182n4, 200n26; as reflection of *salt*, 6–7, 20, 40, 91, 121; "Talas behavior," 175; of women, 89, 95

Bektur Agai. *See* Isakov, Bektur

Benda-Beckmann, Franz von, 6, 182n7, 195n42

Benda-Beckmann, Keebet von, 195n42

besh barmak (noodles with meat), 46, 130

"Best Person of Talas Province" (award), 126

Biehl, Joao, 197–98

bii (leader, rich person), 21, 25–30, 35, 51, 73, 184n9; as distinguished from *aksakal*, 21. See also *aksakal; bash; bolush;* courts; judges; *manap*

birikme (work unit), 48–51, 53–56, 188n12

Birinchi Bolushtuk (encampment), 48–49

Birinchi Mai (work unit), 49

Bishkek, xv, xxiv, 14–15, 26, 39, 56, 58, 62, 99, 122, 132–33, 160; *aksakal* courts in, 63, 65, 190n4; celebrations in, 64, 117; demonstrations in, 113; as seat of government, 60, 79, 127; training for imams in, 107

blessings (*bata*), 57, 85, 102, 116, 119

Bloch, Maurice, 114–15, 196n9

blood (as metaphor), 9, 102, 168, 175, 187n2

blood feud, 186n2

bodily displays, 141

body. *See* metaphors; mortuary rituals

bolush (appointed head), 26, 185n15. See also *aksakal; bash; bii; manap*

border, xxii; control, xxiv, 52

borsook (fried bread), 163

bride kidnapping (*ala kachuu*), 198n4

bride price, 174–75, 186n21

Brusina, Olga, 21, 27

Bukhara, Emirate of, 22, 185n18

Bürgö (descent line), 36–41, 44, 47–48, 53, 56–58, 93–94, 96, 136–37, 169–70, 195

Bürgö Baatyr, 36–38, *37*, 44, 48, 56

burial practices. *See* mortuary rituals

capitalism, "wild" (*dikii kapitalizm*), 127, 166, 169, 206. *See also* market economy; shock therapy

carpets, *90*, 169; in mortuary rituals, 142–43, 153, 156, 162–63, 166; selling back, 152–53; "taking and giving" of, 135–59, 165–67; "taking and giving" of, as against shariat, 148, 151, 153, 155–57; "taking and giving" of, as "squandering," 155; "taking and giving" of, as women's work,

144, 150–51, 200n29. *See also* exchange practices; gift economy; gift-giving practices; *kiit;* mortuary rituals; ritual economy

Carrithers, Michael, 182n3

Chanock, Martin, 7, 184n5

chapan (traditional Kyrgyz robe), 17, 128

Chat Bazar, 58, 117, 119

children, 99–100, 105, 113, 119–20, 124–25; socialization of, 85, 89, 91–94, 96, 147, 149, 182n8

"children of one father" (*bir atanyn baldary*), 21

Chingiz Khan, 43, 197n11

Chöngör (encampment), 188n9, 188n12, 189n14

Chürpö (descent line), 40–41

civilizing mission, 25, 184n4

clothing: according to *salt,* 17; given at funerals, 141–43, 151–52, 157; given for washing body of dead, 137, 162; not according to *salt,* 110–11; tearing of (*see* mortuary rituals). *See also* dress

codification, 184n7; of customary law, 19, 25, 30, 34; of genealogies, 44–45; of *salt,* 6–8, 10, 35, 176

collective farms, 38. *See also* kolkhoz

collectivization, 29, 45, 51, 55, 57, 173, 175

Colson, Elizabeth, 147

Communist Party, 28, 60

communitas, 9

"community of sentiment," 126, 169

competition (Russ. *konkurs*), 166, 170

"comrades' courts." *See* courts

conflict, 7, 96; religious, 15, 160. *See also* dispute

constitution, 16, 32–33, 61, 64, 189n3, 191n20

constitutional reform, xv, 33, 115
consumption, conspicuous, 169
Convention on the Rights of the
    Child, 190n3
corruption, 113, 187n2, 191n14
council, 106; coordinative, 15; of
    elders, 125–26; village (*aiyldyk
    kengesh*), 11–12, 21, 31, 182n9,
    192n26; women's, 31
courts: *aksakal* (*aksakaldar sotu;*
    courts of elders; village courts),
    xv–xvi, xxvi, 3, 7, 11–12, 14, 30,
    33–35, 61–78, 80–89, 97, 99–101,
    104, 161, 177, 187n28, 189n1,
    190n4, 190n9, 191n13, 191n15,
    191n18, 191n20, 192nn21–24,
    197n15; *aksakal,* cases, xvi, 4, 12,
    14, 31, 33, 62–72, 74–76, 83–84,
    87–88, 97–98, 100, 190n9,
    191n17; *aksakal,* fee in, 74–76;
    aksakal, registration of, 190n4;
    aksakal, as state-like, 61, 70, 73,
    81; of *biïs,* 25, 33; city, 63, 67, 98;
    "comrades'" (*tovarishcheskii sud*),
    31; *kazy,* 25, 27, 184n14; military,
    25; people's, 25, 31; regional,
    12, 62–63, 66; state, 7, 12, 14,
    63–65, 67–76, 78–81, 84, 86–87,
    98, 100, 116, 191n13, 191n16
"cultural intimacy," 175
culture, 179; clubs, 184n4; ethnic,
    165; house of, 195; invented, 176;
    Kyrgyz, xxiv, 6, 130; national, 16
custom, xvi–xix, 20, 28, 34, 40, 96,
    177, 179; "according to" (*salt
    boiuncha*), xvii–xviii, 4–8, 11, 40,
    43, 53, 61, 68, 81, 87–88, 91–92,
    95–96, 100, 112, 114–15, 121,
    123, 126, 130–33, 148, 157, 163,
    166, 176, 178; invention of, 20;
    invoking, 3–18, 65, 176, 200n25;
    force of, xix, 136, 164, 174–75;
    public discourse on, 20; relation-
    ship to Islam, 16–18, 32, 101, 107,

164; taming, 155–71. *See also* law;
    salt
customization, xix, 9–10, 22, 32,
    35, 38, 45–46, 51, 57–58, 80–81,
    121–22, 178, 186n26; of shariat, 17

dastorkhon (cloth used to set food on),
    145
daughter-in-law (*kelin*), 47–48, 57,
    67, *90,* 94; expectations of, 48, 91,
    138–40, 144
*davaatchi*s (proselytizers), 106,
    195n40
death, 21, 136–37, 141–42, 145–46,
    198n3. *See also* funerals; life-cycle
    rituals; mortuary rituals
debt, 152, 199n14
decentralization, 33, 63, 80, 136
decrees, 17, 25, 31; presidential, 15.
    See also administrative ruling;
    fatwa*;* legal act
democracy, 26–27, 32, 35, 174
demonstrations, 89, 113, 125,
    127–28. See also *anti-meeting*
descent, 125, 184n6, 187n2; great de-
    scent line (*chong uruu*), 41, 43, 188
    n4; group, xvi, 19, 36, 39, 44–45,
    58, 178; line (*uruu*), xxiv, 21, 24,
    30, 36, 39–41, 43–44, 48, 85,
    90, 177, 188n10; settling, 36–58,
    187. *See also* genealogy; lineage;
    sanzhyra; sanzhyrachy
development initiatives, 136
Dikokamennyi Kirgiz ("Stone-Age
    Kirgiz"), 183n2
disputes, xvi, 4, 6–7, 21, 24–27, 62,
    68, 85, 87–88, 93–96, 118, 177,
    190n9, 191n16; over land, proper-
    ty, 54, 62, 88, 94–96
dispute management, 6, 25, 30–31,
    101, 185n18; *aksakal*s' role in, xv–
    xvi, 4, 7, 12, 21, 24, 27, 62, 85, 87,
    94; alternative (ADR), 64
"dispute watching," xvi

divorce, 65–71, 74–76, 98, 100, 191n16

documents, xxiv, 15–17, 19, 45, 68, 71–72, 79, 98, 155–66, 190n9, 191nn14–20, 201n3. *See also* administrative ruling; decrees; fatwa; legal act

doing "being elder." See *aksakal;* performance

doing "being ordinary," 192n2

dress, 16–17; national, 110. *See also* clothing

drinking, 99, 101, 104, 145, 150, 195n34; being able to drink, 149; being drunk, 149. *See also* alcohol; vodka

eating together. *See* food sharing

education, 30, 91; Islamic, 106, 159–60. See also *medrese*

elders, 4, 26–27, 33, 53, 82–84, 87–88, 91, 116, 192n1; doing "being elder," 83–86, 91, 161 *(see also* doing "being *aksakal")*; female, 89, 91; as "guardians of cultural knowledge," 176; "village elder," 185n16. See also *aksakal*

election, 25–27, 62, 89, 116, 133–34, 166; for *aksakal* judges, 98, 184n13; of imams, 108; parliamentary, 99, 119, 166, 190n8, 194n24, 197n10

emancipation of women, 30

"emotion management," 200n20

"emotion work," 147

emotional displays, 136, 144–45, 200n16

emotional practices, 126, 135–36, 141, 146–49, 170–71, 198n3

emotions, 135–36. *See also* harmony; pride; shame; shame-anxiety

encampment *(aiyl)*, 21, 46, 49–51, 58, 188n12, 189n13. See also *artel'; birikme; kyshtak*

encampment-turned-work-unit, 50–53

Engels: kolkhoz, 50–52, 188nn11–12; village, xvii, xxiv–xxvi, *xxvii*, 3–4, 10–11, 20, 29, 36, 41–43, 49–52, 55–6, 84–86, 91, 97–106, 110, 122–24, 130–33, 169, 174, 181nn3–4, 188nn9–12, 189nn15–16, 202n12

"enlightened false consciousness," 154

essentializing strategies, 175

ethnographers, 19, 21, 30, 32, 194n7. *See also* anthropologists

Evans-Pritchard, E.E., 37, 176

evidence, 10, 63, 72, 81, 191n20, 202n6

excessive spending, 101, 164–66, 175. *See also* consumption; squandering

exchange practices, ritualized, 8, 48, 101, 131, 136, 141, 197n3, 199n10, 200n15. *See also* carpets; food sharing; gift exchange; *keshik; kiit; koshumcha;* mortuary rituals; ritual economy; *tasmal*

extremism, 15–16, 108

family, 47, 54–55, 133–34, 137, 139–40, 142–46, 150, 152, 164–6, 169–70, 185n20; disputes, 62, 95. *See also* daughter-in-law; descent; household; in-laws; relatives

family disputes, 62, 93–95

farmers' association *(dyikan charba)*, 48, 53–54

fasting, 104

fatwa, 31, 107–8, 110, 201n3; the "President's fatwa," 14–17. See also administrative ruling; decrees; legal acts

feasts *(toi)*, 47, 148; "bad" feasts *(zhamanchylyk toi)*, 135; "good" feasts (*zhakshylyk toi*), 151–53, 167, 170. *See also* life-cycle rituals; mortuary rituals; *toi; tülöö*

feeling rules, 147. *See also* emotional practices

Fergana Valley, 22, 26–27

feudal overlords (*kulaks*), 29

fieldsite, xxi, xxiv, 15, 26, 36, 55–56, 65, 68, 72, 78, 80–81, 96, 102, 166–67

fieldwork, xv–xxvi, 8, 17, 19, 36, 54, 67, 80, 102, 139, 174–75

fine. *See* punishment

food, xvii, 39, 46–47, 57–58, 88, 112–14, 130, 136–41, 145, 148, 192n21; sharing of, xxvi, 4, 6, 11, 41, 58, 81, 136–41, 199n10. *See also* exchange practices; *keshik;* mortuary rituals; ritual economy; *tasmal*

foreign investment, 78

Fortes, Meyer, 197n20

forty stones (*dalil,* prayer ritual), 159, 201n6

freedom, 64; of religious belief, 15

Frunze, 52

fundamentalism, 16

funerals, 31, 43, 54, 58, 89, 101, 104, 136–54; expenses related to, 156–165, 175, 178, 195n34. *See also* death; mortuary rituals

Gamliel, Tova, 200n20

Geertz, Clifford, xvi–xvii, 6

Gellner, Ernest, 175

gender: boundaries, 138; and emotional practices, 136, 198n3; roles, 31, 150–51, 175; segregation, 138

genealogy, 38, 43, 57, 82, 177, 187n2. *See also* descent; lineage; *sanzhyra; sanzhyrachy*

"generalized Other," 200 n26

"geographical identity." *See* identity

Gift, The, 199n10. *See also* Mauss, Marcel

gift economy, 153, 170; monetization of, 170–71. *See also* carpets; food sharing; gift-giving practices; *keshik; kiit; koshumcha;* mortuary rituals; ritual economy; *tasmal*

gift-giving practices, 128–29, 138, 140–58, 170–71, 199n11, 200n30; as competition, 166, 170; gendered dimension of, 136, 138, 149–51, 200nn30–31. *See also* carpets; food sharing; gift economy; *keshik; kiit; koshumcha;* mortuary rituals; ritual economy; *tasmal*

"global postsocialisms," 174

globalization, 10

Gluckman, Max, xvi, 179

godparents, 47–48

Gorbachev, Mikhail, 172

gossiping, 89–94, 147–49, 158

governance, 178; local self-, 31–34, 61–62, 64, 79, 182n9, 190n4, 192n26; precolonial, 51

government, 98; of Kyrgyzstan, 15, 54–55, 63–64, 73, 79, 114–17, 125, 127–28; and relationship to religion, 160–61; Russian imperial, 25; Soviet, 29, 73. *See also* administration; state

Governorate-General of Turkestan, 24

graves, 202 n9; digging, 137, 143, 157. *See also* mortuary rituals

graveyard, 45, 54, 138, 142, 159, 163. *See also* mortuary rituals

grazing: regulations, 88; transgressions, 62, 68, 88

"Great Transformation," 172

grief, 145–46, 200n16

Grodekov, Nikolai, 19, 193n5

guests, 130, 162; hosting of, xvii, 58, 130, 137–41, 148, 152, 157, 163, 170, 197n19, 201n4

Gullette, David, 187n2
Gurova, Olga, 174

hadith, 16, 31, *153*, 165
hajj, 201
halal, 166–67; *halal toi*, 167
Hansen, Thomas Blom, 116
harmony (*yntymak*), xv–xvi, 40,
43, 100, 155, 170; demand
for, 151; drinking as an act of,
150; "harmony ideology," 100;
"harmony money" (*yntymak
akcha*), 137, 142, 169; invoking,
81, 88, 114; 116, 132, 176; living
in, 78, 107, 119; maintenance of,
15, 154; as name of restaurant,
170; need for, 113, 118, 175; in
organization of rituals, 135–42,
171; "our relative's harmony,"
170; performing, 114, 116–21,
132, 139, 177, 196n1, 196n9;
praying for, 39–40. *See also* gift
exchange; *salt*
Haroche, Claudine, 181n1
Heady, Patrick, 136, 173
herding. *See* animals, grazing, livestock, transhumance
Herzfeld, Michael, 80, 175
hierarchical relationships: gendered, 31; generational, 31, 82,
96, 126, 131–32, 177; in seating
arrangements, xviii
hijab, 17, 108, 110
history: instrumental use of, 20;
invention of, 20, 31; local,
28, 124, 175, 177; of Islam in
Central Asia, 110; of the Kyrgyz
people and Kyrgyz customary
law, 6, 19–35; of legal systems,
10; rewriting of, 187n29
Hobsbawm, Eric, 20, 184n5
Hoebel, E. Adamson, 179
Homo Sovieticus, 51
household, xxiv; 1937 survey of, 49;

disputes within, 54, 93–96; head
of, 53–54, 85, 89–96, 193n4;
intergenerational dynamics
within, 112, 121; sphere of, 60,
68, 101, 112, 177, 193; as unit for
ritual contributions, 39, 57–58,
137, 139–41, 151, 169, 200n15.
See also family; relatives
hujum (casting off the veil), 186n21
human rights, 64–65, 190

ideal model: *salt* as, 175–76
ideal-typical: definitions, 7; example
of doing "being *aksakal*," 123;
notion of Islam, 30
identity, identification, 56, 175,
202n2; blood as symbol of, 9;
descent-based, 57–58; "geographical," 45–46, 51, 57–58;
Muslim, 110, 150; national, 16,
33, 183n2; personal, 61; political, 114; regional, 187n2
"imaginative construct," 175–76
imagined communities, 175
imam: appointment of, 15, 101–3,
108, 163, 195n34; as differentiated from *moldo*, 161, 195n39;
involvement in mortuary rituals,
138–48, 156–59, 165, 169,
199nn13–14, 201n6; relationship
with *aksakals*, 103–7, 160–63;
salaries for, 14, 16, 108, 186n3;
under Soviet rule, 29–30; as
state employees, 107–8, 186n3;
training of, 107
imperial rule, 26, 28, 184n3
imprisonment, 62; threat of, 66–69,
155
in-laws (*kuda*), 47–48, 92, 138,
141–42, 152, 158, 167. *See also*
daughter-in-law; family; relatives
Inda, Jonathan, 9
independence, xxiv, 38, 55–57, 60,

to be a judge, 73; political, 161; transfer of, 82; technical, 85, 87

Kodol (descent line), 40–41

Kokand, khanate of, 22–24, *23*, 185n18

kolkhoz, 31–32, 35, 41, 60, 73–74, 88, 103, 127, 173, 188n13, 189n19, 196n8; the time of, 21, 45. *See also* Aral; collective farms; Engels; Kommunizm

Kommunizm (kolkhoz), 49–55, 86–87, 98

komuz (stringed instrument), 82, 130, 197n18

koshok (song of lamentation), 144–45, 200n18. *See also* wailing

koshumcha (monetary gift), 141–44, 151, 166–67. *See also* carpets; exchange practices; gift economy; *keshik; küt;* mortuary rituals; ritual economy; *tasmal*

Kozhonaliev, Sabyrbek, 32

Kramer, Fritz, 182n3

Kuchumkulova, Elmira, 200n18

Kudai (God), 11–12, 40, 162

kulak (feudal overlords), 29

Kurban Ait (Muslim holiday), 165

kurultai (people's meeting), 11–12, 21, 182n9

kurut (dairy product), 46

Kushchu (major descent line), 43–44, 118–19

Kuugandy (encampment), 50, 188n9, 188n12

kymyz-közhö (dairy product), 46

Kyrgyz ethnographic dictionary, 8

Kyrgyz Statehood and the National Epos "Manas," 33

"Kyrgyz way," the (*kyrgyzcha*), 4

Kyrgyzstan, *xxiii*, 181n1; Council of Defense of, 15; "a country of human rights," 190n7; government of, 15, 55, 63, 73, 78–79, 114–16, 118, 127, 160–61, 166;

president of, 15, 33, 110, 116 (*see also* Akaev; Atambaev; Bakiev)

kyshtak (winter encampment), 21, 46, 49

Lambek, Michael, 196n9

land, 29, 39, 49–50, 65, 68, 85, 88, 93–96, 99–100, 189nn16–17, 194n21; disputes, 6, 21, 54, 68, 85, 88, 93–96, *95*, 191n16; privatization, 52, 88; reform, 45–46, 52–56, 96, 194n23; rights 99

landscape, 36, 38, 45–46, 49, 56–58, 188n3, 189n14; "imperial," 46, 188n7

law, xv, xvii, 6, 10, 45, 64, 79, 94, 147, 168, 201n1; "combined," 81, 158, 162–63; customary, xix, 7, 9, 12, 14, 17–20, 24–26, 28–30, 32–35, 60–62, 65, 80, 183nn1–2, 184n3, 186n26; customary, codification of, 25, 30; customary, invention of, 19–20, 31, 184n5 (see also *salt*); Islamic, xviii, 22–26, 29–30, 34, 107, 151, 157, 163, 181n2, 184n10; Islamic, "customary Islamic law" (*salttu shariat*), 17, 107; Islamic, knowledge of, 24, 104–6, 110–11, 161; Islamic, relationship to customary law (*salt*) and state law, xviii, 6, 7, 9, 10, 15, 17–18, 22, 26, 29–30, 34, 40, 107, 157–58; 164, 178, 201n1; Islamic, transformation of, 25; Islamic, studies of, 26 (see also shariat); non-customary, xix, 9, 35, 163; *On the Aksakal Courts,* 33, 61–62, 86–87, 187n28, 192n21; *On Local Self-Governance,* 182n9, 192n26; regarding court fees, 65–76; state, xviii; 6, 7, 9, 11, 14, 16–18, 30, 33,

patiency, 6, 96, 101, 182n3, 200n23.
See also agency

peace (*tynchtyk*), 3–4, 26, 31, 39–40,
113, 118–19, 125

people's meeting (*kurultai; eldik
zhiyin*), 11, 21, 165, 182n9

perestroika, 143, 172

performance: as *aksakal*s/elders,
83–84, 86–88, 112, 115–17,
123–32, *129*, 176–77; of authority, 82–111; of cultural intimacy,
175; as daughter-in-law, 48; of
Islam; 103–4; during mortuary
rituals, 136, 145, 148, 150, 166,
200n24; of orderliness, 73, 122;
of relatedness, 38; of *salt*, 7, 9,
20, 88, 96, 112, 121, 148, 178; as
state-like judges, 60, 65, 68–69,
73, 78–81; of *uruu* membership,
56, 58; of *yntymak*, 114, 117–20,
170, 177, 196n1

performative act, 7, 96

performative idiom, 121, 132

performative script, 86

Pionir (work unit), 48–49, 189n18

plof (rice dish), 113

police, 14, 28, 67, 81, 185n18,
190n11; *aksakal*s in place of, 14,
34, 63; invoking, 66–68, 71

political: events, 7, 89, 116–121,
122–131, *129*, 177; instability,
136; knowledge, 161

politicians, 38, 44–45, 55, 85, 98–
99, 112–34, 163, 174, 177, 187n2,
190n8, 193n8, 194n24, 196n4,
197n10, 197n19; performing
yntymak, 117–34, *118*

politics: clan, 187n2; harmony
in, xvi; imperial, 18, 22; local,
188, 192; opposition, 113–114;
religion and, 108, 184n10;
Russian, 19; Soviet, 18; village,
138, 192n26, 194n24. *See also*
authority; political

"post–cold war," 174

"post-postsocialism," 174

"post-post-transition," 174

postsocialism, 173–74, 176; "global
postsocialisms," 174; limits of,
173–74

postsocialist, 60, 80, 172–74; postsocialist nostalgia, 173, 202n2

posture, 181n1. *See also* sitting

power (*biilik*), 100, 185n20, 194n24;
of *bii*s, 26; of blood, 187n2; of
localism, 187n2

pride (*namyz*), xvi, 147

Prior, Daniel, 22

prison. *See* imprisonment; *zindan*

privatization, 45, 51–57, 136, 173,
175. *See also* land; livestock

propaganda, Soviet, 185n20

property, confiscation of, 29, 47;
division of in post-Soviet times,
52–57; theft of, 91. *See also* animals; disputes; land; livestock;
privatization

prosperity (*barchylyk*), 168–69

proverbs, 114, 123, 159, 182n8,
192n1, 197n17; as indirect
communication, 92; reflecting
legal pluralism,10; reflecting
salt, yntymak, 4, 10, 88, 99, 135,
141, 151

punishment, 15, 62, 147; community service, 62; fine 10–12, 31, 62,
71, 73, 100, 138; paying compensation, 4, 12; public apology, 62;
public reprimand, 62

qadi (Islamic judge), 183n15,
184n14. See also *kazy*

Qur'an, 31, 104–5, 110, 138, 162,
168, 191n20

Radloff, Wasilii, 21–22

Ranger, Terrence, 20, 184n5

Rapport, Nigel, xviii

reflexivity, 7–8, 148, 176, 182n4

regulation of *salt* (*erezhe*), 25, 142, 155–56, 202n9

relatives: becoming, 47; expectations of, 69, 85, 91, 133–34, 139, 141–42, 153, 158, 163, 167; sharing among, 3–4, 21, 58, 141; solidarity among, 27, 46, 67; 71, 85, 87–88, 141–44, 170, 193n6. *See also* daughter-in-law; family; in-laws

religion, 163; "close to," 17, 108; freedom of, 15; repression of, 29–32, 186n22; state's relationship to, 14–17, 32, 107–8, 110–11, 155–58, 160, 163, 186; tolerance of, 15. *See also* authority; imam; Islam; law, Islamic; shariat

religious extremism, 15

religious institutions, 14–15, 160, 174, 183n15. *See also* Muslim Spiritual Board; SADUM

remittances, 169

reputation, 4, 6, 90–91, 107, 115, 195n34

respect (*syi, urmat*), xvi, 3, 27, 48, 82, 84–85, 89–90, 92–94, 97, 100, 103, 106–7, 135, 147, 149, 151, 158, 161, 163, 169–70, 177–78, 181n1, 182n8, 192n1; buying, 111–34, 177; *dis*respect, 84, 92–94, 96, 100–101; exchange of, 112, 121, 126, 177; losing, 151, 153; paying, 3, 73, 92, 96, 111–34, 139, 144, 177–78, 197n19

ritual economy, 8, 136, 169, 198n3, 200n15. *See also* carpets; exchange practices; food sharing; gift economy; gift-giving practices; *keshik; kiit; koshumcha;* mortuary rituals; *tasmal*

rituals, 38, 58, 153, 177, 179; appropriation of, 60; elevation of

khans, 197n11; eradication of, 29, 31–32. *See also ash;* feasts; forty stones; life-cycle rituals; mortuary rituals; ritual economy; *tülöö; zhanaza; zhanaza dooron*

Rosaldo, Renato, 9

rules: regarding animal husbandry, 11; for collecting money, 58, 137; feeling, 147; of *salt,* 3–4, 6–7, 10, 34, 176; "for the Siberian Kyrgyz," 24–25; to "tame custom," 162–165, 202n8; village, 3, 14, 58, 137

Russia, 48, 169; postsocialist nostalgia in, 173–74; conquest of Central Asia, 19–29, 76, 110. *See also* Soviet Union

Sacks, Harvey, 192

Sahlins, Marshall, 20, 199

salt, xvi–xix, 6–12, 20, 35, 85–89, 95–96, 98–101, 110–12, 130–33, 146–48, 155, 157, 163–66, 174–79, 182nn6–7, 183n1; "according to *salt*" (*salt boiuncha*), xvii–xviii, 4, 6–7, 11, 53, 68, 81, 88, 91–92, 96, 100, 115, 120–21, 126, 130–31, 148, 151, 155, 157, 163, 166, 176, 178, 199n11; "in the blood," 9, 175; as a burden, 9, 146–47, 151, 153, 166, 168; codification of, 6–8, 10, 35, 176; customization of, 58; efforts to "tame," 155–71; emic perception of, xix, 6, 182n4; flexibility of, 9, 18, 178; formalization of, 178; invocation of, 7–8, 20, 89, 96, 125, 171, 174, 178; in mortuary rituals, 136, 151–55; as ordering principle, xviii, 45, 174; performance of, 20, 88, 112, 120–23; principles of, 82, 85–88; relationship to Islamic law, 10–11,

16–18, 40–41, 103, 107, 110–11, 150, 153, 157, 161, 163–64, 168; relationship to state law, 10–11, 14, 18, 60–61, 76, 78, 96; as "swallowing" noncustomary law 9, 164, 178. *See also* custom; law, customary; harmony (*yntymak*); performance

Salt (working group), 155–57

sanzhyra (recitation of genealogies), 45, 188

sanzhyrachy (elder who recites gene-alogies), 45

Sartori, Paolo, 22

Saruu (major descent line), 43–44, 118–19

Sarytai (lineage subgroup), 58, 137, 170

Scheele, Judith, 26

Schnepel, Burkhard, 182n3

school, 194n17; village, 97, 99, 124–25, 128. See also *medrese*

Schuyler, Eugene, 25

secularism, 30

sedentarization, 29, 38, 45, 57, 173

Sela, Ron, 197n11

self-governance. *See* governance

"self-stereotype," 175

semiotic illusion, 175

Semireche, 24, 184

settlement, 46, 49, 57

Shahrani, Nazif, 100, 121

shame (*uiat*), 149, 200n27

shame-anxiety (*uiat*), xvi, 48, 68, 92, 113, 136, 140, 144, 147–49, 175; as differentiated from shame, 147, 149, 191n16, 193n5

shariat (shari'a), xviii, 6, 110, 148, 151, 167, 181n2, 186n24, 201n1; "customary shariat" (*salttuu shariat*), 17, 107; relationship to custom (*salt*), 7–8, 10, 16–18, 26, 29–30, 101–7, 110, 153, 155–59, 162–63, 168; relationship to

state law, 15–16, 18; *See also* custom; Islam; law: Islamic; religion; *salt*

shock therapy, 56, 169, 174. *See also* capitalism; market economy

Siberia, 24, 29

Siberian Kirgiz, 183n2

Siberian Kyrgyz, Rules for, 24

sin, 159

sitting "according to *salt*," xvii–xviii, 181n1. *See also* posture; *tör*

Sloterdijk, Peter, 154, 201n32

Soros Foundation, 32

Sovettik Kyrgyzstan (newspaper), 104

Soviet antireligious policy, 29–32, 186n22

"Soviet person" (*sovetskii chelovek*), 86–87

Soviet propaganda, 185

Soviet time, 20, 28–30

Soviet Union, 30, 32, 52, 86, 101, 103, 143, 172–73, 181n1

speech acts, 112, 114, 120, 131, 191n20, 196n9

Speranskii, Mikhail, 24

Spiritual Directorate of the Mus-lims of Central Asia (SADUM), 30–31, 160, 186n23

squandering, elimination of, 155

starshina (elder), 26–7

starvation, 173

state, 12, 29–30, 98, 192n25; em-blems/symbols of, 60, 71, 75–76, 81, 117, 155–56, 191n18, 192n23; encountering through docu-ments, 72; imagining, 60–81; invoking, 60–61, 65, 67, 70, 73, 75; Kyrgyz, 16, 33, 52, 156; mimicking, 61, 65, 70–71, 73; relationship to religion, 14–18, 30, 32, 107–8, 155–57, 160–66, 178, 201n1; Soviet, xv, 30, 60, 73; *See also* Kyrgyzstan; Russia; Soviet Union state administration. *See* administration

state atheism, 29

state institutions, 15, 30, 60, 160, 183n15, 197n13. *See also* courts

state courts. *See* courts

state law. *See* law

"statelessness," 61, 73, 78

state-making projects. *See* nation-building

statue. *See* Bürgö Baatyr

stigma, 68, 141, 151, 198n6

stoning, xv, 10, 61

Sufism, 24

Suiunbai Ata (local musician), 122–23

Syr-Dar'ia, 24

Talas: city, 11, *34*, 36, 58, 67, 78, 95, 98, 112; district, 117, 181n3; girls from, 174–75; people of, 174–76; province, xv–xviii, xxii–xxiv, *xxv*, 10, 24, 26; 30, 43, 61, 79, 96, 119, 125–26, 142, 155–57, 173, 181n3, 188n8, 194n13; regional administration, 15, 126, 155–57; restaurant, 170; river, 49; women of, 89

Talas Ala-Too (mountain range), xxii

Talas Entsiklopediasy (Talas encyclopedia), 189n17

Taldy Bulak: encampment, 48; gold mining company, 202n12; work unit, 48

tasmal (food contributions brought to a ritual), 39, 140–42, 152, 170, 200n21. *See also* food sharing; exchange practices; gift economy; *keshik; kiit; koshumcha;* mortuary rituals; ritual economy

taxation/taxes, 14, 22, 24, 26–27, 54, 67, 76, 81, 134, 184n8, 185n18

Taza Suu (water project), 124

Tegerek: encampment, 188n9, 188n12; stream, 189n14

Terek: encampment, 48; work unit, 48, 54

terrorist attacks, 16

toi (feast, celebration), 135, 152, 154, 166–168, *168*, 170, 197n2; *halal,* 167. *See also* feasts; mortuary rituals; rituals

tör (seat of honor), xvii–xviii, 47, 85

Torutai (lineage subgroup), 58, 137, 139, 170

tradition, 6, 33, 86; *aksakal*s as bearers of, 65; invention of, 20, 44; legal, 25

traditionalization, 186n26

traditions of the Prophet, 110. See also *hadith*

traibalizm (Russ.), 119, 187n2

transformation, 27, 172; social, 20, 56; spatial, 56. *See also* "Great Transformation"

transhumance, xxiv, 11, 29; end of, 46–51, 173. *See also* animal husbandry; animals; grazing; livestock

transition, 32, 56, 173–74; the time of, 174

"transitologists," 176

"transitology," 202n3

traur (headscarf worn in mourning), 144, 200n17

tsarist administration, 19, 134

tsarist empire, 19, 24, 30, 184n4. *See also* Nikolai, Tsar

tülöö (ritual), 38–41, *38*, 56–58

Turkestan, 24; Commission, 28

Turko-Mongolian laws, 22

Üch Emchek (kolkhoz, new name for Engels), 52, 123, 181n4, 189n14. *See also* Engels

uiat. See shame; shame-anxiety

ükö (term of address to younger person), 197n17
ulama, 32, 160
United Nations, 63
ürp-adat, 8, 164–65. See also *adat; custom; salt*
uruu. See descent
Uzbekistan, xxii, 33, 186n23, 199n10. See also *mahalla; oqsoqol*

Valikhanov, Chokan, 184n7, 185n18
veterans, 87, 117–19, 123, 126–27, 129–30, 196n7, 197n13
Veterans' Day, 117–19, *118, 119,* 126, 197n19
Vitebsky, Piers, 187n29
vodka, 29, 49, 75, 99, 104, 145, 157, 195n34. *See also* alcohol; drinking

wailers, Yemenite, 200n20
wailing, ritualized, 145, 200n20
washing of the body. *See* mortuary rituals
wealth, 22, 98, 125, 131, 164; in livestock, xxiv, 100
weddings, 101, 152
Werner, Cynthia, 200n15
widows, 89–90; as heads of households, 89, 92, 193n4
Wilde, Andreas, 185n18
witchcraft, 194n15
women's liberation, Soviet policies on, 186n21
World War II, 47–48, 117–18, 175, 188n8

Xinjiang (China), 24, 185n18, 195n43, 199n10
yasa (Mongolian code of law and ethics), 184n10
Yiman Nuru ("The Light of Faith"; local organization of elders), 101, 168
yntymak. See harmony
yrym-zhyrym, 8, 165. See also *adat; salt*
Yssyk Köl (province), 24, 142, 175, 184n8, 193n5, 200n18
yurt, xvii, 21, 46–47, 58, 123, 130, 135, 137, 142, 144–45, 150, 198n7

Zhalal Abad province, xxii; governor of, 98
zhanaza (prayer), 108, 143, 199nn13–14, 201n6. *See also* mortuary rituals
zhanaza dooron (cleansing ritual), 143, 199n14; payment for, 158–59, 162, 199n14, 201n6. *See also* mortuary rituals
Zhangy Turmush (work unit), 48–49
zhek zhaat (male acquaintances), 141–42, 167, 169. See also *kattash*
zheti ata ("seven fathers") 187n2
Zhetigen (major descent line), 41–45, 53–54, 83–84, 118, 123, 128–29, 176, 178, 189n15
zindan (Central Asian prison), 62